Golf Flow

Gio Valiante

Human Kinetics

Library of Congress Cataloging-in-Publication Data

Valiante, Gio.
  Golf flow / Gio Valiante.
    pages cm
  Includes bibliographical references and index.
  1. Golf--Psychological aspects. I. Title.
  GV979.P75V33 2013
  796.352019--dc23
                              2013001572

ISBN-10: 1-4504-3404-5 (print)
ISBN-13: 978-1-4504-3404-1 (print)

The web addresses cited in this text were current as of January 2013, unless otherwise noted.

Developmental Editor: Carla Zych; **Assistant Editor:** Claire Marty; **Copyeditor:** Bob Replinger; **Indexer:** Nan N. Badgett; **Permissions Manager:** Martha Gullo; **Graphic Designer:** Fred Starbird; **Graphic Artist:** Tara Welsch; **Cover Designer:** Keith Blomberg; **Photograph (cover):** Ray Carlin/Icon SMI; **Photo Asset Manager:** Laura Fitch; **Visual Production Assistant:** Joyce Brumfield; **Photo Production Manager:** Jason Allen; **Art Manager:** Kelly Hendren; **Associate Art Manager:** Alan L. Wilborn; **Illustrations:** © Human Kinetics unless otherwise noted; **Printer:** United Graphics

Human Kinetics books are available at special discounts for bulk purchase. Special editions or book excerpts can also be created to specification. For details, contact the Special Sales Manager at Human Kinetics.

Printed in the United States of America   10 9 8 7 6 5 4 3 2 1

The paper in this book is certified under a sustainable forestry program.

Human Kinetics
Website: www.HumanKinetics.com

United States: Human Kinetics
P.O. Box 5076
Champaign, IL 61825-5076
800-747-4457
e-mail: humank@hkusa.com

Canada: Human Kinetics
475 Devonshire Road Unit 100
Windsor, ON N8Y 2L5
800-465-7301 (in Canada only)
e-mail: info@hkcanada.com

Europe: Human Kinetics
107 Bradford Road
Stanningley
Leeds LS28 6AT, United Kingdom
+44 (0) 113 255 5665
e-mail: hk@hkeurope.com

Australia: Human Kinetics
57A Price Avenue
Lower Mitcham, South Australia 5062
08 8372 0999
e-mail: info@hkaustralia.com

New Zealand: Human Kinetics
P.O. Box 80
Torrens Park, South Australia 5062
0800 222 062
e-mail: info@hknewzealand.com

E5756

I was once told that you cannot define love, but that you know it when you see it. In that spirit, I dedicate this book to Melissa Conrad Valiante and Christian Jude Valiante. I can't define it, but I know that pure, unconditional, boundless love exists because I see it every day: A thousand thanks for opening up my world.

I also dedicate this book to Christian David Hoffman, a brilliant, enduring, loyal friend and model of integrity and excellence. *Haec olim meminisse iuvabit.*

Contents

Foreword   vii

Acknowledgments   ix

Introduction   x

Part I
The Golf Flow Experience

CHAPTER **1** Time 3

CHAPTER **2** Control 11

CHAPTER **3** Effort 27

CHAPTER **4** Awareness 35

Part II
Your Flow Toolbox

CHAPTER **5** Skills to Meet
Challenges 47

CHAPTER **6** Mastery Orientation
to Keep Ego in Check 57

CHAPTER **7** Growth Mind-Set
to Adapt to Changes. 65

CHAPTER **8** Resilience
to Overcome Adversity . . . 73

CHAPTER **9** Confidence to Achieve
Sustained Success 85

Part III
Flow on the PGA Tour

CHAPTER **10** Matt Kuchar 97
Loving the Game

CHAPTER **11** Justin Rose. 105
Understanding Your Motivation

CHAPTER **12** Stuart Appleby 117
Developing Appreciation

CHAPTER **13** Camilo Villegas 125
*Maintaining Perspective
During the Highs and Lows*

CHAPTER **14** Sean O'Hair. 139
Being in the Present

CHAPTER **15** Bryce Molder. 147
Playing Your Own Game

Part IV
Ten Keys to Flow on the Course

CHAPTER **16** Study Success 157

CHAPTER **17** Manage Time
Effectively 163

CHAPTER **18** Practice With a Purpose. .169

CHAPTER **19** Achieve a Mastery
Mind-Set 179

CHAPTER **20** Discern Between Real and
Perceived Limitations . . .183

CHAPTER **21** Craft Your Environment. .191

CHAPTER **22** Respond Positively
to Negativity 199

CHAPTER **23** Control Your Body 205

CHAPTER **24** Emphasize Rhythm,
Not Mechanics 213

CHAPTER **25** Play Fearlessly 219

References   224
Index   225
About the Author   228

Foreword

There are many reasons I love golf and have made it my life's pursuit. One of the main reasons is that it tests the totality of a person, the observable, technical, physical skills as well as your mental agility and inner fortitude.

Most of the time championship golf requires a careful, deliberate, dedicated mindset. This was how I won the 1996 Masters, and why I am especially proud of that victory: The game didn't come easy to me that week, and the level of sustained concentration required to coach myself through each and every shot tested the full capacity of my mental toughness.

Those challenging days contrast greatly with days when everything comes together, and golf feels effortless. The first time I remember getting into flow was during the 1987 British Open at Muirfield. I was completely engrossed in my process, and my only focal point was no more than two or three steps in front of me. I especially remember how my 5-iron into the last hole on Sunday seemed to unfold in super-slow motion. I seemed to experience *every single second* of that shot—takeaway, transition, downswing, impact, and follow-through—and I was able to watch the penetrating flight of the ball as it sailed toward my intended target. It all felt so calm and so perfect. Before I knew it, I had been escorted to the 18th green and was holding the Claret Jug. That's how deep my concentration was that day.

Years later I again fell into flow at the 1992 World Match Play Championship. I remember feeling focused, fearless, and confident over each and every shot that week. The result was that I blitzed the field, winning my final match 8 & 7, the largest winning margin in the history of that tournament. If memory serves me correctly, I was approximately 42 under par through 92 holes that week. Such is the power of the flow state.

My experience of flow is similar to what you'll read in this book: I feel confident, relaxed, and patient. I'm aware of my surroundings but acutely focused on each shot, and my rhythm and tempo are in harmony with my mindset and mechanics. In addition to being completely engrossed in the *process of playing*, my thinking is crisp, and I get so in tune with my targets that there is none of the mental interference that often accompanies competitive golf. I see the ball in relation to my target and instantly say, "This feels like a fade" or

"That's a 5-iron." While this is happening, somewhere in my mind I'm also effortlessly registering my environment—dampness in the air, ground angle, breeze, yardage. It is like the old adage: I see it, feel it, react, and execute the shot . . . while running at 100 percent self-belief.

Many people think that I was a very technical golfer, but I don't really see it that way. While I definitely worked hard at my golf swing, when I was playing my best golf my process was simple and consistent with what Gio teaches in this book. I was more into target than technique and was fully immersed in my processes. Even today when amateurs ask me for tips, I default to the mental side of the game. They may ask "How do I chip?" and I will respond, "Never mind the technique. Can you land the ball there, on that spot? Can you see it running to the hole, can you see it go in?" If they say yes, I tell them, "Go ahead and do that." Great golf leads with the mind. Every golfer can choose to think of what to do or what not to do; if you can visualize what you want to do, then you can play well.

While reading Gio's book, I found myself recognizing many of the keys to my own success: the emphasis on rhythm and tempo, and the importance of studying success. For example, when I was a lad of 15, I drove over to Troon for the 1973 British Open. I was there to study Jack Nicklaus, Gary Player, Arnold Palmer, Tony Jacklin, Johnny Miller, and Tom Weiskopf. Afterward I would come back home and play against the greats in my mind. I'd play 3 balls—one of my own, and two belonging to these acclaimed golfers. The benefits that came from these imaginative days were immeasurable. While I didn't yet have full *self-belief*, I knew Jack Nicklaus would hit a booming drive and that Johnny Miller would flush his irons, so while pretending to be them, I developed their habit of being fearless, free, and confident.

Gio also talks about the importance of finding a target on every shot as being essential to flow. When I was growing up in England, my whole practice ground was a single golf hole of about 150 yards, with nothing more than a green, a bunker, and a flag. In retrospect, this minimalist setup was a blessing, because it forced me to craft my mind to hit balls over a bunker, to a target, every time.

In this book you'll read about the strategies that many of the game's top players use to generate flow and play their best golf. You'll be learning the skills Gio's clients have used to amass over 50 professional wins. You'll be joining the legion of golfers who are all seeking that perfect state of mind known as flow.

Sir Nick Faldo

Acknowledgments

As William James said, "It is your friends who make your world." This is certainly true for me, and if I have had any good fortune in life, it is that early on I stumbled upon friends who would remain my companions throughout my life. This book in many ways is largely the result of endless conversations with these autotelic personalities that took place in coffee shops, on airplanes and boats, in hotels and living rooms and libraries, and wherever else we'd collectively pick up the conversations that seem like one big, long talk around a campfire.

Therefore, I'd first like to thank Professor Jack McDowell, Brian Kaineg, Brian Froehling, Dino Doyle, Joe Sora, Ty Underwood, Adam Sehnert, Cory Nichols, Brian Nehr, Andrew Williams, Ben Heron, Rich Shalkop, John Bartell, Kevin Thomas, Greg Pascale, Charlie Sternberg, Jeremy Moore, Walt Rivenbark, Jen and Scott Hayward, Jocelyn and Jason Nettles; the Houle family: Mary, Dave, Ben, Katie, and Joanna; the Lynn family: John, Beth, Tessa, John William, Nick, and James; the Lee family: Gene, Amy, Jamie, and Samantha; the Parra family: Tim, BJ, and Chris; and my newest family: Ryan, Desi, Art, and Anita Conrad.

The golf world is full of enlightened, well traveled, humble, smart, and fascinating people. Those who challenge me and help fashion my thoughts on the game include Roberto Castro, Buddy Alexander, Dr. Craig Davies, Jeff Paton, Camilo Villegas, Jaime Diaz, Tim Rosaforte, Kelly Tilghman, Bryce Molder, Matt Kuchar, Stuart Appleby, Heath Slocum, Charles Howell III, Sean Foley, Jimmy Johnson, Julieta Granada, Steve Bann, Geoff Ogilvy, Notah Begay III, and Justin Rose.

The staff at Human Kinetics has proven to be exemplars of professional excellence: smart, focused, detailed-oriented individuals dedicated to producing the best book possible. Special thanks to Carla Zych, Ted Miller, Jason Muzinic, Gayle Kassing, Bill Johnson, Melissa Steiner, Alexis Koontz, Maurey Williams, Claire Marty, Tara Welsch, Martha Gullo, and Marii Master.

Finally, to my father and best friend, Fred Valiante, and my gracious, brilliant mother, Joanne Valiante, thank you for the unfailing love, guidance, and support.

Introduction

In 2010, golfers I work with won 8 PGA Tour events, completing a run of 10 wins in 12 months. The wins were distributed across 8 different golfers all with different personalities, talents, tendencies, strengths, and weaknesses. This pattern mirrored the 2008 season, in which golfers I'd worked with won 5 of the last 15 events on the PGA Tour.

The results from my work are often dramatic. Justin Rose hadn't won on the PGA Tour in the nine years he'd been competing. Twenty-eight days after our first session, he won The Memorial with a final round 66. Twenty-eight days after that, he won the AT&T National. Similarly, when Arjun Atwal and I first began working together in April 2010, he was ranked 750th in the Official World Golf Rankings and had never won on the PGA Tour. Four months later, he won the Wyndham Championship. Sean O'Hair hadn't won in over two years and when we had our first meeting in July 2011, he had missed 8 of his 10 previous cuts. Fifteen days after our first session, he won the Canadian Open. What's most compelling about these results is that between my first meeting with these golfers and their subsequent wins, not a single one of them changed their golf swing, their equipment, their diet, or their fitness. They simply changed their minds.

If there is any secret to the work that I do, it is that I try to guide my athletes toward what modern psychologists refer to as "flow states," a term that describes a synergy in which all aspects of a person's being—mind, body, will, and intentions—converge to work in perfect harmony. According to the leading researcher on flow, Mihaly Csikszentmihalyi, "The metaphor of flow is one that many people have used to describe the sense of effortless action they feel in moments that stand out as the best in their lives" (Csikszentmihalyi 1997). When this happens, people sense their full potential, achieve excellence, and perhaps even glimpse perfection.

Golfers in flow states enter another realm, as their descriptions attest. They report being able to better see the breaks in greens, more accurately calculate the yardage of a shot, and more fully feel their bodies in space as they intuitively make the necessary adjustments to hit the exact shot they desire. Their walks are more confident, their emotions are softer and more positive, and their perspectives are well suited to the unique round of golf they are playing. The end result for golfers in flow is that they are able to better control the shots they hit, to hit shots that are usually beyond their capabilities, and to shoot scores lower than their handicap would suggest.

Ever since I experienced flow on the golf course first hand more than 20 years ago, I have continued my research into flow as a college professor and a mental game consultant for athletes spanning the spectrum from recreational to professional golfer. I've attended psychology conferences from Vancouver to Boston, and everywhere in between. I have been able to help my clients apply much of what I have learned, and the results have been very rewarding. As a professor and researcher, it has been thrilling to witness the theory come alive in the reality of performance.

One insight that has emerged relates to the way aspiring golfers approach the process of improvement. As young golfers, many in the sport play the game with an unthinking simplicity. Generally, they play well; at the very least, they play mentally free and clear. As they progress and accumulate a deeper understanding of golf, they intuitively seek more instruction and information. Their logic goes something like, "If a little instruction has made me a little better, then a lot of instruction will make me a lot better."

How does this barrage of information influence a brain that is designed, at any given moment, to effectively process seven bits of information (this fact, discovered by scientist in the early part of the twentieth century, is the reason phone numbers have seven-digits)? When you stand over a golf ball, what should you be thinking? What does the brain actually *do* with all the information it has accumulated? The answer depends on the individual, but for a large portion of the population, all that information essentially becomes cognitive gridlock, clogging your brain the way that cholesterol clogs an artery, or too many sheets of paper jam a paper shredder. Too much thinking makes your brain more inefficient, makes you less decisive, and generally distracts you from the simple task of hitting a ball at a target.

Consider this: I have never had a golfer come to me looking for help because he or she was thinking too little, and no one has ever contacted me with the complaint of "there are not enough thoughts running through my mind." Nearly all the golfers who have ever sought my advice have done so because, in one aspect of the game or another, they were having too many thoughts. In an atmosphere of contradicting swing theories and magazines, books, and television shows offering hundreds of conflicting tips, golfers are bombarded with sensory and intellectual information.

All of this affects interpretations, stress levels, and mood, and the emotional toll is enough to overwhelm even the sharpest of minds and to destabilize the purest of talents.

Playing golf in flow is all about doing the simple things required for a golfer to stay out of his own mind, stay out of his own way, and simply hit shots to targets. Consequently, in this book I share with you what cutting-edge research tells us about the flow state and its impact on golfers of all levels, from the high handicapper to the PGA Tour golfer. Fortunately, research suggests that flow is universal (with very few exceptions, everyone can experience flow). My ultimate goal is for you to simplify and refine your thinking so that you can channel your skills and knowledge into simple, effective, repeatable processes that lead to winning golf.

My quest to understand flow, and to apply that understanding, has spanned an entire stage of my life, accompanying me through marriage and the birth of a son, and it has introduced me to a group of athletes with whom I have shared many personal and professional milestones. Learning about flow has not only made me a better golfer, it has provided me with a framework and a perspective that has markedly improved the quality of my life. I hope that this book will bring you the same sense of enthusiasm and excitement that I feel when listening to people describe their flow states and helping my clients get into flow. I also hope that by helping you understand flow, the book not only gives you a clearer view of the game and opens up new ways to improve your play, but also provides some insights that will help you to live a more meaningful and more fulfilling life.

THE GOLF FLOW EXPERIENCE

Peak experiences provide a window into an alternate universe that we visit beyond the covenants of our normal lives and, bound by nothing, are able to sample the energized freedom of our potential. The high that we feel when we are in peak states is like the high that accompanies a moment of courage or important self-discovery. Peak states flood us with the type of joy that teenagers feel behind the wheel of a car as they master the basics of driving or that first-time parents feel when they hold a newborn baby. Athletic endeavors offer myriad opportunities to perform beyond the norm and unleash untapped potential. The common theme of all such experiences is the overwhelmingly positive feelings that emerge from the sense of personal growth and the potential for this breakthrough accomplishment to help us to achieve even greater things in the future.

Researchers studying these peak experiences have found that people consistently use the word *flow* to describe them. Furthermore, they reported feeling no sense of doubt, fear, or distraction; they were completely immersed in the moment.

The past quarter century has brought about a remarkable amount of research on flow states. Two key findings from this research have revolutionary implications for the sports world and beyond. The ability to generate flow states is invariably tied to the overall quality of a person's life, and this ability can be cultivated.

I have found that people often think about flow in the same way that they think about love or luck—as something that happens to them rather than something they do. But just as with love and luck, psychologists have found that people can control many of the factors that improve the opportunity to find flow. Because the factors that determine flow states are things over which people have a measure of control, flow need not be an experience that merely happens, something to wait and hope for. People can learn to identify its characteristics so that they can go with it effectively, nurture it, and get the best out of it when it begins to appear. They can help generate flow!

Aristotle once observed, "We are what we do every day. Excellence, therefore, is not an act, but a habit." Flow is a habit that emerges from a way of thinking about experiences and the meaning that we assign to those experiences. And people who habitually generate flow in other areas of their lives are more likely to generate flow on the golf course.

Now we need to explain in more detail this state of optimal functioning called flow. Flow has been a buzzword for decades, yet it is either poorly understood or, more frequently, misunderstood—even by athletes who know what a struggle it can be to generate flow! But everyone knows it when they're in it. You often hear phrases such as "in the zone," "in the moment," and "dialed in" to describe the experience. These descriptions are accurate, but they don't tell the whole story.

I've spent more than a decade trying to uncover and elucidate the mysteries of flow in golf. This quest took me down unpredictable paths, led me to ask unanticipated questions, and ultimately revealed insights that delighted me and that I hope will also delight you as you learn about them by reading this book.

One fascinating but powerful finding that I uncovered was that golfers usually describe their flow states using seemingly contradictory, or paradoxical, expressions. They report experiencing time moving slowly but the actual event seeming to end rather quickly, gaining control by giving up control, making an effortless effort, and being aware of everything around them while being completely focused on their task!

These paradoxes both define and explain the flow experience in golf, and understanding them is essential to engaging the frame of mind needed to energize flow. Because the main purpose of this book is to improve your golf game by teaching you how to get into flow more frequently, I'll take you through each of the paradoxes. Understanding what flow is and how it works will prepare you to attain it more easily and frequently.

Time

Y ou are alone on the golf course late in the day. The sun is beginning to duck behind tall trees, the shadows are growing long
across the fairways and greens, the air is becoming more still and a
little cooler, and you are walking from one shot to the next with the
easygoing, casual air of a person without a care in the world. There
is calmness in your mind and vagueness about your awareness. You
are paying attention to your game but giving it no more thought than
the attention that you're paying to a breeze, a bird that flies by, or a
squirrel that trots across your path. Without much thought, you gaze
down the fairway and hit the shot that you were picturing. For the
next shot, without a yardage book or any technical thoughts, you
aim and hit the shot toward your target. It comes off with perfection,
leaving you with a feeling of mild satisfaction as you put the club
back in the bag and continue your shuffle down the fairway, toward
the green and the forthcoming 8-footer you have for birdie. You hit
the putt, and off the putter face it feels different in your hands. Pure.
Soft. Happy. Without looking, you immediately know that the putt
was good, that it will be going in the hole.

   As the round goes on, you hit one good shot after another, and
you react with softness as if you are buffered from anything bad
happening to you. You move with smooth, rhythmic movements.
If the ball doesn't go where you expect it to, you don't complain or
get angry. You simply put your club back in your bag, walk down
the fairway taking in the totality of the experience, and hit your next
shot. Your chipping is crisp. Your touch on the greens is perfect.

And your mind is quiet. If you were describing yourself as a piano, you would describe yourself as perfectly tuned. Before you know it, you're walking off the ninth green, and you realize that you haven't made a single bogey, that you've just shot your lowest nine-hole score ever, and that along the way, you'd lost track of your score. Your last realization is that you are also late for dinner because you'd also lost track of time.

Does that sound familiar? I've heard assorted versions of that story from countless golfers over the years. They begin a round of golf with no expectations of shooting a score or playing a particular way. They are on the golf course simply to enjoy the process of playing. To a degree, they mentally check out, and before they know it they are enjoying their afternoon, immersed in their round of golf. They are lost in the moment, lost in the task or experience, oblivious to the pressure associated with passing time. In fact, as they are playing golf, the way that they experience time changes.

BULLET TIME

If you've seen the movie *The Matrix* you are familiar with a special effect that filmmakers use known as bullet time. Bullet time provides the viewer with an alteration of time and space that parallels the real experiences of flow. Bullet time allows viewers to perceive typically imperceptible and unfilmable things (such as a flying bullet) by slowing them down. Bullet time also changes camera angles so that viewers can view the experience from outside themselves—experiencing the moment as both subject and object—all in a slow dimension of time. Generally, golfers in flow experience something akin to bullet time. Time on the course moves slowly, almost eerily so, and sometimes time even seems to stand still, such as when Phil Mickelson won the 2004 Masters Tournament by making five birdies on the back nine:

> *I would certainly go back to what got me here in this event, the Masters, the back nine at Augusta. To shoot 5-under those last seven holes, it was a very slow-motion back nine. Everything was going at a slow pace, and I could see very clearly the shot that I wanted to hit and how I wanted the ball to roll on the greens.*

Note Phil's description of his back nine as a "slow-motion back nine" in which he experienced everything moving at a "slow pace." Phrases like this provide insight into the mental transformation that takes place when golfers get into flow. As with most flow states, the result of Phil's flow state was exceptionally good golf. 12-time winner Justin Leonard describes it this way:

When I get into flow, things slow down a little bit. Your whole process slows. You breathe real easy and there's not a whole lot going through your mind at the time. It just seems like everything slows down a little bit. And you instantly see the shot you want to hit so you're able to play fast. Efficient. You enjoy it as it goes on but once it's over, you're like, "That was over way too fast."

Phil's and Justin's descriptions of their flow states document that golfers do indeed experience time subjectively rather than objectively. They also validate that the transformation of time is associated with their golfing performance; generally, the more time slows down when they are in flow, the better they play. Finally, these descriptions (along with accounts from dozens of other interviews that I've collected) suggest that when golfers are in flow, their brains can experience time as both fast and slow simultaneously (hence the paradox of time). In other words, how we experience time changes from person to person and from moment to moment within the same person, depending on a number of features that I will discuss later in this book.

DOUBLE TIME

Contrary to what happened with Phil and Justin, the subjective transformation of time does not always influence golfers positively. Golfers often tell me that when they're playing badly and are not in a flow state, a round of golf can seem to take forever to end. Additionally, we've all seen golfers who, when they choke, tend to freeze over their shots and take longer than they would when they are playing with confidence. Ironically, although they take longer, their subjective interpretation of time is quite the opposite; even as they take longer over each shot, they feel rushed and jumpy. In these instances, players who are struggling and trying to get into flow begin to feel the pressures that are associated with being out of sync with time. Their minds begin racing, and they are unable to find clarity.

Speaking directly to this point during a 2007 clinic at Mesa Verde Country Club, Tiger Woods talked about facing players who are in situations that they've never been in before:

They are slightly out of rhythm, they give one more look, or freeze over a ball a split second longer, well that's different and if they do that . . . they're uncomfortable. That's fine. I can make them more uncomfortable by playing better.

Certainly that was the case for Nick Watney, who went into Sunday of the 2010 PGA Championship with a 3-shot lead. By the time the day ended, Watney had to birdie holes 16 and 17 to salvage a final round score of 81! Of the major meltdown he recalled, "I was going very, very fast, swinging fast, walking fast, and thinking way ahead." Similarly, Dustin Johnson went into Sunday of the 2010 U.S. Open with a 3-shot lead. His scorecards for the week read 71, 70, 66, 82. What was behind that final round 82? According to Dustin, "Everything started to speed up and I couldn't slow anything down." Think about it: On a golf course where the scoring average for the fields on Sunday was a full shot lower than it was on Saturday, Dustin posted a score that was 16 shots higher! These accounts are not a knock on either of these two golfers, they illustrate how, independent of great talent and perfect golf swing, the subjective speeding up of time can undo even the best.

This insight is worth consideration by people who care about playing their best golf. Two of the best golfers in the world, Nick Watney and Dustin Johnson, went into final rounds with the same golf swings that had put them into contention. Because their minds were not equipped to handle the speeding up of time, their golf swings (as well as other parts of their game) fell apart.

THE POWER OF THE MIND

This point leads us to a fundamental discussion in the golfing world, namely, how important is the golf swing in overall golfing performance? Based on the observations of Watney and Johnson, as well as those golfers who were able to improve their golf game by changing their minds, it seems obvious that golfers who focus exclusively on the mechanics of their golf swings while ignoring the subjective power of the mind put themselves at a disadvantage. They remind me of the story my grandfather used to tell me about an old man who loses his keys while walking in a poorly lit area. Rather than search for the keys in the shadows where he dropped them, he instead searches for them under the lights. When asked why he would knowingly search for keys where he knows that he didn't drop them, the old man responds, "Because the light is better over here." Similarly, golfers often look for solutions to their game where the light is better, but not always where the solution actually resides. They search for the solution where they *want* it to be because they are comfortable in the physical realm. They neglect to search their attitude and mind-set, which is often where the solution lies.

The subjective speeding up of time, as you see from the previous examples, prevents golfers from being able to execute the skills that they clearly possess. In this sense, golf is not exclusively about talent or swing mechanics; it is truly a mental game.

Comparably, the subjective slowing down of time associated with flow often allows golfers to see and do things that are typically beyond their ability. Golfers often comment that they can make necessary adjustments in their golf swings as the swing itself is taking place (a fact that Jack Nicklaus confirmed with me as I was doing research for this book). Their tempo is perfect, and they can feel every moment of the transition from the backswing to the downswing to impact—a flicker of a moment in the golf swing that happens so quickly that it is typically lost.

The transformation of time experienced while immersed in flow states is not limited to golfers out on the course. Any student who has ever spent time in a classroom listening to a passionate, engaging teacher or, conversely, has been trapped in a lecture hall listening to a lethargic speaker with a monotone voice knows that we all experience time on a relative and subjective scale. Experiences that we

Adam Davy/PA Photos

As time slows, golfers in flow find their tempo and rhythm. "Big Easy" Ernie Els is known for his fluid swing.

enjoy seem to end quickly. Summer vacations fly by, and dinner with interesting company invariably ends all too soon. Indeed, although objective time is indeed measureable by clocks and timepieces, our experience of time is always subjective and dependent on our level of enjoyment and engagement.

Although time moves slowly for golfers when they are in flow, it also moves quickly in a positive sense—in the same way that any happy experience seems to end too soon. Their interpretation of quickness is in keeping with the efficient, expedient, decisive behavior that is characteristic of confidence and self-assured certainty. Golfers in flow are quick, but they are in no way rushed.

But time can also move quickly in a negative sense when golfers are not in flow, and here is where the nuances emerge. It is reasonable to interpret Dustin Johnson's explanation as that things felt not only quick but rushed. In these instances, the sensation of quickness is related to an acute awareness of the pressures of time and a sense of being unable to cope with them.

These slow-versus-quick descriptions of the state of flow are where the paradox of time comes into play. How can a person experience something as both slow (a slow-motion back nine) and fast simultaneously?

PUTTING IT IN PERSPECTIVE

Perspective plays a role in explaining the paradox of time. During a round when you are in flow, things are moving in the type of slow motion that Mickelson described. After the round of golf and the accompanying flow state are over, you look back on the experience and find that it seems to have passed very quickly.

Twelve-time PGA Tour winner David Toms captured the paradox perfectly when he reported, "To me as a whole it goes by awful quick, but it moves awfully slow." Compare that with three-time Ryder Cup player and four-time PGA Tour winner Chad Campbell, whose thought-provoking response suggests that he too is uncertain of what to make of his own flow states:

When I am in it, it feels very slow. In a way it's a little bit of both fast and slow. It goes by fast but feels slow. OK, let me try and explain: It feels slow while you are in it, but it goes by quick when you look back on it.

Just like the vacation that ends too soon but during which the days seem long and languid, a round of golf played in flow has hours that seem like minutes and minutes that feel like seconds. These golfers become so immersed in the process of living in the moment that they seem to wake up standing on the 18th hole thinking, "Where am I? How did I get here? Is it over already? What just happened?!" Additionally, golfers in flow describe time using words typically reserved for other dimensions of experience—*smooth*, *quiet*, *peaceful*, *heavy*, and, in all cases, *slow*. A feeling of effortless control over themselves joins this slowing of time over their emotions and over the game itself, and the similarity in the descriptions by professional golfers is remarkable.

LEARNING FROM THE BEST

I've always believed that there is value in studying the best of the best. Whether you're a business person, a student, or a golfer, the process of improvement should always include looking at those who have been successful at the same endeavor that you are seeking to improve. Although this book can help golfers of all skill levels, I have frequently used quotes and passages from PGA Tour players because they have already traversed the obstacles and adversities that the rest of us are seeking to overcome. In that light, let's look at some of the descriptions of flow from PGA Tour golfers:

The zone is both fast and slow. While you are there, it seems slow and effortless and when you look back on it, you can't remember a whole lot of thoughts in your head. When I look back to that last round I was in the zone, it seemed like it took 45 minutes. In fact, everything moved really slowly. I was never rushed.

Bryce Molder, 2011 PGA Tour winner, 4-time NCAA All-American

It seems like you are able to slow things down, but also things seem to be moving slowly around you. You are able to do things quickly, yet they feel like they have a feeling of slowness to them. After 12 holes, it feels like you just played 5. It's hard to explain. It felt like rhythm and timing; everything was just this nice, smooth, mellow tempo. I could do it quickly and still make it feel smooth and mellow and slow.

Jim Furyk, 2003 U.S. Open Champion, 16-time PGA Tour winner

It goes by so fast. Looking back on it, it feels like I teed it up on Thursday and played 72 straight holes. I signed my scorecard on 18 but just went to the next tee. While I am playing, it is more slow. Rhythmic. There is a lot of rhythm when you're in the zone. My energy is even keel.

Zach Johnson, 2007 Masters Champion, 9-time PGA Tour winner

It is when you are content with yourself and the way you are doing things. When I am in the zone, everything slows down. When I am not there, everything seems to be fast. It's just . . . your thoughts seem fast and fleeting. They seem, a lot of things, when you are in the zone, you feel like everything is under control, everything is moving slow around you. To me, I seem to get that way more when I am content with what I am doing.

Hal Sutton, 14-time PGA Tour winner

When I am in flow—in that sweet spot in time—everything kind of slows down. I feel very relaxed, very calm, very confident. I also see and feel shots come to me very quickly. No real swing thoughts, just kind of rhythm and timing. And again, everything just kind of seems to slow down a bit. I can't believe when it's over. I want to keep playing. Time goes by quickly even though you're doing everything slow.

Scott McCarron, 3-time PGA Tour winner

It feels slow. Slow, but not lethargic. The states themselves feel slow but not in a panicky type way. In a calm, relaxed way if you know what I mean.

Charles Howell III, 3-time PGA Tour winner

Despite attemps by golfers to explain it and theories put forth by scientists from various disciplines, there remains some variability in the scientific understanding of the transformation of time. Is there another dimension out there? Possibly. For now, it seems reasonable to say that the transformation of time is both a product and a producer of flow. Being in flow transforms how we experience time. Increasing our awareness of how we experience time increases the probability of getting into flow.

When golfers are in flow, time seems to slow down—to get heavy, leisurely, gentle, and soft as if they have all the time in the world, or at least all the time they think they need. Laced throughout their descriptions is that this transformation of time is also related to the rhythm that they feel, as when Adam Scott observed his state of flow by saying, "I just sort of slide into it, and before I know it I have this great rhythm and focus." These insights have the potential to provide great help for golfers, which we examine more closely in due course.

Control

Eight-time PGA Tour winner Adam Scott generated flow on Friday afternoon of the 2007 Memorial Tournament in beautiful Dublin, Ohio. During that round of golf he effortlessly birdied 9 of his first 12 holes. His 62 was 5 shots better than the next best golfer's 67 and an astounding 11 shots better than the average of the field that day.

To put this performance into perspective, the Memorial is one of four invitational tournaments on the PGA Tour to which only the best of the best are invited to play. That year the field included Phil Mickelson, Tiger Woods, Jim Furyk, Sergio Garcia, Chad Campbell, Heath Slocum, Camilo Villegas, Sean O'Hair, Justin Rose, Steve Stricker, and other dominant names. In short, 120 of the world's best golfers played the same course that day, and Adam was 11 shots better than their collective scoring average of 73.

Adam's flow state allowed him to stand on the 16th tee at 10 under par, staring down the real possibility of shooting golf's magical number of 59 on a challenging golf course. When he was later asked about what it felt like to play those 15 holes, Adam replied,

You have this rhythm in your body and you do everything right. I stood on the 12th tee and just swung an 8-iron and it finishes 10 feet. That's not that easy of a shot. But that's kind of how I do it when I'm going well. I have that much control it seems. Basically, I was just looking at my target and swinging the club and the ball goes there. I just try not to think too much about things and just hit it because the rhythm is just there.

You see again that Adam alludes to the rhythm that we previously talked about. In addition he mentions the amount of control that he has over his shots when he's going well. This notion is not uncommon. Golfers in flow often talk about feeling in total control of their game, able to stroke long downhill putts with perfect speed and hit long irons the perfect distance. Although they always talk about the amount of control that they feel, they universally state that forcing such control is impossible. If you're a golfer, then you fully understand the impossibility of trying to force a shot to go where you want it to go. That is true for golfers at all levels: The act of consciously trying to control is famously counterproductive and produces the kind of overthinking and subsequent tension that makes the control that emerges from mental freedom, and the corresponding flow states, virtually impossible to achieve.

To understand the paradox of control and make a huge leap toward getting into flow with more regularity, ask yourself two simple questions:

1. What is the purpose of practice in golf?
2. Why do professional golfers spend so much time rehearsing their golf swings on the driving range?

As simple and seemingly obvious as the answers to these questions are, I find that few golfers truly understand the purpose of their practice. Understanding the purpose of practice and the way that skills develop helps golfers transfer those skills to the golf course as well as create the best mind-set for peak performance.

As you delve a little further into the neuropsychological explanation of why we practice, you begin to uncover a mystifying and exciting universe—a universe that elucidates and deciphers Adam Scott's 11-shot thumping of the world's best golfers. This universe is inhabited by scientists in lab coats who rarely leave their labs long enough to think of Adam Scott or playing golf. I know, because I've spent time with these self-named lab geeks and have come to find that they are as passionate about their work as PGA Tour golfers are about their work. The result of their passion has been a decade of discovery about how learning takes place at a physical, structural, neural level.

It all begins with understanding a substance in the brain called myelin. Although scientists have known about myelin for years, they've spent much of that time ignoring its role in learning and skill development.

MYELIN MATTERS

To illustrate how learning occurs and why myelin should matter to you, consider an experiment that I recently conducted with a student in my sport psychology class at Rollins College. I set up cameras in the front of the classroom, where I have built a mock putting green. I ask the student to take the putter and try to make a 6-foot (2 m) putt on the artificial green that I've laid over the carpet. With the entire class watching, she lines up over the ball, aims the putter in the general direction of the hole, and makes a jerky, clumsy stroke that hits the ball without any grace or touch. The ball speeds by the hole, missing in both direction (it is left of the hole) and speed (as it rolls 6 feet past). The student pulls another ball in front of her, aims a little better, adjusts her feet, hips, and arms, and makes a softer, less chaotic, and overall better stroke. Although the second ball still misses the hole, it stops inches from the hole, an improvement in both direction and speed. The third try takes her less time to get into an even better position at address, less time to start her stroke, and less time to hit the ball, which rolls with flawless speed into the cup. She smiles and the class cheers.

What the class witnessed was our participant learning through the process of self-correction, with no instruction whatsoever. What's even better for my students is that I've captured it all on film so that the class can watch it a dozen times in slow motion to dissect exactly what happened.

We are able to see several things. As the trials proceeded, the student's focus changed. Rather than look out in the general direction of the hole, her eyes narrow in their focus. In succession, she begins to trace the track that the ball will take on its way toward the hole. With her eyes fixed on the target, she adjusts her hips, feet, and hands so that they are pointing more in the direction of the hole. She adjusts and readjusts her grip a few times until it feels just right. What began as a jerky, recoiled stroke becomes a more committed, determined, complete stroke that follows the ball down the line and into the hole. In the microseconds after the hit, we can see her eyes and head lift, because she is eager to see whether the ball is on line. This habit of peeking is something that I would correct in my clients.

But we are not able to see some of the other things that are happening. Underneath what we know as learning, a neurological process was taking place whereby electrical currents in the brain were firing, traveling down nerve fibers in the brain during every moment of the putting process (think of electricity traveling across the copper wires of an electric cord attached to your computer). One of the key differences between your computer cord and our participant is that the rubber cover around your computer's power cord is fixed. It doesn't change with use; a 1/4-inch (6 mm) cord remains a 1/4-inch cord even after a year's worth of use. For my student, however, the cord that covers the wire is changing. With each successive putt that she hits, an ever-increasing sheath of myelin was wrapping around her nerve fibers. Imagine that each successive pulse of electricity to your computer causes the rubber coating to become thicker. In effect, this is what myelin does to the neurons that create learning.

As we practice an action, myelin wraps and insulates the circuitry, allowing that circuitry to become, in subsequent actions, faster and more efficient. This is the neurological basis for what we commonly know as habit or, in sport terms, muscle memory. This process of myelination cuts across domains and activities. Practicing the piano, rehearsing a speech, and hitting a 9-iron all have one thing in common. They initiate the process of myelin wrapping nerve fibers, and this wrapping makes the neurons fire faster, with more accuracy and more efficiency.

The role of myelin in strengthening habit or muscle memory provides the basis for the adages regarding practice and habit:

Practice makes perfect.

Practice doesn't make perfect; it makes permanent.

We start by controlling our habits. Eventually our habits control us.

First, we make our habits. Then our habits make us.

AUTOMATICITY
AND SYNCHRONICITY

Let's examine more closely how this understanding of myelin and practice applies to golf. The two complaints that I've most frequently heard from golfers over the years have to do with (1) not being able to transfer their skills from the driving range to the golf course and (2) self-sabotaging good rounds of golf.

Research reveals that after a habit is strongly rooted in place, which is to say that after a behavior is sufficiently myelinated, that habit will be the most likely behavior to come out of a repertoire of behaviors. In other words, all by itself with no active, conscious effort, the habits that we create will emerge on their own from the practice and repetition that we've engaged in to help myelinate those circuits. This process is known as automaticity, whereby skills that we initially have to think about go underground and fire without conscious effort (think of how easily you write your name or answer your cell phone—that's automaticity and myelin at work).

As we practice, various brain regions work cohesively in a manner that is consistent with flow. This collaboration by the various brain regions, rather than the dominance of any one region, is responsible for the "quiet mind" that is often reported by athletes after they've been in flow. Flow is such a mentally efficient state of mind that its defining neural characteristic is synchronicity; the various parts work together as one.

AVOID GETTING IN YOUR OWN WAY

As you may have experienced in your life, the fastest way to undermine automaticity and internal cohesion is to try to think actively about the motor task that you are trying to enact. When we try to steer our putter face through the impact area or deliberately think about our club position at the top, we are inviting electronic impulses from our cortex, the part of the brain that is available to conscious awareness, into the temporal region, which is responsible for automatic motor patterns. The transfer of these impulses disrupts the coherence between the various brain regions. By the time that these processes make their way into conscious awareness, they typically come out in the following form of a frustrated golfer: "I feel like I am getting in my own way." What's the answer? Based on what we know about skill development, it could be as simple as this: Practice diligently and then trust your myelin.

A more thorough explanation tying into the paradox of control might be this: You've practiced your game. Through that practice you have deepened the habits by myelinating the neural circuitry. The myelin has insulated those circuits so that they will fire efficiently and effectively. The various regions of your brain work in harmony and become synched up through the myelination of nerve fibers. When you actively try to control the motor pattern (skill) that you are trying to execute, you interrupt the cohesion between the regions and undermine their habitual manner of functioning.

After reading this section, you should now have an understanding of why golfers sometimes experience a sense of the mind turning against itself. In reality the mind doesn't so much turn against itself as it falls out of sync when energizing a different module in the brain—the *thinking* part of the cortex. Focusing on the cluttering details of scores, outcomes, and mechanics energizes the cortex, which is pretty good at reading and doing math but is clueless about hitting a golf shot.

The actual hitting of the golf shot is primarily located in a different brain module, but the key factor isn't really which module is being called upon to what extent (just as it isn't left brain versus right brain, as some psychologists erroneously preach). Rather, it is the cohesion between the modules and across the regions that constitutes mental efficiency and leads to flow. Consciously thinking about and trying to control your golfing motor patterns interrupts the efficiency with

© PA Photos

A quiet mind and a sense of letting go pave the way for good control. Adam Scott regularly demonstrates admirable control on the course.

which your brain communicates with itself—with your body and your perceptual channels. Simply stated, trying to exert conscious control over your game interferes with your brain's ability to control it for you!

So when Adam Scott is effortlessly making nine birdies and is demonstrating total control over his game, he is gaining that control by not trying to control his shots. What is he giving up control of? In short, he is actively giving up trying to control the unconscious—and uncontrollable—region of the brain that learns and executes motor processes such as those used to play golf. When golfers express that they need to get out of their own way, what they are really expressing is the need to quiet their cortex, to allow neural efficiency, and to let the myelin-wrapped neurons do their thing. One phrase that universally resonates with golfers is "Trust it." Translation: Trust your habits, trust your feels, and, most important, trust your myelin.

So far we've established that practice myelinates neural networks to sharpen skills and that the quickest way to interrupt those skills is to think about controlling the movements—the backswing, the putting stroke, grip, posture, aim—that are ultimately beyond our control. In golf the events that lead to the flow-killing overcontrol typically revolve around results. When golfers are not scoring well, they tend to begin thinking and trying to overcontrol their thoughts and golf swings, which is impossible. They begin fighting themselves in the sense that their brain regions are in conflict with one another. The quality of their golf then typically goes into a free fall. For that reason, the mantra of many sport psychologists is "Process, process, process." We have to let go of the things over which we have no control.

IF THE BUDDHA PLAYED GOLF

Thinking about the paradox of control invites us to cross the bridge from neuroscience to philosophy because as much as modern-day empirical scientists want to measure and quantify everything at a structural level, a great deal of debate continues in academic circles about the relationship between materialism, spirituality, and belief. Indeed, research shows that a person's mind-set and beliefs about controllability influence the syncing up of his or her neural efficiency. Research has shown, for instance, that spirituality plays a strong psychological role in helping people control their behavior and overcome their dependencies (Dingfelder 2003). MIT, known as the most research-intensive university on the planet, has sponsored conferences and symposia at the Mind & Life Institute, which explores the relationship between Western science and Tibetan Buddhism.

Through such collaborations, researchers are beginning to report that many monks are able to avoid the typical startle reflex and emotional jolts that most Westerners demonstrate when they hear loud noises. Beliefs serve as the filters of experience, and it is in this area that expert performance will make strides in the coming years.

The implications of the connection between mind-set, or beliefs, and behavior for golfers are many. First, they can learn to disengage from results and exercise vast amounts of patience and composure. For example, when we interpret a bogey as a negative experience, a corresponding physiological effect naturally occurs. The brain sends signals for the body to create stress hormones such as cortisol. Cortisol leads to stress and tension. Stress and tension compromise our ability to swing the club. Conversely, if we are able to exercise the mental discipline to interpret a bogey as just part of golf, to accepting the bogey or laugh at it, we won't get the corresponding doses of cortisol that lead to the levels of stress and tension that compromise our performance on subsequent shots.

In this way the ideas and beliefs that a golfer chooses to construct about the game really do matter. Those beliefs have corresponding physical and physiological consequences. Letting go of overcontrol boils down to trusting that the practice you are doing will ultimately produce greater efficiency and better results. Notice that I said "ultimately." Focusing on results in the short term and expecting too much too soon can throw us off the path of improvement. Because a lag effect occurs between practice and the brain's ability to integrate that practice into a behavioral repertoire, golfers often lose confidence when they don't get immediate results in all areas. I can think of no surer path to self-destruction and deterioration.

Historically, coaches have talked about having faith, having confidence, or believing in themselves. The only thing required is a little patience and understanding of the lag effect of myelination and skill development. After you understand that good habits will show up eventually, remaining patient becomes easier; in golf, the more you can remain patient, the less likely you are to interrupt your habits and ability to get into flow. For instance, Sean O'Hair and I had been working on teaching him how to play patient golf. Before the 2011 season, he knew that impatience was interrupting his ability to play well. But knowing that something is a problem is often a far stretch from knowing how to fix that problem. Knowing *that* and knowing *how* are cousins rather than siblings.

Only after a full year of consistently practicing patience with the same discipline that he practiced his wedge game and putting was

Sean finally able to say that he played four full days of patient golf. By practicing patience independent of results for a full year, Sean was finally able to accept his shots, maintain his rhythm, keep his focus, see his targets with clarity, and have his brain work with him rather than against him in the pursuit of great golf. The result was a T2 at the 2012 Sony Open in Hawaii, a tournament that Sean described as "unrushed, patient, almost easy." The most important aspect of that tournament occurred when he started his third round with a double bogey and proceeded to be three over par through five holes. He used those bogeys as an opportunity to remind himself of the importance of staying patient and of not forcing anything in golf. He settled into the rhythm of his routine and made six birdies coming in for an outstanding finish. Although not all of us have it in us to birdie 6 of our last 12 holes, we can still learn a great lesson: Handling your adversity with the calm patience of the Buddha keeps your mind and body in balance, and that balance enables good golf to follow bad scores.

DEVELOPING PATIENCE AND TRUST

The departure from being a results-oriented golfer to becoming a patient, process-oriented golfer requires more than a quick talk with a mind coach. Because patience applies to all areas of life, becoming a patient human being often requires a full philosophical shift in how we view ourselves, how we view other people, and what our values are when it comes to life itself. My golfers who practice patience not only think about their golf swings and routines but also consider golf in the larger realm of life. My golfers read Gracian, Kierkegaard, Aristotle, and Plato. They consider the fundamental questions in life and the way in which they flow into golf. They meditate on the Greek concepts of eudaemonia and arête—happiness and living an excellent life. In the final assessment, they all conclude that patience truly is a virtue. This philosophical buy-in leads to better golf by enabling the cognitive mechanism required for optimal performance.

Consider Tiger Woods' observation on patience. When asked his strategy for closing the gap on the leaders of a tournament, he replied:

As I said, the art here is just letting the round mature, and there's no need to force it. Just go ahead and just capitalize on certain holes, and just because I'm at 1-under par doesn't mean I need to go force things. As I said, let the round mature. I had plenty of holes left, but the conditions were benign and just go ahead and get it done, and it happened.

What Golfers Can Learn From Steve Jobs

Steve Jobs, the genius founder of Apple computer, was philosophical about his craft. His philosophy of success perfectly captures the paradox of control, the importance of belief, and the virtue of acceptance. When invited to give the commencement address at Stanford University in 2005, he gave a brief but powerful speech titled "Stay Hungry, Stay Foolish," in which he told three stories that summarized the path that his life had taken, a path that allowed him to amass a net worth of over three billion dollars, change the world, and alter the computing habits of a planet.

The first story that Jobs told was about dropping out of college because he couldn't see the value in it. Dropping out of college afforded him the opportunity to drop *in* on things about which he was curious; in this case he dropped in on a calligraphy class. Ten years later when he was designing the first Mac, he included the multiple typefaces and fonts that he learned about in calligraphy. These multiple fonts are now standard on all personal computers. "It was," he said, "impossible to connect the dots looking forward when I was in college. But it was very, very clear looking back 10 years later."

His second story told how he and his friend started Apple in a garage and in 10 years built it into a two-billion dollar company. Soon after a creative difference occurred between Jobs and someone whom they had hired to run the company, the board of directors decided to fire Jobs from the company that he had built. "I didn't see it then, but it turned out that getting fired from Apple was the best thing that could ever have happened to me." The massive shift in his life enabled Jobs to enter into the most creative period of his life, to start the most successful animation studio in the world (Pixar), and to meet his wife and fall in love.

His final story told of being a cancer survivor, an experience that taught him the importance of making every day matter.

Jobs told the story of three experiences that, in the moment, he believed to be dreadful. When looking retrospectively at his life, he realized that they were the best things that could have happened to him, that a purpose was attached to those experiences, although he could not see that purpose as the experiences were happening.

His message at the end of his speech was powerful and seems perfectly tailored to a golfer looking to make sense of the setbacks in his or her game:

You can't connect the dots looking forward; you can only connect them looking backward. So you have to trust that the dots will somehow connect in your future. You have to trust something—your gut, destiny, life, karma, whatever. This approach has never let me down, and it has made all the difference in my life.

I like to use a Taoist parable with my golfers to help them understand the manner in which our reactions play out over the course of time and why underreacting to situations can often be beneficial. The story speaks to the idea of control, but most important, of letting go:

An old, poor farmer in ancient China worked a small plot of land with his teenage son. During this time, horses were considered a sign of rare wealth; the richest person in the province owned no more than a few of them. One day, a wild horse galloped into the town, jumped the old farmer's fence, and began grazing on his land. According to local law, this meant that the horse now rightfully belonged to him and his family. The boy could hardly contain his joy, but the father put his hand on his son's shoulder and said, "Good luck or bad luck, who knows?" The next day, the horse, not surprisingly, made its escape back to the mountains, and the boy was heartbroken. "Who knows what's good or bad?" his father said again, with the same composure. On the third day, the horse returned with a dozen wild horses following. The boy could hardly believe his good luck. "We're rich!" he cried, to which the father replied, "Good luck or bad luck, who knows?" On the fourth day, the boy climbed on one of the wild horses and was thrown, breaking his leg. His father ran to get the doctor; soon both of them were attending to the boy, who was moaning and complaining about his miserable fate. The old farmer wiped the boy's forehead with a wet cloth, looked deeply into his eyes, and said directly, "My son, who knows what is good or bad? It's too soon to tell. Be patient and we'll know in time." And on the fifth day, the province went to war, and army recruiters came through the town and conscripted the eligible young men—except for one with a broken leg.

As the parables suggests, it is true that we rarely know the full value of an experience while the experience is taking place, or even shortly thereafter. Many experiences that we initially interpret as bad turn out, in the fullness of time, to have been a blessing. The terrible summer of golf may be the very thing that propels a golfer to find the proper teacher. An abysmal grade in college may teach a valuable lesson about accountability and rigor.

The opposite is also true. Those experiences that feel like great blessing can, in the fullness of time, backfire if not put into the proper context. Nowhere is this more apparent than in studies of lottery winners. Although the numbers vary depending on which study you read and how you define going broke, estimates are that roughly 70 percent of those who win the lottery or encounter significant financial windfalls will squander their winnings within 15 years. Compounding their financial problems is the fact that they are also likely to alienate their families and lose friends along the way.

Ultimately, the true significance of an experience is always contextual, always to be made sense of in distant time, and as true in golf as it is in life patterns. A wayward drive on Thursday may be precisely what's needed to uncover the swing flaw that allows for the good drive on Sunday. Missed putts may teach us how to be patient or how to monitor grip pressure. Being sidelined with injury may be the thing that provides us motivational fuel for the rest of the season, reminding us how much we love to play the game. Knowing the value of an experience is almost always difficult while, or even soon after, the experience itself has taken place. For that reason, my golfers and I root our philosophy in patience and learning.

There is something freeing about trusting in your life path, and that perspective makes all the difference to golfers both on and off the golf course. You will see this perspective highlighted in a later chapter when you learn about the turning points that enabled my golfers, especially Matt Kuchar and Sean O'Hair, to win their tournaments, but for now the important lesson that emanates and relates directly to flow is to learn how to let go of the uncontrollable factors in your life, to turn yourself over to an experience, and to trust your habits and life path. More directly relevant to golfers is that the confounding double bogeys, the pattern of choking, and the maddening lack of improvement may (and often do) carry important learning experiences that we are wise to look for.

WHY IT'S HARD TO LET GO

Many elite athletes are self-described control nuts who feel a compulsive need to control every aspect of their life and their game. Sometimes, this trait helps breed the excellence that gets them to the highest levels of their sport. Embracing patience and trust means changing their whole approach to their sport.

As described in his autobiography *Open*, tennis champion Andre Agassi was obsessive about every aspect of his game. He never let anyone pack (or, for that matter, even touch) the bag that he packed for a match. He had a place for everything and was able to tell upon picking it up whether it was even a fraction of a pound underweight, which meant that it was missing something essential.

This neurotic, habitual need for control often allows elite athletes to outrace the others in their generational cohort and get to the highest level in the first place. But this trait may also get in the way of the skills that it helps to develop, nurture, and sharpen.

Most successful players have been trained to pay attention to detail, and they've learned that carelessness in golf can mean the difference between a positive and negative outcome. To some extent, the compulsion to control is a big part of a striving athlete's makeup and success. This attribute makes it all the more difficult for accomplished golfers to relinquish the control that they rely on.

But as Sun Tzu teaches, all strengths can also be weaknesses, and this is nowhere more evident than in the metric of control. The urge to control every aspect of the game can often lead to a type of overcontrol that sets the stage for performance paralysis. Golfers who come to me in this state often describe their game as if they are living in a self-created psychological straightjacket.

Can people like this give up control and surrender themselves to the experience? Yes. And just as striving for total control over everything in their lives leads athletes down the path to excellence, when they learn to let go, they get into flow and are able to have greater control over their golf shots.

GOLF LIKE A NASCAR DRIVER

Many professional golfers talk with familiarity and reverence about NASCAR drivers. Because they understand that mistakes in racing end up in dangerous and race-ending crashes rather than mere bogeys, they admire the way that NASCAR drivers performing at the highest speeds must trust their unconscious minds to react rather than vainly try to keep up with conscious thinking. Roberto Castro, who in 2007 won the Byron Nelson Award for being the nation's top golfer while a senior at Georgia Tech, alluded to that metaphor when he was playing well.

Roberto visualizes a racecar going around the curve with two wheels up, just barely. Two wheels are on the inside curve, and two wheels are off the ground. To win the race, you've got to be willing to risk pushing it to the edge. The thrill, as Tom Watson said, is that you don't know whether you can hold it. But that's the thrill! The fine line in golf is that you're going all in on your shots, trying to be fearless without being reckless, and maintaining confidence in the face of a humbling game. It is in this zone of proximity where the flow state hides, waiting to be gently, discerningly beckoned.

Other golfers also use the racing metaphor when they describe golf. When they overcontrol the game, the disastrous metaphors are telling: "I was steering the ball around," "I was squeezing the wheel too tight," "I was holding on too tight," and "I couldn't let it go" are phrases that I often hear from professionals and amateurs alike. Obviously, this counterproductive kind of control is precisely the type of mind-set that golfers need to learn how to prevent.

I talk more about how to prevent this obsessive focus on control in later chapters, but for now it may be helpful to listen to the voices of those who have made it a lifelong vocation to explore the finest details of the game. Here are some examples of how top golfers describe the flow experience when they are finally able to relinquish control.

It tells you what to do. You don't have to think about it. You certainly can't control it so you go along for the ride.

David Toms, 13-time PGA Tour winner, 2001 PGA champion

You go back to the basic fundamentals you've been working on. You just focus on those and go ahead and trust it and make a good swing. I guess in a way it happens so fast you have to give that control away a little bit and go ahead and trust it.

Jim Furyk, 16-time PGA Tour winner, 2003 U.S. Open champion

One of my keys is to give up control to gain control. When I'm swinging, just go ahead and get it up and swing and hit it. More often than not, it's going to go where I am looking. If I try to control a shot too much, to keep it in the fairway or keep it in bounds, my body gets tense, my muscles tense, and I don't make a flowing swing.

Scott McCarron, 3-time PGA Tour winner

You have to give up, free yourself up a lot. Say to yourself, "I have worked hard, I know what I have to do, and I am good at it, now I am going to let myself go do it." It is hard to let yourself play golf, especially when your confidence is low. For me, I have to sometimes give myself permission to relax and go play.

Davis Love III, 20-time PGA Tour winner

When we get it in golf, I am out here 200 yards from the green, but I know where my ball is going to go and I know how it is going to get there. And there is no second-guessing. It is just going to happen. It will happen! And it does. And it's neat.

Curtis Strange, 17-time PGA Tour winner, 2-time U.S. Open champion

There is no thinking involved whatsoever. No extra thinking. Just very calm. A sense of knowing. I don't hope or wish. I just have a sense of knowing. Even before I hit the shot, I know where the ball is going to go. I am not trying to hope it there, or wish it there, or guide it there. There is this sense that I know where it is going to go and that it is going to be good. One hundred percent I know where the ball is going to go. I know the club I've pulled is the right club. I know exactly where the wind blows. It's a bit uncanny but you really do feel that certain . . . in that much control.

Charles Howell III, 3-time PGA Tour winner

The more that you try to control things, the further away you tend to get from having control. Consequently, overcontrol leads to clutter, to tension, and ultimately to poor golf shots and even worse putts. What are you supposed to make of the great clichés of golf, such as "Free it up," "Let it go," or "Let it happen" rather than "Make it happen"? We all know what coaches are alluding to when they say these things, but how do we get beyond the metaphorical? PGA Tour player Bryce Molder helps us refine our understanding:

I want to focus on making a good swing and not caring where the ball ends up. I don't want to get in the habit of trying to guide a ball anywhere, so I have to care about trusting my swing without caring, per se, where it lands.

Hence, the most control that you'll ever have in golf is by giving up trying to control outcomes and trying to overcontrol motor patterns such as putting and golf swing—an oxymoron in any language but also a truism. On this note of puzzlement we move to the next paradox in the flow states of PGA Tour golfers: the paradox of effort.

3

Effort

Whether they play the game regularly as competitive golfers or play for recreational or social reasons, all participants of golf agree that golf is a difficult game. People may use words like *beautiful, fun, complex, maddening, sublime, addictive,* and even *fulfilling,* but few players ever use the word *easy* to describe golf on any sort of long-term, regular basis.

Of course, many people believe that certain people were born to play golf, that the game comes easily for them, and that some athletes are simply naturals. Indeed, many people view golfing royalty much like other royalty and assume that the throne was conferred upon superior players as a birthright or a happy accident of genetics. Those who excel at golf are viewed in the same manner as kids who are considered child prodigies in music or academics.

The media have fueled this misperception. Images of a two-year old Tiger Woods hitting golf balls on the *Mike Douglas Show* in 1978 are now part of our collective consciousness. More recently, video of a young Rory McIlroy swinging a golf club in his living room at the age of three was shown on television, and his swing then was compared with his current swing. The conclusion seemed to be that Rory was born great, that he was born with the swing that was winning him all those tournaments. A common assumption is that greatness is conferred upon our top golfers rather than earned through hard work, practice, and dedication and that these players are exempt from setbacks, adversity, slumps, and the full spectrum of distractions and emotions that regularly plague golfers all across the world.

Nothing could be further from the truth.

When he met Tiger at the 2010 Ryder Cup, McIlroy realized that even he had bought into some of the hype:

You put him on such a high pedestal. And then you meet the guy. . . . Before I'd met him, I thought he was super human. But once you meet him, you realize he's just a normal guy who works hard on his game, and gets the most out of it.

In a landmark paper that is widely studied in the arena of performance psychology, Anders Ericsson popularized the concept of the 10,000-hour rule. Ericsson argues that expert performance is the result of a tremendous amount of deliberate practice. Specifically, according to Ericsson, it takes 10,000 hours (20 hours for 50 weeks a year for 10 years = 10,000) of deliberate practice to become an expert in almost anything. Although debate continues within academic circles about the exact numbers, researchers generally agree that the only path toward expert performance is through abundant repetition, deliberately crafted, over long periods.

I have spent 15 years traveling with, teaching, learning from, and studying the world's greatest golfers. I can attest that they all worked hard for a long time. Players do not excel at the game because the game comes more easily to them than it does to everyone else. They have become the best in large part because of their ability to persist and to absorb the difficulties of bad golf better than those who fail to achieve excellence. In other words, regardless of talent or pedigree, no one is immune from golf's inherent difficulty. If you plan to improve, you shouldn't expect to avoid adversity; rather, you should prepare your mind to absorb adversity. Anyone who doubts this fact should track the careers of the top 100 junior golfers over a 20-year period. If excellence were primarily inherited, then the attrition rate would not be as large as it is and the game would not leave behind so many casualties.

This explanation is not meant to be negative or discouraging. I simply believe that the best way to improve at golf is to be realistic and accurate about the inherent nature of the game so that you can effectively prepare for the implicit ups and downs. What do you say, for instance, about a game in which one of the best players in the world, Sergio Garcia, can make a 12 on a par 4 (as he did at the 2012 World Golf Championships at Doral)? What do you say about a game in which another one of the best players in the world, Ryo Ishikawa, can shoot an 85 at the 2011 PGA Championship in a round that included five double bogeys, no birdies, and one triple bogey?

In a book titled *Extraordinary Minds*, Harvard educator and psychologist Howard Gardner dismisses the notion that greatness can ever emerge solely from genetic traits. He points out that Mozart practiced so hard under the tutelage of his father that his skill was myelinated just as any other skill would be. Further, Gardner explains, to move forward, "Mozart had to make sharp and difficult breaks—a break from his teachers and models, a break from the accepted practices, and most painfully, a break from his father."

Similarly, besides spending a great deal of time honing their craft, all top golfers whom I have met have had to endure painful experiences and failures. Outstanding players not only suffer occasional defeat in competition but also face adversity on a daily basis. In their hours of regular practice, golfers miss shots they "should" make and keep right on practicing. Through this relentless dedication to work through adversity, golfers become more resilient.

Like any other habit, resilience is strengthened through experience and practice. Albert Bandura, former president of the American Psychological Association, coined the term *normative failure* to explain why successful people are generally those who fail the most and keep on persisting. "When failure is the norm," Bandura contends, "resilience becomes second nature."

Renowned for beating balls until his hands bled, Ben Hogan was famous for his work ethic and his success: 64 PGA Tour wins, 9 major championships, World Golf Hall of Fame membership. Common golfing lore has it that, while he was alive, Hogan would have a recurring dream in which he would make 17 hole-in-ones, only to lip out on the 18th hole for a 2.

Golf torments and teases golfers of all levels. Just when you are ready to quit, that magical round appears. Then with newly raised expectations, you can't putt, can't drive, or can't chip. You go through stretches where you hit it pure, but can't make a putt and as soon as you figure out your putting, your driver takes a vacation. With rare exception, these are the recurring, agonizing tales of golfers everywhere.

In terms of the mental suffering involved, golf shares commonalities with distance running, cycling, and triathlon. A client once told me that golf does to the brain what boxing does to the body!

GOLF IS NOT AN EASY GAME— EXCEPT WHEN IT IS

Against this backdrop of overwhelming challenge we find the anomaly of the flow state. When golfers describe playing golf while in flow, they almost universally report the game as being effortless. Even more interesting is that the aftermath of effortless flow leaves golfers feeling exhausted and in a state of fatigue that we see only after an athlete has expended enormous amounts of energy and effort (this is the reason why it is often difficult to follow a great round of golf with another great round of golf).

Thus the paradox: The round itself feels energized and effortless, but afterward players realize how much vigor and effort they used to energize their flow state. The abundance of focus and mental sharpness aligns with physical exactness to produce a result that feels unforced, almost transcendent. Golfers feel at one with their task, and that task, whether it's putting or swinging, feels as natural as breathing and walking—as easy as "seeing it and doing it."

A great deal of preparation goes into setting the stage for flow, but when they are in flow, golfers describe the process as effortless. Flow awakens in people the feeling that, at that particular time, they are capable of anything to which they set their minds. Words like *smooth*, *rhythm*, *calm*, and *natural* abound in descriptions of the effortless sense that flow provides.

Scott McCarron said, "When I am in flow, golf is effortless. It is unleashed. Smooth power, however you want to call it. It does not look or feel like I am swinging hard, but I am actually hitting it farther."

Similarly, 2011 U.S. Open winner Rory McIlroy reflected on a flow state that happened to him when he was 16 years old.

> *I shot the course record 61 at Portrush when I was 16, so that was a pretty good round. But you know, it was very funny, on the golf course—I can still vividly remember that 61. I can remember nearly every shot. And today I got myself in a very similar state of mind. I don't know what to call it, call it the zone or whatever you want to—but I was just seeing my shots, I was hitting them. If I put myself in tricky spots; I was getting it up-and-down. I was seeing putts go in. I was reading the lines. It's pretty cool when it happens because it doesn't happen often.*

In 2003 14-time PGA Tour winner Kenny Perry shot a 61 in the third round of the Colonial. After the experience he made the following statement:

> *My rhythm is better this week than I've ever had it in my life. I feel like I'm swinging real easy at it and the ball is really going far. And it was just very simple out there for me today. I don't know, I guess it was what they talk about, the zone thing, and whatever it was, I was in it today. It was just very easy for me today.*

How can we reconcile the conventional wisdom that golf is a brutal, merciless, mind-bogglingly difficult game that gets the best of even the most gifted, diligent golfers in the world with the descriptions of the game provided by players such as Adam Scott, who confessed, "Basically, I was just looking at my target and swinging the club and the ball goes there"? Think about Rory McIlroy's description of shooting that 61 as being as easy as walking in the park and Kenny Perry's use of the words *simple* and *easy* to describe the 61 that he shot.

At this point I hope that I have only slightly confused you. In penetrating the mystery of flow for the past 15 years, I spent many nights feeling somewhat confused as well. But I can tell you that although these paradoxes may seem confusing, if you keep trying to understand the essence of flow, your pursuit will be justified.

BECOMING ONE WITH THE CLUB

Consistent with the unforced effort that golfers describe, athletes in flow often report feelings of attachment with their equipment and the tools of their particular trade. For instance, cyclists describe the bike as feeling like an extension of their own bodies, almost like an exoskeleton. For rowers in a regatta, the oar feels like an extension of the body and they can actually feel the water better. Golfers who have been in flow often describe the golf club as being an extension of their hands and arms. Their sense of feel with the club is as sensitive as it is with their own hand.

If you've ever been in flow while playing golf, you are familiar with this phenomenon. You have this overall sensation of being connected to every aspect of the process of playing golf. Everything . . . flows. Your thoughts flow, and various parts of your body—shoulders, arms, torso, legs, hands, eyes—work in unison. Everything, including your equipment, works as a cohesive unit. Although it is crazy to think about the golf ball making decisions on its own, a sense of destiny and cooperation materializes between golfers and their equipment as they pick the right club for the right shot. And when they pick the club, they do so with confidence, with no second-guessing. And when they put the club into their hands, the fit, length, weight, look, and feel are all perfect. In my camp, that is, among the golfers with whom I work, we refer to this occurrence as a time when the machine is working, an analogy that captures how machines function smoothly because many parts are working together in unison.

U.S. Open winner Jim Furyk captured this aspect of flow perfectly:

The club just feels good in your hands. My hands feel different on the club. My hands feel long and thin rather than short and stubby. It makes the grip feel small, yet really comfortable. You can place the ball right where you want to, and be so confident about it . . . and be able to play effortlessly.

Nick Potts/PA Photos

Even for pros like Keegan Bradley, the sense of effortless effort experienced by golfers in flow comes only after a great deal of conscious, deliberate practice.

British Open champion Steward Cink reported similar impressions:

I don't feel like I have a club in my hand, rather, everything, including the club and my body, feels like one in the same. It is almost as if I am tossing the ball where I want it to go. It is that easy.

This sense of connectedness and ease is automaticity at its best, and it's a function of the thousands of hours of deliberate practice that myelinate our habits. We practice for precisely that reason: So that when it comes time to be on the golf course, we select the right club, go through a routine, execute the appropriate shots, and accept the results without engaging in a whole lot of extraneous thoughts. The impression of the club being an extension of ourselves is a sign that the brain that is working optimally. The brain has built-in filters that block out nonessential information and key in on the things that matter. There is nothing extraordinary about this, because we do it every day. When you first learn a physical task such as roller skating or riding a bike, you have to think about how to balance, steer, and brake. Over time the physical tasks require less conscious thought;

they become natural and automatic. The real fun comes when you feel so connected to your skates or your bike that you move as one!

For the golfer in flow, the brain filters the extraneous, zeros in on the task, and provides us with the wonderful perception of being in easy harmony with the equipment and the game itself.

ENERGY AND EFFORT

When you spend a lot of time traveling with golfers, one of the things you notice is that people involved in the traveling show known as the PGA Tour become road weary around the end of June. By the time September rolls around, many of the world's best golfers are walking around like zombies with dead eyes. Flow states noticeably diminish in frequency. The hope, energy, enthusiasm, motivation, and effort characteristic of late spring and early summer are replaced, for many, by a limp to the finish line. This state of psychological atrophy is the antiflow.

Although flow states seem effortless, the body and mind are actually working extremely hard. Think of driving a V12 Ferrari Testarossa with 390 horsepower. As you accelerate in the Ferrari, it may seem as if the car isn't expending any energy at all, but in fact it is burning a great deal of fuel. Similarly, an F-16 fighter jet can fly with effortless lift, but that level of performance burns an enormous amount of fuel. These two analogies fit the flow state on many levels. Flow states are the most premium and optimal of mental states. They are best in class. They are also efficient and powerful. And like the Ferrari and the F-16, they consume a great deal of energy, though you don't feel it at the time.

The energy used to fuel flow needs to be restocked, and if it isn't, golfers fall into antiflow. For that reason, many of the world's best players vary their playing schedules. They often choose to play three or four weeks in a row and then rest for a couple of weeks so that they can replenish their physical and emotional energy in the hope that they can generate flow during the next cycle. Johnny Miller and Phil Mickelson, who both preferred to play many early season tournaments, garnered few of their career victories in the second half of the year.

The links between subconscious control and effort are abundant. By trusting your habits and engaging in implicit (rather than busy and verbally explicit) thinking, you are essentially reducing the communication between motor and nonmotor regions of the brain. A gradual withdrawal of conscious, particularly verbal, thoughts about the golf swing occurs as a golfer slides into flow. As control gradually rises, the game of golf should feel more effortless.

Because the purpose of this chapter is descriptive rather than prescriptive, I will wait to expand on how you can harness the power of this effortless effort. For now I simply ask that you make sense of effortless effort and appreciate your brain's ability to myelinate and ultimately, the power of automaticity.

Here are some other descriptions of flow that reflect the sense of effortless excellence that golfers experience.

> *When I'm in it, golf is effortless. Things just seem to happen rather than you working hard to make them happen. It becomes a more natural, more rhythmic flow to your game or your stroke or your swing than trying to be repetitive and mechanical.*
>
> **Davis Love III, 20-time PGA Tour winner**

> *You get over it, and there is really not any doubt in your mind how you want to play the putt for whatever reason. You just look up and you are seeing right where you want to putt it. Every putt that has break, you are just seeing right to that point where you want to putt it until it breaks and your speed is really good. It is kind of like playing with the bank's money in Vegas. You just don't feel like you can lose. You got the big "cush."*
>
> **John Huston, 7-time PGA Tour winner**

> *Effortless. 100 percent effortless. I'd say effortful is trying too hard. Every shot feels forced. There's a "try" element in the game, in the shot. Flow is totally effortless. There is no try. There is no anything. It just is. It's absolutely zero trying. No effort. Zero. It just happens.*
>
> **Charles Howell III, 3-time PGA Tour winner**

> *To me when things are flowing, things seem to go so easy, it is effortless. Calmness, no panic, everything is under control. I think it is when effort and talent come together is when you reach flow.*
>
> **Hal Sutton, 14-time PGA Tour winner**

What an elegant insight Hal provides: "when effort and talent come together." In a sense, that combination is precisely what generates flow—a great deal of past effort combined with the inherent talent, and the trust in both the effort and the talent—to allow the combination to pay off.

Awareness

Everything about golf indicates that the athletes are in pursuit of an objective. Whether it is to shoot a particular score, win a match, or practice a certain shot, golfers behave as if achieving their objective is all they have in mind. This purposeful, outcome-oriented behavior is even more prominent in competition in which diversions that draw attention to the score are plentiful. On the PGA Tour, money lists, leaderboards, and various statistics that measure every possible outcome abound—scoring average, proximity to the hole, putting averages, which side of the fairway tends to be missed, up and down percentage, strokes gained putting, and FedEx Cup points!

In this results- and outcome-driven context the paradox of awareness emerges. Although people are going after outcomes, they completely lose track of the outcomes, get lost in the moment, and turn themselves over to the experience that they are having. In these cases, playing golf becomes almost ancillary to enjoyment of and immersion in the experience of the moment.

Consider the case of Matt Kuchar at the 2002 Honda Classic, where he shot a final-round 66, including a back-nine 30, to claim his first PGA Tour victory. Here are the facts. Matt signed up for the tournament. He drove to the golf course every single day that week and practiced. He was in a competitive frame of mind. He knew where he stood at the end of each day. He was, by all measures, engaging in what psychologists call purposeful, goal-directed behavior. He was there to achieve a desired, measureable outcome: winning a PGA Tour event. All of his explicit behaviors that week demonstrated that Kuchar had an outcome in mind and was working toward it.

But during that final round of golf, a change took place. Matt's awareness shifted to a quiet, calm, transcendent state of being immersed in the totality of the experience. Instead of becoming more focused, more intense, and more attuned to his score, Matt went blurry. He relaxed, zoned out, and detached from the intensity and pressure of the back nine on Sunday. And because he turned himself over to the experience, Matt won his first PGA Tour event.

To gain insight into the shift that took place for Matt Kuchar, let's examine the following passage from his postround transcript:

> **REPORTER:** *Take us through the emotions of the day when you started the final round. You had Joey in front of you and Mike Weir, and you knew it was going to be a shootout today, didn't you?*
>
> **MATT KUCHAR:** I wasn't paying much attention to any of that. To win the event, I was sure I needed to go low. But I never put a number in mind. I never paid attention. I didn't really look at what scores the leaders shot, how many back I was. I went out there to the first tee and I hit the first tee shot. I didn't look at a leaderboard and didn't know how I stood. The 17th green is the first leaderboard I looked at.
>
> Actually, I got in the scorer's tent and I'm adding up my scores, and, of course, you go hole by hole. And I add up my scores, compared to what the scorecard says on each nine, and I see I shot a 35 on the front. And I add up the back nine on the little marker's scores of my notes, and I see "1-under, 2-under, 3-under, 4-under, 5-under." Is that right? I had to triple-check that I shot 5-under on the backside. I didn't even know that I went that low on the back. I must have triple- or quadruple-checked that that was the proper score. And sure enough, going about it just like Coach Heppler said my freshman year, six years ago. And I came out with a victory. It was exciting for me.

Note that some of Matt's observations seem to be in direct opposition to his goal-oriented behaviors.

FOCAL AND PERIPHERAL AWARENESS

Like Matt, golfers in flow pay close attention to the task at hand, take in events around them that are helpful or neutral, and are immune to distractions and pressures. Strange as it may sound, the ability to do this isn't unusual. Let's look at the science.

Consciousness theorists often refer to two states of awareness: focal and peripheral. Focal awareness occurs when we concentrate on something at the forefront of our awareness. For example, someone watching a Hitchcock film in a darkened theatre is usually demonstrating focal awareness, especially during the most dramatic and suspenseful scenes. Peripheral awareness occurs when we track marginal or background events while focusing on something else. Using the same example, the person watching that Hitchcock film might be marginally aware of the smell of popcorn, spot an imperfection in the screen, or notice that the temperature in the movie theatre is a little chilly.

When golfers are in this zone of peripheral awareness, when they are attending to things other than their score or the mechanics of their swing and letting automaticity take place, they often have their best rounds of golf.

When discussing their flow experiences on the golf course, golfers often report feeling hyperaware of everything around them, even though their attention is focused exclusively on the task of playing one shot at a time. Thus, the paradox of awareness in flow is that athletes' attention focuses like a laser on the only thing that really matters: the current shot. While they are hyperfocused, however, they are also able to process, on some level, many features of the surrounding environment—a breeze, a change in temperature, a shadow, a distant sound—or any subtle change in their internal states, such as metabolism, mood, energy, rhythm, or the tempo of themselves or their playing partners.

Curtis Strange, 2-time U.S. Open champion, 17-time PGA Tour winner, and NCAA champion, describes the experience this way:

Everything slows down. Honest to God, I am so aware of everything, but then very little matters, if that makes sense. Everything slows down. The positive thoughts are there, and there are no secondary thoughts.

LOOKING INWARD AND OUTWARD

Flow researchers suggest that the merging of awareness is not only between focal and peripheral but also between internal and external. Specifically, they suggest that people go through their lives with their focus largely attuned to one of two things: their internal frame of mind or the physical undertaking that is right in front of them. In other words, people are either internally self-focused or externally task focused. This idea may explain why golf can be so simple for young golfers. In the tender years before they've developed a full sense of themselves, they can simply focus on the task in front of them. They don't have the attention or ability to do much more beyond that.

When golfers seek my help because their once-quiet minds are now full of clutter and confusion, they often talk about having moved from task orientation to self-orientation. Specifically, they report that they used to stand over a shot and be aware only of the shot itself. Whether it was a drive or a putt, the shot itself was what mattered. The shot occupied both their focal and peripheral awareness.

After a few years of getting emotionally battered and beaten up by the game, golfers stand over those same shots and instead of thinking about hitting a shot at a target, they think of themselves, their lives, and what the outcome of that shot would mean to them (What happens if I don't pull this off? How will I feel? Will I be embarrassed or frustrated? What do I get if I succeed?) As you might imagine, focusing on the self and the consequences of playing well or poorly rather than on the shot itself does not help anyone consistently hit quality golf shots.

According to Mihaly Csikszentmihalyi, the Hungarian psychology professor widely acknowledged as the architect of the concept of flow, during the flow state these two things—self and task—fuse together so that who you are and what you are doing become one in the same. In certain respects, you become one with what you are doing.

HEIGHTENED CONCENTRATION

The flow state is characterized by a seamless marriage of self and task. Golfers in flow are usually aware on some level that they are playing well, but that is as far as their attention to the results or the score tends to go. They are aware of the quality of their play, but their attachment remains weak and vague enough to prevent anxiety. They rarely know their exact score or the exact score of their opponents. In this sense, they lose self-consciousness while increasing self-awareness and awareness of events around them, a feature of flow that Jack Nicklaus captured in the following description.

In the 1960 World Team Championship, you could have fired a cannon between my legs as I stood over a three-foot putt and I would have stroked it right down the heart without missing a beat. My concentration that week was at its peak, and for a very good reason. Every golfer at his or her own level occasionally experiences, usually out of the blue, a spell when everything feels absolutely right—grip, aim, posture, takeaway, backswing, downswing, impact, follow-through . . . and the result is a mind totally free of concerns about technique or ball striking, and therefore a mind applied exclusively to competitive strategy and course management.

Week in and week out, professional tournaments have different qualifying standards. Some provide sponsor exemptions, whereas others go off money lists, past status, or other various qualifications. In 2003 golfers could qualify for the Tour Championship in only one way—by being in the top 30 on the money list in the week going into the tournament. Thus, the golfers who were in the field of the season-ending tournament were the best in the world. It was, and remains, the most fair and difficult field in the world. Against this field of excellence Chad Campbell put on a virtuous display of golf by shooting a 61 on Saturday, which put him in position to go on and win the tournament the next day. To put this Saturday round of golf into perspective, consider the high quality of the competition and then that the cumulative average of the rest of the field that day was 70. Here is what Chad said about the 61 that he shot in those blistering conditions:

> **REPORTER:** *About what hole did 59 start creeping in your mind, or how hard did you try to keep it out of your mind?*
>
> **CHAD CAMPBELL:** I didn't try. I really was telling the guys outside, it sounds funny, but I never really knew exactly how many under I was. I knew obviously I was playing good, but it doesn't really matter. I kept trying to hit good golf shots and keep making birdies. When it's going good you just try to stay out of your own way. You're hitting the shots and making the putts. The worst thing you can do is start thinking about it and just start playing safe. Only bad things can happen then.
>
> **REPORTER:** *So when did you find out you were leading?*
>
> **CHAD CAMPBELL:** I don't even know. I guess when I went in the booth or after that. I don't really know. I wasn't paying attention. I was kind of focusing on my own game and wasn't worrying about it much.
>
> **REPORTER:** *You do realize you're leading now, though?*
>
> **CHAD CAMPBELL:** Yes. I don't know who is in second or anything like that, though.

This multilevel of awareness and the merging of self and task provides for perfect automaticity, which, in turn, affects which features of the experience that a person actually remembers. Adam Scott could recall with precise clarity many features from a round in which he achieved flow: his targets, the softest breeze, the nuanced slope on the green 150 yards (135 m) away. Simultaneously, he could not recall other, more obvious features: which clubs he selected, his playing partner, or his score, all which were out of his realm of awareness. Those aspects of the experience were at such an automatic level of functioning that they were difficult to recall later. "When I'm in that place where the game is effortless, I am not thinking how I am feeling," Scott said. "I am just feeling. I am into it. It just happens—slowly at the time—and then it's sometimes hard to remember details."

Similar to Adam Scott, despite being immersed in the experience at the time, neither Chad Campbell nor Matt Kuchar were aware of their score or their position in the tournament. Matt had to "quadruple-check" his scorecard to make sure that it was right, and Chad wasn't aware "how many under I was," until he was notified by an official as he walked off the golf course. Even so, he was unaware of who was in second.

Certainly, this was the case for Anthony Kim at the 2008 Ryder Cup when captain Paul Azinger had sent Kim out first to go head-to-head against Sergio Garcia, whose Ryder Cup record in the preceding years had been so stellar that he was considered the heart and soul of the European squad. Young Anthony Kim, 22 years old at the time and in only his second year on the PGA Tour, was just naive enough not to know what he was in for. He simply did what he always did in competition: He honed his concentration to a sharp edge and played aggressively against the golf course. After making a 10-foot (3 m) par putt on the 14th hole, Kim began walking toward the 15th tee to tee off, unaware that the par putt had closed out the match. He was so involved in his process that he was unaware of where the match stood.

I've time and again heard similar experiences from golfers including Matt Kuchar, Chad Campbell, Stuart Appleby, and Justin Rose about their stellar rounds of golf. In fact, everyone who gets into flow almost universally describes this transformation. What follow are some observations on the flow states of golfers in which they observe the automaticity of their decision making and their transformed awareness.

You are just so aware of so much. For me I am able to do so much in my head—figuring out how to play the next shot, being totally certain of the current shot. Like I'm thinking about the day at Doral I shot 62 in the wind—it was better than the next best score that day by like 5 strokes. It was extremely windy so I was calculating yardages and computing what the wind was doing and how it would affect the ball flight. Whether to fade or draw the shot into or with the wind . . . I was able to calculate that very quickly and very, very confidently. It becomes so clear and makes sense. You are able to look at the yardage, look uphill, factor in the wind, think about what is going on the green, where you want to place the ball, and know exactly how hard you want to hit that shot, and do it in a relatively short amount of time. Yet throughout, it all felt slow, if that makes any sense.

Jim Furyk, 17-time PGA Tour winner

I don't remember if I was 12 or 13 when I first got into flow. I had 10 birdies and 8 pars. I won the tournament. I didn't even think about what happened until afterwards, signing my scorecard, and shot 62! It was like I blacked out. I didn't know what I was doing. I just kept going through the motions.

Bubba Watson, 2012 Masters Champion, 4-time PGA Tour winner

I got done with the day and had shot 61. It was my best day ever. I actually had a chance to shoot 59, or 58, or something stupid. I got done and I realized that I did not know what had happened. It was the most unbelievable feeling of my life. For the rest of the week I was trying to re-create that. You know, just go blank for eight holes. Don't remember what you did.

Brandt Snedeker, 2012 Fed Ex Cup Champion, 4-time PGA Tour winner

But it's weird, you get in the zone, and you even forget about how many under you are when you get that low. You kind of forget what you're shooting. I had no idea, really, what I shot. The hole looked like a bucket today. I was just trying to make every putt I looked at. Almost did, too.

Tim Heron, 4-time PGA Tour winner

The times when I've gotten into it, I forget how many under par I am, or where I am in the tournament. Like in a match play, how many up or down I might be. You lose track of all that. Again because your focus becomes so narrow, you know, consciously you know all that but it isn't part of your thought process. And you're not thinking about those outside things that can be detractors. Your focus goes from the size of a basketball to a pin needle and nothing that goes on around you matters. You don't hear things that go on. Your focus gets so narrow on what you're trying to do. Your focus is so narrow, you're just walking up to your ball and seeing the next shot and pulling the club and doing it. And after that's over, you're just walking up to your ball again. You're not fighting through thoughts like "what if I hit it here or there?" You don't fight through any of that. It all just disappears.

Justin Leonard, 12-time PGA Tour winner

There's a great attention to detail about yardage, wind, club selection. All of those factors are just automatic. It isn't lethargic, though, so that it's a slow routine. It's definitely not fast or rushed. When you're not in flow, it's a little bit more contrived. Having to try to focus. In flow my focus just happens. I am not trying. Internally there's a knowing, a calm, relaxed knowing. Nothing can shake my focus at that point. My focus is softer. It's softer. Like soft ice cream—soft but intense. It is hard to describe because it isn't a "trying" focus. There's no trying in this state. It's all just happening and you're sort of . . . you're sort of rolling with it.

Charles Howell III, 3-time PGA Tour winner

ENLIGHTENED PUTTING

The opposite of unthinking simplicity is the active, chattering, indecisive mind that becomes aware of too many things, particularly things that don't matter. We alluded to this in chapter 2 in discussing the sensation of the mind turning on itself. More information often amplifies whatever thoughts golfers have, and the amplification places a drag on automaticity, compromises perceptual channels, and interrupts the flowing sequence of mechanics. For example, Sergio Garcia's putting woes have been well documented. When asked about the talented Spaniard, his friend Geoff Ogilvy, 2006 U.S. Open champion, made the following observation:

I like Sergio. We play together all the time, but his putting has gone a bit awry. It's odd. He's so analytical about his putting and not about everything else. I remember playing against him when he was a 16-year-old amateur. You could almost tell him to pick it up from 15 feet. It was a joke how good of a putter he was. He was the best I had ever seen at that stage. So somewhere along the line something has changed. It looks to me as if there's too much thinking.

What is worth noting is that Geoff Ogilvy is one of the best putters in the modern era. Tour players regularly tell me, "I want to learn to

Murray Richardson/Icon SMI

To be successful at golf's highest levels, golfers must be able to adjust their awareness to an optimal level. Geoff Ogilvy excels at this.

putt like Geoff Ogilvy. Not his stroke, but just his whole attitude." The numbers confirm what his peers see in Geoff. He is a big-time player with a big-time game. At the time of this writing he's won seven times on the PGA Tour, including the U.S. Open, two World Golf Championships, two World Golf Championship Match Plays, and an Australian Open. Additionally, he consistently leads the Tour in important putting statistics; he regularly makes more 3- to 5-footers (1 to 1.5 m) than anyone on the Tour. My point is that people who know about putting, who are themselves good putters, are typically the best sources of information for those who don't make putts. The reason is that more than likely they've already traveled the road required to get to that point. They've made and corrected the mistakes and have arrived at a place where they finally get it.

One of the great putters in history, Loren Roberts (aka "The Boss of the Moss"), says that in the moment between taking his final look at the hole and beginning his stroke, he intentionally allows his vision to become blurry, his physical trigger for letting automaticity take over. I've heard similar reports from scores of PGA Tour golfers who putt well with their eyes closed. Of course, sensory information often interrupts automaticity, so these reports make sense.

Indeed, automaticity theorists would argue that greatness in golf—in fact, greatness in any endeavor—boils down to the ability to turn oneself over to automaticity and let awareness fade out to the blurry periphery where automatic processes lead to greatness. *We must be sure, however, that the habits we've turned over to the automatic pilot of our subconscious mind are excellent habits that have been formed and nurtured through careful preparation, execution, and effort.* Indeed, when the magic influence of flow on awareness is combined with the paradoxes of control, effort, and time, the result is the uncanny ability to make highly complex decisions quickly and efficiently. Tiger captured all four—time, effort, control, and awareness—in the following summary:

> *The best way to describe it is that is the only thing that's going to happen. The ball will go in the hole. I think when my concentration is at its absolute peak . . . I have what I would describe as a blackout moment, where I don't remember later actually performing it. I would never say that I have tele-kinesis, but I do think when I am in that moment when my concentration is the highest, when it's at its peak, I see things more clearly, and things happen slower, and I think they happen easier.*

The paradox of awareness is characterized by being completely focused on the task at hand while also being vaguely aware of discreet features that seem unrelated to the experience itself—a breeze, a memory from childhood, the sound a leaf makes as it is stepped on. This concept is not new.

Buddhists use the term *kensho* to describe the sudden bursts of enlightenment that people sometimes feel. As with flow, one of the characteristics of kensho is the realization of nonduality of subject and object or, to put it in flow terms, the merging of the individual with the task that he or she is doing so that the person becomes one with the task. Finally, kensho is characterized by a blissful realization whereby a person's inner nature, the originally pure mind, is directly known as an illuminating emptiness. Although flow is a present-day construct that lives under the scrutiny of modern science, with all its empirical demands and technologies, the historical references to kensho provide a rich, descriptive, and timeless understanding of this transcendent state.

YOUR FLOW TOOLBOX

Flow states emerge from disciplined processes, a focus on the present moment, high levels of awareness and emotional control, and commitment to energizing the right frame of mind.

But flow is not simply a cognitive activity. We don't just think our way into flow. Although flow is partly a cognitive change in the sense that we think differently about experiences, we also have to feel and behave our way into flow.

Sustained hard work, a sincere desire to master the task for its own sake, willingness to evolve as an athlete and person, commitment to persevere in the face of difficulty, and a firm belief in yourself and your abilities are the tools for flow highlighted in this section.

Flow has a motivational component in that the quality of our experiences is tied to the underlying reasons why we are engaging those experiences in the first place. Flow maximizes the skills that you've developed, but there are no shortcuts when it comes to developing those skills. A special kind of motivation is required to continue working on something, such as skill development, that doesn't provide an immediate, highly pleasurable reward. Practice sessions don't always go as planned. Some days you show up and you are hooking it. On other days you are slicing it. Some days you're skulling it, and on others you're hitting it fat. But to improve, you have to force yourself to stay there on the driving range, digging it out of the dirt until you find something that works.

To be truly successful, you have to love the game, and not just the rewards or accolades, because in golf we all go long stretches without any tangible, external rewards. Those who play for glory fall victim to distractions and often fail to achieve what they seek. Intrinsic motivation and love for the game fuel the long journey to expert performance in golf. More important, and more relevant to this book, they also set the stage for flow.

Flow is an active process. Rarely if ever will a golfer get into flow while simply sitting in the clubhouse before a round. It is through active engagement, consistent challenge, and total focus that flow blossoms. We will talk in this section about what the Japanese call *kaizen*—the process of continual, escalating self-challenge. Engaging challenges that force people to push themselves galvanize the factors that often lead to flow.

Golf is said to be the game for a lifetime. Unlike sports such as football or wakeboarding, golf is a sport that you can improve at until your twilight years. In 2012 I was at a PGA Tour event in which 63-year-old Tom Watson competed in the same field as 22-year-old Harris English. Only one of them made the cut, and it wasn't Harris English. My point is that as we get older, as we gain experience and perspective, we change in ways that affect the way that we play the game. Therefore, at its most fundamental level, great golf over the long term requires that we grow and adapt.

As you read this section, you will understand why I tell my golfers, "People will call you many things; don't ever let them call you fragile." Golfers break down into two camps: those who know how punishing golf can be and those who are going to find out. Improvement in golf rarely follows a straight line. You will have to endure zigzags, twists and turns, good shots paired with bad bounces, and subtle cruelties in the game as you strive to get better. Rather than rail against this fact, successful golfers recognize difficulties as opportunities.

The final component that you're going to read about, one that is essential for your mental toolbox, is confidence, or what you will come to know as self-efficacy. Perhaps no psychological construct is more important, or more elusive, than confidence. All golfers know that they won't get far without it, yet they regularly do things that cause their confidence to deteriorate. We will discuss the sources and effects of confidence, and specific strategies that you can engage to strengthen yours.

So as you turn the page, prepare to answer the following question: Why do you play golf?

Skills to Meet Challenges

When I was growing up, my father used all sorts of sayings and quotations to teach life lessons to my two sisters and me. If I slept in on a Saturday, he would wake me by saying, "You can't soar with eagles if you hoot with owls." In advance of school exams or Little League games, he would say, "Failing to prepare is preparing to fail." When it came to our chores, he said, "Well done is better than well said." At the time, these always seemed corny to me, but over time I realized their value. I've come to appreciate the power of these simple words of wisdom to provide guidance even in complex matters, like the game of golf.

One saying that Dad repeated many times across various situations was simply, "You get out of it what you put into it." I've found this to be true of my undertakings in life, and it absolutely applies to flow. Getting into flow is not something that happens all by itself. Passivity and laziness will not bring it about. Flow requires that we make regular, active investments in ourselves, in our lives, and in the attitudes that we cultivate about how we play the game of golf. It requires the development and maintenance of a solid skill set and a commitment to seeking out challenging experiences to expand that skill set. The probability of flow increases when solid mental tools are paired with sound physical technique. Because flow states happen when we default to automaticity, it behooves us to develop sound mental and physical habits that we can rely on when we are on the golf course.

The sport of downhill snow skiing provides the perfect metaphor through which to understand the flow state. Those who ski know that mountain terrain is rated by level of difficulty. A typical mountain has terrain that contains four levels of difficulty that are designated by color and shape of symbol: green circles, blue squares, black diamonds, and double black diamonds. Green slopes, often referred to as bunny slopes, have only a slight vertical incline, whereas double black diamonds are extremely steep and designated for only the most capable skiers.

Green circles—beginners, easy bunny slopes.

Blue squares—novices, medium difficulty.

Black diamonds—experts, steep.

Double black diamonds—extreme expertise required, very steep, frequently icy or ungroomed, high danger.

Now answer the following questions:

How would an expert skier feel spending the day on green bunny slopes?

Bored

Alert

Excited

Frightened

How would a novice skier feel on a double black diamond?

Bored

Alert

Excited

Frightened

How would a novice skier feel on a blue slope?

Bored

Alert

Excited

Frightened

Finally, how would an expert skier feel on a black diamond slope?

Bored

Alert

Excited

Frightened

Answers:

1. Because bunny slopes do not offer enough challenge, the expert skier is likely to feel bored.
2. Because black diamonds are difficult, the novice skier is likely to feel frightened on such slopes (and likely to get injured).
3. Because blue slopes offer reasonable challenge, a novice skier is likely to feel alert or excited.
4. Because black diamonds offer extreme challenge, an expert skier (with extreme skills) is likely to feel alert or excited.

This exercise demonstrates that, when a skier's level of skill does not correspond with the appropriate level of challenge, the skier is likely to experience a negative psychological state. In examples 1 and 2, expert skiers on bunny slopes get bored and novice skiers on double black diamonds get frightened.

Conversely, look at scenarios 3 and 4. When the level of challenge effectively matches the level of that person's skill, the skier feels energized, excited, and generally alert. In other words, when challenge and skill correspond with one another, the skier feels an assortment of positive emotions. Within the confines of this metric, where correspondence is present between challenge and skill, flow states are most likely to occur.

The challenge–skill (C–S) correspondence works across many domains of functioning, athletic and otherwise, from childhood through adulthood. If you walk into any elementary school classroom where reading instruction is taking place, you will notice that most schools organize student reading levels to correspond with C–S so that students read books that are at the appropriate grade level, as the jargon goes. Students who are able to read at a third-grade level become frustrated when given books written for readers who are functioning at a fifth-grade level. In fact, many motivation and behavior problems are not inherent in the child but rather emerge from classroom practices that do not stimulate and challenge students at an appropriate level. Too much challenge often leads children to become discouraged and subsequently causes behavior problems.

Similarly, students reading at a high grade level are frequently forced to read books that don't provide enough mental stimulation or intellectual challenge. Although the students who are challenged too severely get frustrated, students who are insufficiently challenged get bored. Their attention wanders, they are not engaged, and they too have behavior problems.

As a frequent consultant to schools, I have seen firsthand how providing students with just the right level of interesting challenges turns their focus away from mischief and toward their academic studies. Only when teachers are able to find the sweet spot of learning where the academic challenge corresponds with or slightly exceeds the students' skills does the learning environment turn out happy, engaged, productive students who love to learn.

The C–S correspondence extends into adulthood. We choose books, movies, careers, and hobbies that are challenging and interesting to us. Similarly, we enjoy thought-provoking conversations that push us to the edge of our intellectual capabilities. We tend to gravitate to people whose perspectives we find pleasantly stimulating. Indeed, it is human nature to strive for the type of challenge that leads to growth. According to William James, we are all born with an innate impulse toward better understanding and mastery, which is why the feeling of personal growth—spiritually, intellectually, or physically—is one of the greatest feelings in human experience.

ZONE OF PROXIMAL DEVELOPMENT

I teach classes not only in sport psychology but also in educational psychology, where I familiarize my students with a Russian psychologist by the name of Lev Vygotsky. Vygotsky is famous in educational circles for a variety of reasons, but perhaps his most enduring contribution has to do with a psychological construct that applies to sport as well as education, which he called the zone of proximal development, otherwise known as the ZPD (figure 5.1).

The ZPD is defined by the distance between the level at which a student can solve problems independently and the level at which that student could potentially solve problems with proper guidance. Although he conceived the ZPD over 50 years ago, Vygotsky was discovering what flow researchers would finalize many years after his death, namely that the sweet spot of learning and performance

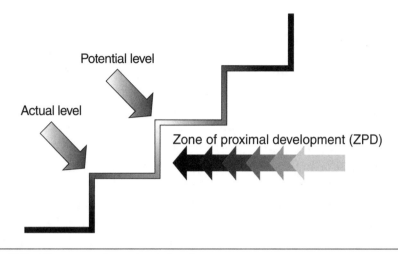

Figure 5.1 The zone of proximal development.

requires enough challenge to stimulate the brain to pay attention but not so much challenge that the brain shuts down and freezes. In schools, this sweet spot exists where students are challenged at a level just a fraction beyond their capabilities, a level just beyond their mental fingertips that requires them to reach, stretch, and strive.

Just as mental challenges at a level slightly beyond peoples' current capabilities stimulate cognitive growth, physical challenges at the same level stimulate physical growth. Those who desire to improve their physical strength often use slightly more weight than they can independently lift. Readers familiar with physical fitness and strength training know exactly what I am talking about: The best way to gain strength is to try to lift more weight than you can, all the while having someone spot you to avoid injury. It is through challenging the muscles that growth occurs. Brain and muscular development follows the same principles involved in aerobic and anaerobic development.

So vital to the flow state is the challenge–skill correspondence that Csikszentmihalyi called it the golden rule of flow. With that said, at this point it is important to note an important detail regarding the relationship between C–S and the flow state.

Many challenges are subjective in nature, and in the grey area of subjectivity people actually have a measure of control over whether they get into flow. By framing such situations in an adaptive manner, people can set their own personal level of challenge to correspond with their level of skill. For instance, golfers who want to increase their chances of getting into flow by balancing their C-S ratio may set a goal for the day to get into a routine on every single hole, to pick a target on every shot, to par every hole on a challenging golf course, to commit to every shot. That is, they may set their short-term goals as anything that gets and keeps their attention while simultaneously establishing a healthy level of vigor and challenge to stimulate flow.

I previously noted that people who are able to generate flow states in other areas of life are more likely to generate flow on the golf course. This tendency is related to the way that they view what they are doing as well as the activities that they choose to do. Csikszentmihalyi identified certain activities as being *autotelic* activities, which are activities that we "do for its own sake because to experience it is the main goal" (Csikszentmihalyi 1997). People who spend a lot of time performing self-rewarding activities tend to get into flow frequently.

People who frequently get into flow fall into two categories. The first consists of people who know themselves well enough to understand which activities bring them flow. After they identify those

Michael Tureski/Icon SMI

To get into flow frequently, golfers must first develop their skills by embracing challenges. Hunter Mahan has been displaying his considerable skills on the tour since 2004.

activities, they hone in on and spend a lot of time doing them. An example would be the high-level surfers I've met whose motto is "Live to surf." This phrase is more than a catchphrase to them; they mean what they say and spend little time thinking about anything but surfing. When good waves are predicted, everything else—jobs, other hobbies, the news—takes a backseat.

The second category of people who spend a substantial amount of time in flow is made up of those who possess the uncanny ability to become deeply involved with and committed to almost anything they are doing. They don't need a particular domain, per se, because their minds are so strong that they can use many activities as bridges to flow. These people possess adaptive traits rather than simply adaptive skills. What I mean is that they have learned to bring curiosity, competitiveness, joy, and enthusiasm with them into almost everything that they do. These traits buffer them against the toxic emotions—boredom, apathy, negativity—that plague many others. Indeed, as I've mentioned, these are the types of traits that I work to develop with my clients so that they are more fully in flow off the golf course, which makes flow more habitual and easier to generate when they are on the golf course. When at work, they are fully immersed and engaged at work. When they are home with the family, they are present and fully involved in their family lives. When they are on the golf course, they are deeply attentive to, and immersed in, that particular round of golf. The same is true for most activities in their lives. They are seldom distracted with thoughts from the present or the past, and they seldom concern themselves with the what-ifs of life. Those who can concentrate and find the sweet spot of their minds across various domains are said to possess autotelic personalities. This ability to become deeply immersed in the totality of an experience on that fine line where challenge meets skill is the hallmark of people who get into flow.

POLISHING YOUR SKILLS

I began this chapter by suggesting that generating flow requires us to make regular investments of time and effort into ourselves. People frequently ask me how they can actualize this process. How do we make investments in ourselves? The answer, as it usually is with the pursuit of excellence, is simple: with consistent, thoughtful, deliberate practice.

I help my golfers hone their mental and physical skills by engaging in this type of practice. We work to develop calm, focused minds, and we actively strive to be our best selves in word and deed, in the same way that Buddhists, Christians, and people of all beliefs do. I don't simply remind my clients to be grateful. Rather, we actively practice gratitude through words and deeds. My golfers regularly list things that they are thankful for. During interviews, they use positive words of gratitude and enthusiasm. They react to bad shots with curiosity and to difficult situations with excitement rather than discouragement. On the driving range, whether at a tournament or at home, we stagger our practice sessions, do our drills with discipline and enthusiasm, and practice in rhythm. We are detail oriented as we practice our routines, we accept our shots, and we cultivate the habit of physical and mental freedom.

In addition, my golfers generally wake up early, eat healthy, read and study, and immerse themselves in the process of continual growth. If you ever go to a PGA Tour event, you can spot my golfers from across the fairway. They are usually the ones who walk with energy and enthusiasm, who smile and take time for fans, and who fully commit to every shot. These are not merely the thoughts of exceptional achievement. These are the behavioral habits of those who would achieve excellence.

By performing these actions on a daily basis, my golfers prepare themselves to default into flow when they are on the golf course. I believe that this is the main reason that they've been able to achieve more than 45 wins in the past 10 years.

SETTING THE STAGE FOR FLOW

You can take a few lessons from this chapter that can be helpful for finding flow.

First, because so many cognitive, physical, and situational features need to come together to get into flow, we have only a measure of control over when and how frequently we get into flow, on and off the course.

Second, because we have that measure of control we have some influence over our flow states, and we can increase the probability and frequency of flow by applying that influence. The primary way that we can influence getting into flow is by taking control of our attitude regarding the idea of challenge. I am not suggesting that everyone needs to thrive on challenge with the same extreme intensity of professional athletes and autotelic personalities, but a fundamental shift in perspective to engage and enjoy challenges is certainly helpful for those who want to increase their probability of getting into flow. This quest for and love of challenge should permeate their personal, professional, and recreational lives. By inviting challenges as pathways to growth, people are also inviting a good deal of mental stimulation. They have opportunities to read their reactions in competitive situations, to practice patience and composure, and to process information more deeply, including information that is relevant to playing great golf.

Third, the level of challenge that we encounter in life is under our control. If you buy into the C–S rule, then you can begin to take charge of establishing the goals that you have for various areas of your life. By setting short-term, challenging, achievable goals for a variety of areas of life, you are focusing on your interests and developing the habit of working toward goals. The habit of excellence that Aristotle referenced is a habit of mind that will enhance both your golf game and your life!

On the final hole of the 1950 U.S. Open, in one of the most storied shots in golf history, Ben Hogan flushed a 1-iron that led to his eventual victory that year. Hogan later made the following observation:

The view I take of that shot is markedly different from the view most spectators seem to have formed. They are inclined to glamorize the actual shot since it was hit in a pressureful situation. They tend to think of it as something unique in itself, something almost inspired, you might say, since the shot was just what the occasion called for. I don't see it that way at all. I didn't hit that shot then—that late afternoon at Merion. I'd been practicing that shot since I was 12 years old. After all, the point of tournament golf is to get command of a swing which, the more pressure you put on it, the better it works.

In this statement, Hogan brilliantly captured the marriage of mind and body that emerges from effective, careful, deliberate practice. He further illustrates Jack Nicklaus' belief that golf tournaments are won before they are ever played. You may not be playing for PGA championships, but if you've bought this book, then you love the game of golf and you're trying to improve at it. Take a page out of Hogan's playbook and practice properly for whatever challenges you face. The more care that you take in developing your habits, the more likely it is that they will be reliable when you need them.

Mastery Orientation to Keep Ego in Check

As Jack Nicklaus described, flow is that state of effortless action that we feel when everything is going just right. But as I've discussed in this book, flow states rarely just happen out of the blue. More commonly, they are the product of a constellation of psychological and physical factors that come together in an emergent manner, which is why flow is as much something that we have to *let* happen as *make* happen.

The first step in the process that leads to flow begins with the reasons that golfers choose to play the game. Whenever golfers come to visit me for the first time or pull me aside to ask my advice, I typically first ask them to explain why they play golf. It's really not a trick question. In fact, it is rather straightforward. Despite the simplicity of the question, however, many golfers have a remarkably difficult time explaining why they play golf.

Great golfers, on the other hand, never have difficulty answering that question. They are crystal clear about why they play golf. As the legendary Jack Nicklaus remarked, "I had no visions in my head of fans and trophies. Basically I sought three things from the game: to improve at it, to compete at it, and to *win* at it." Tiger Woods plays the game "to be the best I can be, to challenge myself, and to win every single time I tee it up." Golf's pioneering proponent of *kaizen*, the Japanese term for continuous, incremental improvement, Ben Hogan, said, "I don't like the glamour. I just like the game." Clearly, each of these gifted golfers was driven to win, but it is the desire to master the game, to be challenged by it, and to improve at it that causes champions to fall in love with it.

As I often explain to golfers, if you can find clarity regarding your motivation in the game, you'll be able to unlock a significant portion of the psychological mystery that surrounds golf and overcome many of the psychological obstacles of the game. The nature of a golfer's achievement goal orientation determines whether she or he will be able to remain calm and focused under pressure or become edgy and nervous. Not to be confused with the more popular outcome goals that answer *what* a person wants to achieve, achievement goals focus on the *why* that drives behavior.

Because seamless thinking and a quiet mind characterize flow states, achievement goals provide clarity about a person's motivation. Conflicted motivation results in conflicted thinking, whereas clarity of motivation sets the stage for peak performance and ultimately for flow. Therefore, before reading any further, you should ask yourself that simple question that I pose to all golfers: Why do you play golf?

Take a moment to write down your answers. If you've written, "Because it's fun," then push yourself a bit further and ask, "Why is it fun?" If you answer, "Because I like competition," then push yourself and ask, "Why do you like competition?" Take a moment and write down the reasons with the intent of connecting with the internal motivations that the game nourishes in you. Next, see which of the following two psychological categories those reasons fall into.

MASTERY ORIENTATION

The first achievement goal orientation is called mastery orientation. A mastery golfer is one who is driven by the love of the game, the challenge of the round, and the desire to improve. Mastery golfers become absorbed in the details of the game, and they launch themselves into exploring and understanding those details. Their motivation to play is often guided by the same simple and basic motivation that guided them when they first picked up a golf club as children: curiosity, interest, challenge, enjoyment, fun, excitement, and enthusiasm.

Mastery golfers engage the idea of kaizen, and they view their work as long term and never ending. They not only accept the fact that golf is a challenging, fickle, unpredictable game; they savor it. They thrive on the challenges that are inherent and implicit to the game. They love the challenge, the eternal struggle, the fickleness and unpredictability, the high highs and low lows, and the sensitivity to marginal differences in their moods, bodies, and concentration. They love playing golf, rather than some version of golf in which every bounce goes their way, in which every well-struck shot results in a good lie, and in which the conditions are always consistent and perfect.

Jack Nicklaus was the archetypical mastery golfer. I've profiled Nicklaus closely throughout the years. I've had the chance to dine with him, to play golf with him, and to interview him for this book. His ideas are mastery to the core. In *My Story* (Nicklaus 1997), he wrote,

> Meeting such challenges is never easy, but to me the urge and the struggle to do so are what competing at sports is all about. That's because, when I succeeded . . . the emotional high was the single biggest thrill of my life. And the reason, of course, is not that I have whipped up on all those other people, but that I have conquered the toughest opponent of all: myself.

The reasons for playing that I hear from mastery golfers are typically consistent: love of challenge, opportunity to test themselves, and continual refinement of skills. Most want to take their learning, understanding, and ability to execute golf shots as far as possible. They genuinely want to know their own limitations and are willing to test those limits through relentless learning, practice, instruction, and competition.

A unique characteristic of a mastery golfer is the view that there are two players in every golf contest: the golfer and the course on which he or she is playing. Except when dictated by common sense during head-to-head formats, mastery golfers do not compete against other golfers. They never obsess about a score or compete to impress or show off to others. Because the matchup is always the same—the golfer versus the golf course—the mastery golfer is buffered against external distractions and finds it relatively easy to get lost in the process of playing that course one shot at a time.

EGO ORIENTATION

The second achievement goal orientation is called ego orientation. In contrast to intrinsically driven mastery golfers, ego golfers play for extrinsic reasons that center on others. Usually this takes the form of wanting to impress or otherwise gain recognition from other people by shooting low scores or winning so that others will look at them in a more favorable light. Ego golfers enjoy playing well to the degree that others know that they played well. They don't enjoy the game of golf as much as they enjoy the status or ego-fulfilling characteristics that come with playing golf. In many cases, ego golfers play golf to make themselves feel better (about themselves) and to show that they are better than others. Ego golfers value the attention, compliments, accolades, envy, and respect that accompany good golf as much as, and often even more than, actually playing good golf.

Like mastery golfers, ego golfers also know that there are two players in every golf contest. But unlike mastery golfers, for whom those two players are the golfer and the course, the two players that ego golfers see are the golfer and other golfers. Ego golfers do not play the course. Instead, they constantly measures themselves relative to others, be they a tournament field, their business colleagues, or even their friends and family.

The greatest players in the game have all been mastery golfers. Bobby Jones spoke of Old Man par. And it would be hard to improve on Jack Nicklaus' ideas on the subject:

> *I developed an ever sharpening awareness that one's true opponent in every golf contest is never another player, or even the entire field, but always the course itself—a realization, I am now sure, that has been common to all great champions and, I believe, a major contributor to their success.*

A mastery outlook is often what allows promising young golfers to separate themselves from their peers. Consider Zach Johnson's reflections on winning the 2007 Masters:

> *I didn't look at the boards. I really didn't know what was going on, which was a good thing. I was able to maintain my focus and maintain an even keel and, you know, I stuck to my guns. I played my own game. I knew if I just kept doing what I was doing, staying in the present and putting well, I had a chance. . . . I really felt like I just tried to maintain my focus, and maintain my game plan.*

By contrast, because ego-oriented golfers tend to experience a round of golf as a chance to show off, their confidence is held prisoner to the success that they experience doing so. For ego golfers who wish to—who *need* to—impress, any misstep is a potential embarrassment in front of the people whose approval they crave.

© PA Photos

Mastery golfers like Zach Johnson commit to the internal, process-oriented goal of achieving their best possible level of play.

Ego golfers are confident to the degree that they feel themselves successful in achieving their goal, whether that goal is shooting a certain score, beating a certain player, or impressing a certain client, coach, or observer.

Imagine, however, the anxiety, stress, and tension that invariably chaperone the need to earn the approval or admiration of others. Imagine the discomfort and dread that must accompany the fear of failing to impress. Imagine the irritation that follows a missed shot or an exercise in poor judgment. Playing a round of golf with an ego mind-set requires handing other people the keys to our feelings and emotions. For an ego golfer, satisfaction and growth can never come from within. Instead, it must be purchased with the accolades of others.

When their confidence begins to waver, ego golfers go into what's called an ego-avoid mind-set. When they are in ego-avoid mode, ego golfers play to avoid failing or to avoid making mistakes. Rather than playing to achieve personal excellence, they become motivated not to make mistakes, not to get worse, not to be embarrassed. The inner self-talk that ego-avoid golfers use typically takes the form of desperate phrases such as "Don't slice," "Don't choke," "Don't miss," and "Don't hit it into the water." This mind-set of trying to avoid the negative is based on fear, which is the source of the physical tension that often produces the very results that it aims to prevent.

Working Toward Mastery Golf

Here is an e-mail that I sent to my golfers to illustrate how mastery golf is actualized:

Just a reminder about the purpose of our Mondays:

The longer we stay in this game, the more chance we have that the bad stuff can accumulate in our minds and either deflate our motivation or clutter our minds with unnecessary information. Thus, on Mondays we want to accomplish the following:

1. *Dump any bad experiences, bad emotions, or memories that do us no good from the week before. This process is called clearing.*

2. *Learn one or two simple lessons that can help us improve and grow. These lessons can be technical, personal, or anything that goes into the overall mix that makes us healthy, energetic, mentally free golfers.*

3. *Summon a sense of gratitude for the process. We all function better (and freer) when we are grateful and appreciative of (rather than feeling entitled and presumptuous about) what we're doing and those who assist us in that effort.*

It is [calendar date], and I'd like you to reflect on the year so far. If you are carrying any negative emotional baggage, root it out and discard it. If you have learned any great, simple lessons so far, identify them, record them in your file, and be prepared to use them constructively.

A lot of great golf courses lie in front of you. Each site and round of competition represents a ripe opportunity to demonstrate your passion for the game and to become fully engaged in the event. Remember, golf is a process of long-term learning, and the knowledge that you gain each week adds to your self-awareness and strengthens your game.

ORIENTATION SHAPES EXPERIENCE

On the professional tours that I frequent, the characteristics of mastery golfers and ego golfers manifest themselves in interesting ways. Mastery golfers approach a round of golf with the mind-set of trying to play the golf course the best way they know how. They are consistent in their mannerisms and motivations; their Thursday preparation is the same as their Sunday preparation. Their effort level remains constant whether the shot is for a birdie, par, or bogey. Their challenge is to get into their routine, stick to their game plan, and commit to every shot regardless of the circumstance. Mastery golfers treat every situation with the same focus and intensity, and they realize that when they are thinking properly, there are no easy shots and no hard shots. There are only golf shots.

On the other hand, ego golfers tend to play with the aim of making the cut or, sometimes, not missing the cut. When near the lead, their energy and intensity feeds off what other golfers are doing. Because their efforts are focused on the competition rather than getting the most out of their game, they tend to play to the level of the competition. Frequently, this tendency manifests itself as playing down to the level of their competition and scoring worse than golfers with inferior skills and abilities. Their confidence and stress levels change according to how other golfers are playing and from the results of their own shots. As such, they finish a round of golf emotionally drained and feeling that they have no control over their own confidence—which, of course, they don't.

Playing golf with a mastery orientation is deeply and fundamentally important because this mind-set buffers golfers against the type of panic triggered by the changeable nature of the performances and approval of others. Playing for mastery reasons rather than to feed or protect the ego makes it possible for golfers to absorb the natural fluctuations inherent in the game. Regardless of how much progress they find themselves making, mastery golfers engage continuously in the process of learning, refining, and improving. Their commitment to this process does not waver. Regardless of the surprises and disappointments of the game, they continue to view golf as a challenge and focus their attention on the golf course rather than on the other golfers, the score, or the crowd. For mastery golfers, the process and motivation remain constant.

Ultimately, becoming a mastery golfer requires a pure type of motivation. Because golf presents endless and novel challenges, success at the game requires the type of person who derives satisfaction from kaizen, who has a love of challenge. Consistent with the love of challenge, mastery golfers have a love of experience and a love for learning and growth independent of performance outcomes. As a golfer moves higher up the golfing ladder, the measure of improvement is typically delayed and fickle, often coming long before it is reflected in scoring. This outcome is especially true for more skilled golfers, for whom improvement comes in smaller and more nuanced increments. Of all the reasons to become a mastery golfer, perhaps the most important is this: Research studies have shown that a mastery orientation is significantly related to the ability to generate flow.

Growth Mind-Set to Adapt to Changes

Despite the degree to which they help us transcend ordinary abilities, flow states are real and happen to normal golfers all over the world. This idea suggests that human beings are walking around every day of their lives with untapped reserves of potential. Like an overlooked gold mine with reserves of bullion, people have untapped reserves of energy, alertness, clarity, and potential.

Many psychologists use assessments and intervention methods to gauge and guide clients toward normalcy. They give personality tests, IQ tests, reading tests—all to discover how individuals compare with the norm. When people stray too far beyond acceptable, conforming behaviors, the psychological community labels their behaviors as abnormal, deviant, or extreme. Efforts are made to standardize behaviors and performance. This preference for normalcy may help a society become more psychologically homogeneous, but it does nothing to stimulate exceptionalism. Rather, steering everyone to average functioning and performance only encourages mediocrity.

Having spent time studying the life paths of extraordinary people, I have seen firsthand that people come into their own during different stages and phases of their lives. Furthermore, those who become known for extraordinary achievements rarely follow a well-trod path but instead accumulate the battle scars that come with being wholly, boldly, uniquely themselves. Steve Jobs, the founder of Apple Computer, was a college dropout. Sigmund Freud was a writer and physician before he created the field of psychoanalysis. Albert Einstein failed the entrance exam to the Swiss Federal Polytechnic Institute, and when he couldn't find a teaching position, he spent two years as a patent clerk. PGA Tour winners Matt Kuchar and Will McKenzie left golf in their 20s, Matt to work in finance and Will to film snow-skiing videos, before they zigzagged their way back to the game. All these exceptional characters had the courage to follow their intuition, to live their own lives, and to let personal growth be the guiding light to lead them through adversity.

Golfers who achieve flow function consistently beyond the normal; they are at the far end of the bell curve. They deviate from the norm so that they can unleash their full potential. They celebrate the things about themselves that are unique and uncommon. As such, when exploring flow, people are essentially choosing to live their lives at the fringe of their capabilities, or at least looking within to explore and expand their internal potentialities (and break through the limitations).

Excelling at anything in life, including golf, requires us to make decisions that allow the kind of personal growth that lends itself to flow. People who want to grow (in the deep, meaningful, psychological sense of the word) have to be willing to look at themselves honestly without the filtering lens of the ego. They have to be willing to become comfortable with being uncomfortable. They have to be willing to trade illusion for candor, to replace idle comfort with difficult challenge, to face fear rather than avoid it, to love what is most difficult, to acknowledge personal weaknesses, and to relish the uncertain outcomes that accompany great endeavors. To live in flow, you must make a decision to adjust your mind-set in a specific and uncommon way to become the best you possible.

Many people live their lives in such a way that they never get into flow. Their belief system—the psychological mechanism that filters experiences and influences how they subjectively experience the world—creates a state of mind that is antithetical to flow. They live narrow lives confined to the conventions of the status quo. They are prisoners to the evaluation and validation of other people. By being risk averse, they make themselves averse to feeling the joy that accompanies living life at the edge of potential. They never find themselves, and even sadder, they are afraid to try.

Conversely, the autotelic personality described in chapter 5 engages the world in such a proactive way that it fills their psyche. In that regard they find life fulfilling in the literal sense of the word; their minds fill with the joys of the world. In all cases, the ability to get into flow is dependent on a belief system or a way of seeing the world and the game of golf in a manner that allows flow.

ACTIVE STATE OF CHANGE

Based on all accounts, flow is a state change more than it is a simple emotional change or a departure from conventional thinking. You can't think your way into flow, although you can certainly think your way out of flow. But you can choose to focus on a few key ideas that invite flow to happen.

Flow states have what biologists describe as emergent properties, in the sense that flow involves simple entities coming together to yield more complex behaviors. Examples of emergent properties include the way that flocks of birds or schools of fish organize. You might also think of tornadoes and hurricanes, disparate energies in which unique individual properties converge, self-organize, and create a larger, more powerful symbiotic form.

Within the framework of our mind-set, we need to understand golf from a developmental perspective, that is, to be aware of how we experience golf throughout the life cycle. Although our brains are designed to give us a sense of sameness and consistency from day to day, the reality is that we are in a constant, perpetual, and eternal state of change. We are all in the process of growth and of becoming someone new. Because every observer of the human condition, from Aristotle to James to Piaget to modern doctors, acknowledges that the human condition is one of continual biological, psychological, and physical change, it serves us well to accept that fact and enjoy the ride. Those who resist this fundamental feature of reality often become stuck—stuck psychologically, stuck emotionally, and stuck in the ruts that are characteristic of narrow-minded golfers.

Sean O'Hair's 2011 decision to "let go and let God" reflected his willingness to turn himself over to the development that was emerging from within him. At the age of 30, he was not the same golfer that he was at 17, and his acceptance of this truth is what enabled him the freedom he needed to play better golf. On this note, I find that too many golfers aim to remain static. They resist the fact that life—at biological, physical, and psychological levels—is a process of change. By accepting and embracing this fact, we can better understand how and why golfers should give up trying to overcontrol their destinies in golf and instead play with the momentum of their lives. When they do this, their golf begins to take on emergent properties that allow for the serendipitous collision of factors that leads to the complex and exceptional state of flow.

Perhaps the most vivid example of emergence and symbiosis is life itself. Scientists know at a material level what makes us uniquely human. Generally, you, me, Ernie Els and the rest of the seven billion people who inhabit the planet are composed of roughly 65 percent oxygen, 18 percent carbon, 10 percent hydrogen, 3 percent nitrogen, 1.5 percent calcium, and trace amounts of phosphorous, potassium, sulfur, chlorine, sodium, magnesium, iron, zinc, and iodine. Armed with this knowledge, scientists should be able to combine these elements in such a way as to create life. Combine the elements, cook them to the right temperature, shake them up, and create a living being! Sounds easy, right?

But following this recipe, as scientists in the past have done, produces nothing but a soupy mixture of disparate elements. Even when placed in an environment conducive to creating a living being, these ingredients don't become a person. Although scientists can identify the building blocks of life, they cannot create life. Life is, by all measures, an emergent process.

Our bodies are constantly renewing themselves. At a molecular level the human body fully renews itself every seven years. Other than your teeth (which do not repair themselves) every organ and cell you have now is entirely different from ones you had seven years ago. We generate a new taste bud every 10 days, an entirely new skin about once per month, and a new skeleton every three months. Every hour about one billion cells in the body must be replaced.

"That's interesting," you may be saying to yourself, "but what can this possibly have to do with golf?" The game of golf is played by people, and just as peoples' lives are a dynamic process of growth and regrowth, golf is a dynamic game that requires growth and regrowth of our perspective, beliefs, and sense of self.

LETTING YOUR GAME EVOLVE

Many golfers get to a place in their game where they prefer remaining stagnant to evolving with their game. They often reach this point when they are playing well. They feel good about their game, they are swinging and putting well and naturally, and they want to remain in that place of playing well. In my opinion, this tendency to want to stay put is a mistake that leads to stagnation and is counterproductive to growth. To try to stay the same while your physical and psychological selves are undergoing change would mean that you're using an outdated swing and mind-set for your current self.

You wouldn't dream of playing in the clothing and shoes that you wore many years ago, or using the clubs or balls that you used when you first started in the game, or playing the level of course that you started out on. If you are an adult reading this book, you probably don't react with the same temperament you did as a teenager, having adopted a perspective that allows gratitude and patience to come more quickly.

Golf requires such evolution. Just as our bodies change, our beliefs evolve over time, as do our cognitive processes and personal motivations. As such, if you plan to be a competitive golfer, you need to develop the mind-set of growing with the game and letting your game evolve as you evolve as a person. Thus, the overarching mind-set to get into flow is, quite literally, to *flow* with your own growth, development, and change.

Steve Stricker understands the need to evolve. His name is probably familiar to most readers of this book. Steve has won 12 times on the PGA Tour, has 20 professional wins worldwide, and has been a member of three Ryder Cup teams and four Presidents Cup Teams. After joining the PGA Tour in 1994, Steve had seven good years before falling into a deep and well-publicized slump. After all but disappearing from the PGA Tour scene for a number of years, he was granted a sponsors' exemption in 2006. Making the most of it, he went on to earn seven top 10 finishes that year. He was PGA Tour comeback player of the year in both 2006 and 2007.

What happened behind the scenes, during the years when Steve was off the radar, is instructive. Of those dark days he admitted,

There were no physical injuries, but mental injuries there might have been, I'm not sure. I was obviously struggling with confidence and everything that goes when you're not playing that well. I just put in a lot of time this winter. I worked hard at it.

In 2006, when his game began showing signs of life again, he was constantly asked about his slump. It seemed that every time he was asked about it, he delivered some sort of lesson that he'd learned

© PA Photos

To let their true talents emerge, golfers must often be patient and let their game evolve, as Steve Stricker has done.

along the way. At the 2006 Booz Allen Classic, Steve provided some insight:

> *I just continued to practice the things that I was doing this winter. They're starting to click. It makes sense to me. I'm understanding my swing again, what I'm doing, what I'm not doing. It's almost like another phase. I mean, you can take any player, you kind of go through phases out here. A friend of mine was telling me last week, we were both talking about it, I started off my career and had some success, I was building up, then I kind of went into another phase where I kind of went to the bottom, had some good years in between. I'm starting to feel like my game's coming around, my attitude's coming around. I think it's just the whole feeling or perception that I have about my game, my family, everything, is going in the right direction. Kind of a combination of things.*

As his game began to build momentum, he would sit in the press rooms and discuss how his perspective on the game had changed, what he'd learned about his swing, how important it was to play one shot at a time, and what it felt like beating balls from out of a trailer, out into the frozen Wisconsin snow. Through his adversity, Steve evolved technically, emotionally, and intellectually. He rolled with the ups and downs of the game and kept playing. By his admission, his motivation came from his love for the game.

GOLFING TODAY FOR TOMORROW

Our development as people travels through time. Although people have many perspectives on the exact nature of time, one of the more popular has to do with what is called the relational theory of time, which suggests that events do not take place in time, but rather that it's the other way around. Time is defined by the order of the events that take place. As such, life becomes the main aspect of existence, rather than time.

Einstein was aware that time is not what it seems, which is why his theory of relativity suggests that time is not only relative but also variable and flexible. Scientists who study time closely are convinced that time is not unidirectional and that, mathematically at least, time can be slowed and may even be able to be reversed.

But for now that all remains theoretical, and for the purposes of this book we can say that time interacts with our psyches and with the game of golf. And here is something that is worth thinking about. For all the space that I've dedicated in this book to time, there is no such thing as now. Beyond an abstract concept, now does not exist because as soon as you think of a moment, that moment has become the past. In the words of Kai Krause, "Everything is about the anticipation of the moment and the memory of the moment, but not the moment."

I recall sitting in a lecture with a former teacher of mine, Professor Frank Pajares, who gave me an analogy that works: NFL quarterbacks do not throw the football at a streaking receiver. Rather, they anticipate where the receiver will be at a future point in time. That's where they place the ball.

Similarly, golfers need to view themselves as emergent beings with emergent properties and realize that the habits of mind that they cultivate today will emerge at some future point in time. Beat yourself up today, and you will feel the effects down the road. Practice sloppily today, and those habits will emerge down the road. Savor the opinions of others too much today, and you'll be a prisoner to their validation in the future.

That realization is the best way to integrate the sense of emergence into your mental toolbox. Focus on the now, but realize that the habits we create—habits of patience, attitude, kindness, acceptance, and humor—really matter because the things that we do today will show up down the road when we are on the golf course. To quote Oliver Wendell Homes, "I find the great thing in this world is not so much where we stand, as in what direction we are moving."

Resilience to Overcome Adversity

One area where the differences between mastery golfers and ego golfers are especially obvious is in the way in which they deal with setbacks and adversity. Because image and validation from other people is the barometer of success for ego golfers, as we discussed in chapter 6, they tend to interpret bad scores as bad golf. When they don't play well, and by that I mean when they don't score well, ego golfers typically feel embarrassed, frustrated, and angry. They hold little funerals each time their results are less than perfect. Their negative reactions penetrate their psyches and seep into other areas of life in the same way that a chemical leak can pollute groundwater. These cycles often metastasize into self-doubt, and they begin to reinterpret not only their most recent failure but also everything they've done to date. Their failures begin to loom larger as their past successes drift further out of sight. Their self-criticisms jump from attacks on their golf game to attacks on their identity. Rather than saying, "I played bad golf," they say, "I am a bad golfer," and the more they say it, the more self-fulfilling that prophecy becomes. Attributions change, stress levels rise, motivation diminishes, and before you know it, they've talked themselves into a slump, all the while never taking any responsibility for the situation that they themselves have created.

Conversely, score is not the barometer of success for mastery golfers. Because they view the game in terms of long-term improvement, they use score as a measure of improvement, but not the only measure of improvement. Whereas insecurity is at the heart of ego golf, learning and growth are at the core of mastery golf. Mastery golfers gauge a performance as much by what they have learned through the round as by what score they shot in that round. Mastery golfers know that if they focus on learning, they can apply those lessons next time and be a better golfer day after day, week after week, and year after year.

Mastery golfers often respond to bad scores with curiosity. Because their motivation rests on continued learning and improvement, they reflect on their performance, identify what went wrong, and approach the next round with increased determination. Because they are driven by the love of challenge, they strive to rise to the challenges that the game provides. Ego golfers ruminate in a tangled mess of misery, embarrassment, doubt, and frustration.

As such, after a good round, mastery golfers typically don't brag, gloat, or peacock. After bad rounds of golf, they don't lose their temper, berate themselves or other people, or relive every bad shot in their minds. In either case, good score or bad score, mastery golfers default to the learning possibilities that they just experienced and wonder how they can apply what they've learned to become better down the road. They live according to one of the truisms of life: It is all right to make mistakes so long as you learn from those mistakes. This maxim is as true in golf as it is in other areas of life.

In my experience, the game of golf rewards this approach of learning from your mistakes. Much of the success that I have with golfers is not because I steer them away from mistakes, but because I teach them how to learn the right lessons from the mistakes that they make. In this way, my golfers tend to improve over time. Because this belief is foundational to their mind-set, they are able to shed the emotional baggage that accompanies the game of golf and stay relatively positive, happy, balanced, and motivated about the game.

Nowhere in the psychological spectrum is the distance between knowing and doing as vast as the gulf between mastery golf and ego golf. Most golfers leave my Fearless Golf Academies feeling charged up about playing mastery golf. Frequently, they go on to play much better golf in a short time. That said, they also frequently acknowledge that they struggle to flip the switch from ego golf back to the mastery golf that they enjoyed in their youth.

This difficulty is understandable for the simple reason highlighted by prominent self-concept researcher Herbert Marsh (1994) in an article titled "The Importance of Being Important." Marsh and other self-concept researches have argued that we all have an innate need to develop a self-concept that we can be proud of. Certainly, playing good golf puts us in good stead in front of our friends and peers. But this human need to be proud of ourselves sets the stage for the internal conflict and resistance to mastery golf. Those who are able to win this battle tend to play freer and more fearless golf. Those who attach their identity to their golf scores often play with the fear of damaging that identity.

The reality is that all people have it in them to be both mastery and ego oriented to various degrees. The key thing is to find the healthy balance that works for you, knowing that you will be better on some days than others and not beating yourself up too much on the days that you fail to achieve pure mastery.

A TALE OF TWO GOLFERS

I am often asked why I don't just buy into the fact that some golfers have "it" and some don't. And I am frequently challenged on my opinion that talent is overrated in golf. To address these doubters, I ask them to ponder the following example. See whether it convinces you that you can immunize yourself against adversity.

Suppose that two 10-year old golfers live in parallel universes. Golfer A undergoes five positive experiences per day. In other words, throughout a given day, that golfer takes the time to practice gratitude, to identify a positive thought, to energize his or her mind with small goals, and to engage the people in his or her life with encouragement. At the end of the day, golfer A takes time to review the day and identify things that he or she has learned.

Now imagine that golfer B generates five negative experiences per day. Golfer B begins the day complaining, criticizes breakfast or lunch, and replays bad shots from the previous day. Rather than learning anything that could propel him or her forward, golfer B mentally checks out and passively winds down the day in front of the television.

You can classify positive learning experiences as cutting across areas of learning. As I tell my golfers, it doesn't matter how, or about what, we are learning and improving so long as we are learning and improving. Eventually our lessons will converge, and we will become better. Thus, during our routine exercises, I ask them what they've learned about golf, about parenting, about their physical and spiritual health—anything to keep the positive momentum of life.

Over a given year, golfer A will have had 1,825 positive and growth-enhancing experiences. Golfer B will have had 1,825 negative, suppressive experiences, resulting in a total disparity of 3,650 experiences. When you extrapolate these events out over five years, the disparity between learning useful, encouraging lessons and learning unhelpful, discouraging lessons becomes even more severe: 9,125 positive experiences for golfer A and 9,125 negative experiences for golfer B, a disparity of 18,250 experiences.

Before reading any further, take a minute to ponder the effects of this disparity. After you do this, you can better understand why great golfers aren't born and why a golfer like Matt Kuchar has been able to think his way into the upper echelon of golf. Consider whether you are ready to begin to change your perspective, your golf game, and your life.

On the eternal timeline, having the proper mind-set tends to be more important than talent in golf. While innate traits like size, talent, and strength tend to dominate during the early years of the game (i.e., junior golf), the philosophical approach that golfers take into their careers tends to separate the wheat from the chaff over time.

FACING THE GAME'S CHALLENGES

On this note, every PGA Tour golfer I've ever spoken with has a story about a junior golfer they knew who was loaded with talent but lost his or her way. Talented junior golfers to whom the game comes easy never learn how to compensate effectively, to absorb adversity, or to manage their weaknesses (largely because their weaknesses are not yet exposed). Those golfers who are able to traverse the obstacles of the game learn to approach golf with a mind-set of long-term learning. They train themselves not to get embarrassed because it is widely known on the Tour that not even the most technically sound golf swing can be repeated when a person's mind is clouded with the prospect of embarrassment. Tour players seldom get angry because anger blocks the brain's ability to learn and distorts the ability to make the adjustments required to get better. They view setbacks as opportunities and interpret bad scores as the game showing them areas that they can explore, refine, tweak, and improve. And they always listen closely to the game, seeking opportunities for constant growth and improvement.

Much of the mastery philosophy that I teach my golfers anticipates that they will eventually need to learn how to cope effectively with setbacks and failure. Mastery athletes in general, and mastery golfers in particular, realize that the game requires them to take risks continually to test their limitations. Because pushing their limits to the point of failure becomes an end in itself, failure is a key variable in the equation of success. More accurately, becoming comfortable with failure and learning the valuable lessons that result becomes paramount.

Golfers sometimes encounter difficulties beyond the usual challenges. Scott Verplank is a prime example. While an amateur at Oklahoma State University, Scott won the 1985 Western Open (becoming the first amateur to win a Tour event in 30 years). He has won 5 times on the PGA Tour, been featured inside the top 20 in the World Rankings, played on 2 Ryder Cup Teams, and earned more than $27 million dollars on the PGA Tour.

Two bullet points on his impressive resume are often overlooked. In 1998 he was awarded the PGA Tour Comeback Player of the Year, and in 2002 he was awarded the Ben Hogan Award, which is given to the player who "has continued to be active in golf despite a physical handicap or serious illness."

Jack Carroll/Icon SMI

In golf, as in life, adversity can trigger the growth and improvement that leads to greatness. Scott Verplank's career is an inspirational example of resilience.

Not only did Scott have to face the usual challenges associated with professional golf—golf swing, putting stroke, physical aches and pains, self-doubt—Scott also endured a serious back injury for much of his career. On top of that, he has battled a left wrist injury, which prevented him from competing for much of the 2010 and 2011 seasons. And he has waged a lifelong battle with serious diabetes.

Consider the following stories of other PGA Tour golfers who have squared up and met adversity head on:

As a junior, Scott McCarron was kicked off the UCLA golf team, lost his scholarship, and returned the following year as a walk-on, putting left handed as an attempt to cure the yips. After graduation, he joined a failing business venture with his father that broke them both. After taking out an $8,000 loan, he failed to get through Qualifying School the next two years. In 1996, $2,000 in debt and on the verge of bankruptcy, he won a tournament in New Orleans (and $270,000). Midway through 2001, he had earned over 5 million dollars on the PGA Tour, had secured three victories, and contended in several of golf's Majors.

When Bob Jones first came out to watch Nicklaus play the 12th at Augusta, cool, calm Jack proceeded to shank his shot over their heads. He went on to win 6 Masters and amass a total of 70 PGA wins.

After being struck by lightning as an amateur golfer in South Africa, Retief Goosen had to overcome an array of ongoing health hazards. As if that weren't enough, he suffered a broken left arm in a skiing accident in Switzerland prior to the 1999 golf season (a year in which he beat Sergio Garcia in the World Match Play Championships, had 11 successive wins in the Dunhill Cup, and won the Novotel Perrier Open). Retief also won the 2001 U.S. Open and has a total of 4 career PGA wins.

In 2005, when deciding whether to turn pro, LPGA player Julieta Granada's car broke down. The repairs of $600 cost more than all the money she had in her bank account. She had to take a taxi to the golf course each day. Had she not earned enough that week, she would have been stranded in a small town with no money and no car. She finished 2nd, earning $6,500 (and her car back).

At the Milwaukee Open, Tiger Woods' first tournament as a professional, he recalled being so scared he couldn't breathe. He parred the subsequent hole, finished tied for 40th, went on to win 6 Majors in 4 years, (14 overall), and broke a host of PGA records. As of this writing Tiger has 74 career PGA wins.

As a sophomore in college in 1979, Fred Couples made the cut in the U.S. Open and was paired on Saturday with Lee Trevino, then the number-one player in the world. Of the experience he said, "I was so nervous I couldn't even see my ball on the first tee." Fred shot an 80 that day, but has since gone on to win 14 PGA tournaments, including 2 Masters.

After a stellar 1994 season in which he won the Masters, Jose Maria Olazabal was forced to withdraw from the Ryder Cup due to severe foot pain after which he was diagnosed with rheumatoid polyarthritis. He was unable to walk without excruciating pain for 18 months and was forced to miss the entire 1996 golf season. After months of treatment and therapy, Jose came back to win the 1999 Masters and has a total of 5 PGA wins.

After emerging as one of golf's brightest stars, Hal Sutton went winless for eight years after 1986, with his low point coming in 1992, when his earnings fell to $39,324. He then won 6 tournaments between 1997 and 2001 and has 14 PGA wins to his credit.

Bob May's life in golf began inauspiciously as he bounced around from tour to tour, failing to qualify for the PGA Tour 7 times. He went to Asia, then played the Hogan tour, got his tour card, lost it, went back to Asia, then spent three years on the European Tour. He kept grinding, practicing, and competing and finally, in 2000, played against Tiger Woods in one of the greatest finishes in Major Golf history at the PGA Championship at Valhalla.

Your growth and development as a great competitor essentially mirrors the process of the growth and development of muscles when you engage in weight training. To grow, muscles have to be pushed to failure. In sport, as in life, the natural consequence of pushing your personal limits is the risk that you will fall short of what you're trying to accomplish. But by falling short we come to learn the methods, strategies, and techniques required to propel us beyond the edge of our limits. This advanced understanding that setbacks, failures, and lulls in performance are a key part of ultimate excellence is what prompted Jack Nicklaus to coin the term *so-called failure*.

One of the best self-assessments on the subject of failure comes from Michael Jordan (Goldman & Papson 1998, p. 49):

I've missed more than 9,000 shots in my career. I've lost almost 300 games. Twenty-six times, I've been entrusted with the game-winning shot and missed. I've failed over and over and over again in my life. And that's why I succeed.

I cannot overemphasize the importance of looking at golf as a game of continual learning and thus embracing failure as "so-called failure" and ultimately as a valuable teacher. Bad golf is not the golf gods picking on you. Bad golf doesn't mean you stink. Bad golf doesn't mean that you're a bad person. And bad golf ought not to be frustrating. What is commonly thought of as bad, or sloppy, golf is typically the game giving you objective feedback, telling you, "Hey, you're not doing something properly here. Reflect on your game and figure it out." Through such reflections growth occurs. Ultimately, golf is the fairest of games. It punishes you when you do a thing wrong and rewards you when you do it right. What could be fairer? Although there is a degree of luck in golf (a bounce here, a breeze there, the occasional ball in a divot), as in all of life's endeavors, it evens out in the end.

Sometimes I'll say to a golfer, "The game is giving you exactly what you need to improve." This line usually comes after they've played a poor round of golf or are otherwise experiencing the game in a manner that is frustrating to them. What is interesting to me is how frequently golfers turn away from the exact experiences that have the greatest potential to make them better. This idea is important for you to hear, so let me say it a different way: Golfers frequently actively avoid the very experiences that can make them better. Instead, they prefer to find their answers in the easy, obvious, or convenient places. To give an example, in 2010 I met a golfer who was not patient. His self-assessments spoke to the fact that he didn't consider himself patient or able to play a mature round of golf. "If I do nothing else this year but become more patient on the golf course, it will have been a good year," he said to me.

Although he recognized that he wasn't patient, he exhibited a different pattern in his game when his wedge play began to deteriorate. Specifically, despite hours of practice, he was not hitting his wedges close in tournaments. Imagine a golfer who refines his game to such a level that he's able to do the "difficult" parts of the game well. He is able to drive the ball long and straight, to flush long irons close to the pin, and to shape the ball with different flights in different weather conditions. When faced with a standard wedge shot from 50 yards (45 m), however, he can't seem to hit it close no matter what he tries. After rounds of golf, he laments his poor wedge play, and finally, when he can take no more, he loses his patience for the last time.

This point is critical for this golfer because now that he has lost his patience, he is going to practice his wedges, but he is going to do it with a sense of urgency, a sense of desperation. He will practice with quickness and tension—the very opposite of patience. This golfer is impatiently trying to improve his wedges, not realizing that the weakness in his wedges is an opportunity to improve the other part of his game that is failing—his patience. What this golfer doesn't realize is that the problems in his wedge game are exactly the opportunity presented by the game that would enable him to improve his patience. If only he would look at it that way.

During our first conversation, this golfer told me of his impatience. A few calls later, he called me in a heated state of mind, impatiently railing against his poor wedge play. "Can't you see," I asked, "that the game is giving you exactly what you need to improve? The game is doing you a favor, giving you something that tests your patience. This is a great opportunity to improve!" He didn't want to hear it. "So," he asked bluntly, "tell me what to do to hit my wedges closer." I replied, "To hit your wedges closer, you have to get better at not hitting your wedges closer. You have to respond to your adversity with patience. You have to accept."

I did not hear from this golfer again for six months, when the game of golf had finally backed him into such a corner that he was on the verge of losing his Tour card. When he finally bought into the idea that adversity was something to value rather than lament, his game began to turn around almost immediately. So it goes with the game of golf.

VIEWING SETBACKS AS FEEDBACK

Setbacks (which I ask my golfers to interpret as feedback from the game) are a key ingredient in the recipe of improvement. Although results are no doubt important, the process of continual learning and improvement has to be considered an integral part of any golfer's development. Too much focus on results interrupts this process. Too much focus on results forces golfers to exchange long-term improvement for short-term fixes, which may buy immediate results but tends to lead to long-term disasters. Experimentation and pushing oneself to the limits will surely produce some bad results along the way. What we make of those bad results is what matters in the end. Great athletes, like all accomplished professionals, push their limits, fall and falter, and learn from their mistakes rather than dwell on them. "Failure should be our teacher, not our undertaker," said Denis Waitley. "Failure is delay, not defeat. It is a temporary detour, not a dead end. Failure is something we can avoid only by saying nothing, doing nothing, and being nothing."

Mastery athletes often count on teachers to help point out where they can improve. Jordan considered it an important key to his career (Goldman & Papson 1998):

> The mental skills came with the education of the game that either I learned from Coach Smith or I learned in the course of the coaching staffs that I've been involved with. Tex Winter was the most helpful because he was probably the one who would criticize my game more than anybody, and to me that's a plus and driving force.

Critiquing a pupil is an essential task of great teachers. Nadia Boulanger was the first woman to conduct several American symphony orchestras and was the principal influence on such greats as Aaron Copeland, Quincy Jones, and Elliot Carter. When asked about the teacher–student relationship, she provided one of my favorite quotations about developing excellence in people: "Loving a child doesn't mean giving in to all his whims; to love him is to bring out the best in him and to teach him to love what is difficult."

You can approach a double-breaking, downhill-sliding putt as a fun challenge rather than an irritant. You can approach rainy, windy conditions as a chance to test yourself in various weather conditions. You can choose to interpret a month of poor scoring as a way that the game provides you feedback on your weaknesses and then view your task as a fun challenge to identify and correct that weakness. The bottom line is that golf is a game full of endless challenges, and you have the choice to decide how you want to approach those challenges.

Some of those challenges are obvious, and some are not. We go through stretches of playing poorly because we are steep with our irons. We know the cause, and we go about correcting it mechanically. Just as often we go through stretches of playing poorly and have no idea what is causing the erratic drives, the inconsistent irons, or the off-line putting. Those times can certainly be frustrating, but they can also provide the impetus to learn the hidden details and nuances within our game and within ourselves. Contrary to what some cynics think, the game doesn't pick on people, although I do understand the sentiment. In a game that is partly determined by luck, it can often seem that we're getting none of the favorable bounces, that we're always hitting into the wind, or that we're always getting the unfavorable side

Laying Down a Pattern

The following is an e-mail that I sent to a golfer during the 2011 season. It depicts how mastery golf is actualized, how we try to absorb adversity, and what types of things we consistently do to keep our mental tools sharp and functional.

You always hear me say how I want you to "lay down a good pattern" or "pay attention to the pattern you're laying." I realize that you may not know exactly what I mean when I say that so I thought I'd give you a quick explanation.

A popular saying in psychology goes something to the effect that "behavior causes behavior." What we mean is that human behavior has a tendency to repeat itself, and it doesn't need any help to do it. It's an interesting thing to consider, especially from a golf perspective. Think of the following: people who are nice are generally and consistently nice. The "niceness" repeats itself. People with a quick temper tend to have a quick temper consistently. Freud actually coined a term, "repetition compulsion," to describe this repetition of behavior and life patterns. I am sure you would be surprised if Steve Stricker began throwing clubs, if Matt Kuchar began scowling, if Shaquille O'Neal began making free throws, or if politicians began to make good decisions. Why? Because behavior leads to more of the same kind of behavior, so the habits that we develop are important to pay attention to. Generally, they are going to repeat.

This is why it is important to ignore results (especially early in the year) and pay attention to how you are "seeing the game" (another thing you always hear me say). If you spend the first month really working on the rhythm of your routine, how free you can be, and not getting negative, then you can see how going deeper into the season you can just get better and better. That's our plan—to get you right back where you were your first few years on Tour. Get back to (1) finding your feels, *(2) feeling* free *(forget score), (3) working really hard to lower your* expectations, *and (4) forgiving* yourself.

I am so happy to see you getting back into form. . . .

of a draw. This frustration with the randomness of the game can be exacerbated as we watch an opponent's ball bounce off a tree into the middle of the fairway or see his mis-hit drive somehow stay in bounds. The truth of the matter is that golf is a fair game and no one gets a free pass.

The great American author Gore Vidal once observed that, on an eternal timeline, "everything happens to everyone if there is only time enough." And so in golf, given enough time, everyone goes through just about every experience the game can offer: the goods, the bads, the highs, and the lows. During some rounds we get every bounce and every break, and in other rounds we get none of the breaks. At times we turn a 68 into a 74, and at other times we turn a 74 into a 68. An important turning point for many golfers comes when they stop trying to find ways to make the game easy and instead turn their attention to learning how to manage the game's difficulties better. In that regard, no one has the responsibility (not me, not a swing instructor, not the competition committee at your club) to make the game easy for you.

The best thing that I, or any teacher, can do is make you comfortable with the fact that golf is often fickle, unpredictable, and difficult and then provide you with strategies to enable you to manage yourself and your game through the variability. But as precarious as the game is, it is also honest, fair, and rewarding. On an eternal timeline, golf will reward good thinking as surely as it will punish bad thinking. And if you can be comfortable with the idiosyncratic, unpredictable, demanding nature of golf at the advanced level, then you will have taken an important first step toward allowing yourself to get into flow.

Confidence to Achieve Sustained Success

The most important tool in an athlete's psychological arsenal may be confidence, or what psychologists now call self-efficacy. The importance of an athlete's confidence has become so accepted in athletic domains that it borders on being a worn-out theme. Haven't we all recently watched a sporting event in which the announcer, at a critical juncture in the contest, takes a moment to inform us that the losing team or athlete seems to "have lost confidence" or that a reenergized competitor has "regained her confidence"?

Despite such clichés, confidence in sport is essential to success. Boston Celtics head coach Doc Rivers has spoken eloquently about the importance of constantly feeding and strengthening his team's confidence, a tactic that has no doubt contributed to the six division titles and the 2008 NBA Championship that the Celtics have won under his guidance. College football coach Urban Meyer, who through 2009 had the highest winning percentage in the history of the NCAA, has advocated fast-paced offenses. When asked why he slowed his offense down with quarterback Tim Tebow at the helm, he spoke to the importance of allowing his players to stay in the huddle as long as possible with Tebow because his confidence was contagious to the team.

As important as confidence is in basketball and football, I believe that it is amplified in the game of golf. Here is how Jack Nicklaus put it:

> *What I do know is that inner certitude about one's abilities is a golfer's primary weapon, if only because it's the strongest defense against the enormous pressures the game imposes once a player is in a position to win. Golf's gentlemanly code requires that you always hide self-assuredness very carefully. But hide it or not, you'll never get very far without it.*

Although the importance of confidence in sport has always been acknowledged, it wasn't until relatively recently that psychologists were able to isolate and categorize the specific types of experiences that develop confidence, as well as the particular channels through which it enhances performance. Because of those breakthroughs, we are no longer restricted merely to stating the obvious, which is to say that confidence is important. Now, we can specify why it is important. Even better, we can explain how confidence is developed and how it can be nurtured and maintained. Great leaps have been made in the field of psychology by researchers who spend time exploring this mental judgment.

Although human beings are born with varying personality traits and temperaments, self-efficacy is something that we acquire as we navigate through the tasks and activities of life. When we succeed at something, particularly at something difficult, the feeling that accompanies that success is naturally accompanied by the belief that we can probably do that again, and probably faster and with less effort. After all, in doing it the first time we learned the skills required, and we can now make use of that knowledge to quicken the process. We probably also believe that we can do something a little more difficult, something that requires refining the skills that we have acquired or even learning new skills.

Self-efficacy in the form that matters to golfers results from certain types of experiences that happen as we develop (e.g., successes and failures) as well as our interpretations of those experiences. To the degree that we are willing to invest time making the best sense of our experiences, we can have far more control over our confidence than you might think.

INTERPRETING AND WEIGHTING EXPERIENCE

The first and most important type of experience that helps create and nurture our self-efficacy beliefs is the success that we have attained in a particular endeavor. In the simplest terms, success breeds confidence and failure diminishes it. The more you win, the more confident you become. While you are standing over a 5-foot (1.5 m) putt, your mind at some point will ask itself, even if unconsciously, "Can I make this putt?" It will then look back into its archive of experience, into its mental diary, and the question will be answered by whatever page in the diary you open at that time. If you've made a lot of 5-foot putts, then the answer is, "I can make this putt," and your brain goes about its usual business of telling your body what to do and how to do it. If your body is up to the task, it responds accordingly, and, all things being equal, you are likely to sink the putt. The process of the mind dipping into its diary of experience to search for a self-efficacy judgment works the same for you and me as it does for Adam Scott, Phil Mickelson, or Annika Sörenstam. Here is how it works for Tiger Woods:

What happens to me is that whenever there is a touch of pressure, I can tell myself something very important. I can say, "Hey, I've done this before." That's very reassuring. You feed on it. It's a powerful statement to say to yourself as you're coming down the stretch and you have a chance to win that you've done it before.

Drawing on prior success is what allowed Jim Furyk to build his self-efficacy and rise to number two on the PGA Tour money list in 2006. When asked why he feels confident that he can win a U.S. Open, Furyk noted,

Well, I think it's definitely a confidence builder. It was the difference between thinking I have the ability to win the tournament and knowing I have the ability. I've always had a lot of confidence in myself and my ability, but already winning one makes a difference.

But confidence does not simply emerge as the aggregate, or mathematical average, of your successes minus your failures. A number of things complicate that equation. First, it's not the success itself that raises self-efficacy. Rather, it is your interpretation of that success. Think about it. There is no real objective indicator of what is or is not

Todd Kirkland/Icon SMI

Confidence comes from a positive mind-set as well as positive experiences. Jim Furyk's success on the tour has increased his confidence, but his belief in himself and his positive mind-set led to that success.

a success. What we believe can count as a success depends on the expectations that we brought to the activity. And these expectations differ between people. A PGA Tour golfer and a recreational golfer with a 25 handicap will certainly have different interpretations of a round of 90 played on a beautiful day on a course that rates 70. The Tour golfer will likely have his confidence bruised by such a score, but the recreational golfer will think that he'll soon be ready to join the big boys.

Expectations can also differ for the same person across time. As a golfer improves, the scores interpreted as indications of successful play will similarly shift. The implications of rising expectations for achieving flow are powerful, and we will visit them later in the book.

Another complication in the success and failure equation of self-efficacy is that an initial failure, or even repeated failure, need not result in loss of confidence. The role that success and failure play in shaping confidence has much to do with how much weight we give to each experience, and this weight is often determined in complex ways. The occasional failure, no matter how severe, is unlikely to weaken our belief in our capability if that belief has been powerfully nourished across time and experiences. For example, poor rounds and distant finishes in particular tournaments were unable to jolt Jack Nicklaus from the conviction that he could win any tournament on any course. That same hardy and unshakeable self-efficacy is evident in Tiger Woods today.

BLAME YOUR AMYGDALA

Human beings are more likely to have their confidence undermined by failure than to have it boosted by success. The feelings that accompany success are frustratingly fleeting, whereas the self-questioning and angst that accompany failure, particularly public failure, can undermine our self-confidence for a long while—often for a lifetime. The reason has to do with a little almond-shaped module in the brain called the amygdala. During negative experiences such as missed putts or drives that sail out of bounds or into the water, the amygdala uses hormones and neurotransmitters to highlight the experience. In the same way that students use yellow highlighters to emphasize important parts of a text, the brain uses those neurochemicals to emphasize negative or painful memories (which is why it can be so penetratingly difficult to forget and get over a breakup, the death of a loved one, or a childhood trauma). This highlighting process is at the heart of posttraumatic stress disorder. The phenomenon explains why, when asked about a missed 3-footer (1 m) on the 72nd hole three weeks after the event, Boo Weekley said, "That putt, still to this day, that three-footer, that still gives me a little bit of a jitter."

Golf history is strewn with examples of tremendous players who nonetheless suffered permanent blows to their confidence from traumatic losses. Tony Jacklin admitted that he was never the same after he followed Lee Trevino's unlikely chip-in on the 71st hole of the 1972 British Open with a three-putt from 18 feet (5.5 m) that cost him the championship. Arnold Palmer was badly shaken after losing a seven-stroke lead to the ultimate winner, Billy Casper, on the final nine of the 1966 U.S. Open. Greg Norman never again contended in a major championship after entering the final round of the 1996 Masters with a six-stroke lead only to collapse.

Research has also shown that whereas we often remember positive experiences as a general sensation, we remember negative experiences in richer and more complex detail, and for a longer time. Hence, the more negative experiences that a golfer remembers, or the more intensely and emotionally the golfer remembers even a single bad experience, the bigger the effect is on the golfer's self-efficacy. The mind's diary has good recall for pain.

DON'T FERTILIZE YOUR FAILURES

An elite-level amateur golfer who had made playing competitive golf central to his life came to see me one day. He explained to me that two years earlier he had been in contention on the final day of a tournament when he came to a par 5 that began with a demanding tee shot. He had missed the fairway the previous day, and that was on his mind on the last day of the tournament. While trying not to drive right as he had the day before, he drove right, just as he had the day before. Out of bounds. He began feeling even more nervous, so he teed up another ball. Now fully conscious of the trouble right, he tried again to guard against hitting it right. He opened his stance, aimed way left, and sliced it right again. Out of bounds. He rushed to put another ball on a tee, made a swooping swing, and pulled it left. Out of bounds. He then hit a 5-iron into the fairway and walked away from the hole with a 14. He followed that up with a 9 on the next hole. Since that experience, he hasn't been able to play a competitive round of golf. And although he was a USGA 1 handicap at the time, he hasn't broken 80 since.

Despite all the success he had experienced up to that fateful tournament, a single experience undermined his confidence in himself and in his ability to hit shots that he was clearly capable of hitting. If our success experiences can be thought of as the bricks with which we can build our self-efficacy, then the interpretations that we make of those experiences, as well as the memories that we store of them, can be thought of as the mortar required to build our confidence with the bricks that we acquire.

Successful experiences can enhance and build our confidence only if we can recall them and keep them alive in memory. In the end, the measure of control that golfers have over their confidence is directly related to two mental strategies that bear nurturing. The first is how committed they are to keeping their success memories alive and at the forefront of their mental life. The second is how effectively they are able to put away the perceived failures and disappointments so that they do not exercise their memorable functions. And as I will explain, these two strategies are directly related to how effectively golfers can generate a flow state.

The traumatized amateur golfer who came to see me is an exemplar of one with a problematic frame of mind. As I questioned him, I learned that he was ego oriented to the game, more concerned with how others viewed his play than with the play itself. He didn't compose himself on the golf course and did not default to his routine; he beat himself up for days afterward and relived failure memories over and over in his mind. He essentially took a negative experience and fertilized it so that it grew wild and destructive. It wasn't long before weeds took over his mental garden. As a result, he became incapable of cultivating that garden. Most golfers rebound from their experiences, but the lesson is clear: Negative experiences take their toll on self-efficacy if you allow them to.

TRAIN YOUR BRAIN

What should this golfer have done? Because self-efficacy is rooted in perceived success and perceived success is rooted in the memories that we make of our successes, the first lesson is to learn how to manage frustrating and disappointing experiences in golf through selective memory. Tiger Woods had the misfortune to three-putt two of the last three holes of the 2007 Deutsche Bank tournament. When asked by a reporter if he could recall the last time he had done that, Tiger replied, "No, and I don't care to either." Tiger well understands that after he has learned from his errors and missteps, there is no profit to keeping failures in memory.

To minimize the damage from our failures, we must also get the most benefit we can from our successes. The way to use your mind in golf is to work hard to remember all your good shots. Because the brain is wired to stamp in the negative, you must proactively try to imprint good shots and positive experiences. When it comes time to hit a shot and the brain is looking around in its mental diary, all champion golfers are good at using their memory in such a way that an entry pops up telling of the time that they made a great shot under similar circumstances.

When asked to explain what he thinks about before hitting a 5-iron in competition, Fred Couples insisted that he tries to remember the best 5-iron he's ever hit. Similarly, legendary putter Brad Faxon said that he approaches every single putt in competition as if he'd just made the same putt 1,000 times in a row. In this sense, visualization is a tremendous asset. No matter what caliber of golfer you are, the time spent after a round of golf replaying great shots and positive

Creating Episodic Memories

An exercise that I often do with the PGA Tour golfers who consult me is designed to enhance their confidence. I ask them to write me e-mails highlighting the best shots that they hit during a given week. Regardless of how their week went, I ask them to recall their 10 or so best shots in precise detail. Here is an example from a golfer during the 2005 Honda Classic:

1. *On Thursday with a right-to-left wind on 17 from 259, I put a 3-wood up a little in my stance and aimed just left of the flag. I hit the purest flat fade that cut up into the wind, straightened out, and then softly fell to about 6 feet behind the hole. I barely felt it hit the face it was so solid.*

2. *On Saturday on 16 with a right-to-left into wind, I hit a driver off the tee and aimed at a tree through the fairway, trying to hit a fade of the left bunker. I put the ball a little more forward and had a clear picture of the ball's trajectory coming off the face and starting at the right edge of the bunker and fading back at my target through the fairway. I hit an effortless feeling pure tee shot exactly where I wanted. I had the same wind on Sunday and hit the same shot with just a little higher ball flight.*

3. *On Thursday on 2 with a left-to-right into wind off the tee, I hit a 3-wood trying to hit a little draw into the left center of the fairway just right of the top right edge of the left bunker. I made a smooth swing with no rush and hit a pure slight draw exactly at my target. Very solid.*

4. *On Saturday on 2 I had about a 12-footer right of the hole. I had a great routine, had a clear picture of the line, and hit a very instinctive stroke that did exactly what I thought and went exactly in the center of the hole. It would have gone in a thimble.*

5. *On Saturday on 2 from 147 yards with some helping wind, I hit a slightly choked pitching wedge to a back center hole location. Two days before I rushed my swing and hit it over the back, so I got rid of that thought and focused on the flag's shadow about 7 or 8 feet right and a little short of the hole. I told myself 90 percent and hit it exactly how I wanted to, except it was about 4 feet right of my spot.*

6. On Sunday on 14 from 202 with a back left hole location and an into wind and a little out of the right, I decided not to fade it back into the wind. I decided I would make a freer swing if I choked up and just hit a low, flighted, straight shot at the middle of the green and let the wind take it to the hole. I made a smooth aggressive swing, and it started right at my target and drifted to about 6 feet short right of the hole.

7. On Sunday on 11, I hit a bad 4-iron into the left bunker and hit a mediocre bunker shot to about 15 feet. I told myself that these are the putts that I have not been making lately, so I committed to every cell in my body being focused on my spot on the hole. I hit a pure putt with perfect speed and made it.

8. On Friday on 12 from the front left bunker, I had about 35 yards to the flag with the green running away from me to a bowl off the green that dropped off about 12 feet behind the flag. I made an aggressive swing and thumped it. It landed perfect and then spun to about 6 feet behind the hole.

9. On Saturday on 14 with a right-to-left crosswind, I choked up on a 3-wood and hit a flat little draw with the wind off the left edge of the first right bunker. It drifted to the center of the fairway to the perfect spot at the top of the small rise. It was instinctive, a free swing, and it felt effortless.

10. On 15 on Sunday with a back right hole location and the wind coming slightly off the right and in my face, I hit a controlled 6-iron with a slight fade about 3 feet left of my target which was 10 feet left of the hole. It was the perfect distance and it was smooth without any rush.

Note that this golfer recalled not only the shot but also the circumstances of the shot as he was experiencing it at the time. This point is important because the brain creates what are called episodic memories, which are memories of the events, or episodes, that make up our lives. Those memories are critical to building self-efficacy. By actively recalling, writing down, and re-creating those episodic memories, this particular golfer is enhancing his self-efficacy. In this case, he not only finished well in the Honda Classic but also began an upward cycle of good play that continued throughout the spring and summer, largely because he took control of his mind and his confidence.

memories will pay off with better shots in the future. In the event that they made no great shots that day, athletes can still visualize good shots that they've made in the past or envision what future great rounds of golf would look and feel like.

Let me emphasize that golfers can replay their successes even after a poor round of golf in which it seems that they hit every shot badly. In fact, replaying successes is especially helpful after playing poor rounds. At those times it's critical to work hard to find and focus on the bright spot: the good putt, the soft chip, the committed drive, or the perfectly released 7-iron. Good shots happen even in the worst rounds, and we have much to learn, and to recall, from them. Look hard enough, even at your bad rounds, and you'll realize that there are some bright spots in there! And in the rare case that you can't find a bright spot, look to your future and create—yes, create—your destiny by using your imagination to paint a picture of excellence.

Jackson and her colleagues found that high self-efficacy (e.g., high confidence) is a critical factor for facilitating flow states. Of all the psychological variables they tested, self-efficacy had the strongest relationship with flow. Athletes who believe in their capabilities are more likely to experience a balance between challenge and skills, even when the challenges of their sports are high. Golfers who not only love the challenge of difficult tasks but who also believe in their ability to overcome those challenges tend to perform the best. Their belief system serves as a psychological breeding ground for optimal functioning in the form of flow states.

Generating flow is impossible without a robust sense of self-efficacy. Remember that self-efficacy, or confidence, is essentially your belief in your capability to achieve an outcome. The good news is that science has validated that consistently applying the specific techniques outlined in this chapter can over time strengthen that confidence and measurably improve performance and the ability to experience flow.

FLOW ON THE PGA TOUR

I'll never forget the first time I witnessed flow on the PGA Tour. During the 2002 season, Davis Love III and I had become pretty good friends. Entering 2003 we would talk regularly, discussing various aspect of golf, especially as they related to the mental side of the game. After coming off a winless 2002 and a four-year stretch with only a single win, Davis was certainly open to new perspectives and ideas. With the Tiger Woods phenomenon in full effect, Davis really took to the idea of mastery golf and playing the golf course rather than the score, field, or opponent. Heading into the final round of the Players Championship that March, he had a lot of things working for him. He had picked up an early season win in California, his confidence was high, and he was deeply committed to applying the principles that we'd been discussing.

I walked with Davis on that drizzly Sunday, and for the first time I witnessed flow on the PGA Tour. The memory is etched into my brain, and I am sure I will never forget it. As the round was unfolding, Davis began to walk differently than he usually did. Gone was the nervous energy that typically characterized his Sunday rounds. In the place of that nervous energy was steely resolve and calm focus. Although he was playing with his good friend Fred Couples, Davis' attention seemed elsewhere. My notes from that day describe him as being "both internal and external at the same time."

Then, as the transformation unfolded on the 7th hole, a par 5 at TPC Sawgrass, Davis made a birdie. He didn't celebrate the birdie but gently pulled the ball out of the hole. He calmly proceeded to add birdies on holes 8, 9, 10, 11, and 12 for a string of six consecutive birdies. He added an eagle a few holes later for a final round of 64, which was 10 shots lower than the scoring average that day.

In the pressroom afterward, Davis commented, "I'll remember this round of golf for the rest of my life because it's something I've been building up to the last few months." Davis was referring to his evolving attempts to play mastery golf, to ignore leaderboards, and to play one shot at a time. Like all of us, he struggled internally to ignore expectations and results, but eventually he won the battle and it paid off:

> *I was trying as hard as I could not to look at the scoreboard. . . . I really stayed away from thinking about score . . . trying to stay focused on what I was doing, playing each shot and picking targets and not worrying about the score.*

As I've stated throughout this book, flow is a multidimensional experience that is the culmination of several aspects of a player's game coming together. Davis' 64 was the first time I was able to witness self-efficacy and mastery golf converge with physical and technical excellence and synergize into flow.

Since that magical round, I've been fascinated by the construct of flow, and I've been fortunate to witness it many times over the past decade. Many times these flow states have been produced by players I work with, and just as many times I've stumbled into them as a happy coincidence of being in the right place at the right time. Sometimes the flow states last for several holes, and sometimes they last for entire rounds of golf. One thing I'm certain of is that flow is real, and you know it when you see it.

What follow are stories from the past few years that illustrate flow states and what I've learned about the mental preparation that enabled those golfers to generate flow. Each story highlights one critical dimension of flow. I hope that, through these stories, you will see a bit of yourself and learn lessons that will help you continue to grow, refine, and improve yourself as a golfer and increase the chances that you'll be able to play golf in flow.

Matt Kuchar

Loving the Game

Cooper Neil/Icon SMI

Matt Kuchar entered the final round of the 2009 BMW Championship in Chicago paired in the final group and had a legitimate chance to win the tournament. The stakes were high during this inaugural season of the PGA Tour playoffs: Play well, and earn a spot in the following week's Tour Championship in Atlanta; play poorly and be eliminated.

Everything about the possibility of playing the Tour Championship excited Matt. As a Georgia Tech graduate and Atlanta resident, Matt loved the prospect of playing a home game in front of family, friends, and neighbors. During his time in Atlanta, he had played East Lake often enough to know that he loved the course. He believed that his experience there might give him an advantage. Finally, Matt had recently reversed a trend in his career. Up until 2009 he'd established a pattern of starting the year strong only to fade after June. In 2009 he had finally found the consistency that he was looking for; he was playing well late into the summer and wanted to keep it going.

All this anticipation led to a final round 75, which dropped Matt from 1st place to 10th place for the tournament and eliminated him from the Tour Championship. As you can imagine, Matt was initially disappointed. When dealing with experiences such as this, every golfer has a choice to make. Indeed, there is reality and there is what you do with that reality. Matt had a choice to make.

During times like this many golfers focus on the emotional letdown of a bad round. They feel bad, and they beat themselves up so much that they keep feeling bad. They want it to hurt. In many cases, they may even escalate the self-defeating attitudes by making their personal attacks more, well, personal. Rather than simply focus on the emotion, they make the conceptual leap from attacking the performance to attacking their own character: "You're not good enough to win. You're a loser. You don't have what it takes."

I see talented golfers do this sort of thing all the time. Apparently, they are angry because they didn't perform well and they hope to perform better in the future. But because beating yourself up is antagonistic to good performance, I've always wondered how much these people actually care about getting better. They say they want to improve (e.g., "I'm mad because I really, really want to improve"), but if they really wanted to progress, they would manage their emotions better. At least that's the way I view golfers who lose their temper and chalk it up to a self-proclaimed strong desire to improve.

Although these golfers are wallowing in self-pity and engaging in self-abuse, the great champions of the game have already turned their attention to becoming better. The champions move on and focus on taking steps toward improvement.

By this measure, Matt Kuchar is a great champion.

Matt decided to frame the situation in 2009 as well as he could and to turn every negative into a positive. This task wasn't difficult for Matt because he is by nature a positive person. Specifically, Matt turned his negative into a positive by focusing on three things: the things he did well, the things he could build off, and most important, the things he could learn from the experience.

WHAT'S LOVE GOT TO DO WITH IT?

More than being positive, Matt has a deep love of both competition in general and the game of golf in particular. This love has allowed him to become one of the most consistent players on the Tour over the past several years.

You might ask what Matt Kuchar's love of competition and golf has to do with flow and great golf? The answer is that it has everything to do with his ability to get into flow and to play well on the Tour!

One of the most defining and enduring characteristics of flow states is that they almost always occur when people are doing their favorite tasks—the things that they love to do for the sake of doing them. People commonly experience flow when they are doing things such as gardening, cooking, playing sports, swimming, sailing, painting, playing video games, or even having an engaging conversation or going on a long car ride. The objective task doesn't necessarily matter, so long as the activity is something that generates positive feelings. Think about it. Have you ever been in flow doing something that you dread? The answer is probably not. An activity or experience that fragments our thinking or fails to capture our full attention creates a splintered, atrophied state of mind that is the exact opposite of flow. This is consistent with John Dewey's famous observation that "there is no greater enemy of effective thinking than divided interest." Whatever the task is, it has to capture your attention and bring positive feelings.

When I use Matt Kuchar as a common example of a golfer who gets it and who therefore often gets into flow, a common reaction is this: "Well, how hard can it be to love golf—especially when you're playing for million-dollar purses every week?" This reaction misses the point entirely and flies in the face of abundant research that shows the diminishing effect of external rewards on motivation and performance. The reality is that succeeding at Matt's level of play requires so much time, commitment, sacrifice, and dedication that external rewards, in the absence of love for the game itself, would never produce the type of golf that Matt produces week in and week out on the PGA Tour.

The more acquainted you become with the game, the more you realize how frustrating it can be for many people. Golf often begins as a love affair between the person and the game. How many of us, in our youth, would stay on the golf course or driving range until dusk or dark, often hitting balls into the blackness of the night and looking for them with a flashlight? When I was in my early teens my friends and I spent many evenings playing golf at night. We'd hit the ball and say, "That one felt like a push." We'd go look for it with a flashlight, prepacked in our bags in anticipation that we'd be unable to drag ourselves off the course at dusk. I know many golfers who fell hard for the game at a young age and couldn't get enough of it

This love affair eventually turns bittersweet as we enter periods of high effort without seeing any improvement (the game turns on all of us at times). We find ourselves in the dreaded slump, which often devolves quickly into hating the thought of ever playing golf again. How golfers respond to this phase of development powerfully shapes their future development. In this regard a philosophical approach to the game can be helpful.

While mired in the midst of his slump in 2003, Steve Stricker commented, "This game is so fickle. You can just find it from one tee to the next or lose it from one tee to the next, so you've got to keep plugging away and keep working at it." As his game progressed and he began playing better, he reflected, "I think it's the nature of the game, and that's what I've come to realize."

FOR BETTER AND WORSE

Over the years that I've been working with golfers, I've heard more than my share of stories of golfers breaking golf clubs, throwing their clubs into a lake, and vowing to quit the game altogether.

Frustration is part of the game. The fact is that you can work relentlessly to improve your game, but you will not progress at a predictable, steady pace, nor will you ever fully master the game and be able to perform perfectly in every outing.

The frustration that plagues recreational players is not lost on the best players in the world. As we discussed in chapter 8, the best players probably got there not because they don't ever play poorly or get frustrated, but because they absorb those experiences better than others do. Think of how you feel after a missed putt or a drive that sails out of bounds. Now imagine having those feelings thousands of times, week in and week out. Compound that with week after week of airports, rental cars, hotels, blown leads, missed cuts, chokes, snipes, and slumps. All told, living the life of a professional golfer can be weary, dreary, and exhausting.

Yet some players stick it out, embrace the highs and lows of the game, and enjoy great success.

Matt Kuchar's mind-set buffers him from developing a negative attitude. In 2010 Matt offered some insight into how he thinks about the game:

> *I love the game. I love playing golf. I love practicing. I love everything about it. I love having chances. And even when the chances don't go your way, I think it makes you tougher, makes you stronger. If you don't get beaten up by it, if you keep on stepping forward, all those close calls, they're going to make you better for opportunities in the future. It's fun. I have a great time out here. I have my family traveling. I've got a great family. I enjoy life as a professional golfer. I think it's a great life. It's a great way to make a living. And I feel awfully fortunate.*

The crucial point here is that Matt doesn't only love golf when he's playing well. He loves everything about the game—the highs and the lows, the challenges and the successes. To put Matt's remark into perspective, realize that he made it after a disappointing finish.

Also note that he won a PGA Tour event in 2002 and promptly went into a prolonged slump. It was during this slump that he decided to revamp both his golf swing and his attitude.

When people say that they too would love golf if they made a million dollars a year playing it, they're guilty of reverse causality. Matt doesn't love golf because he makes money at it. Matt makes money at golf because he loves it. He loved it when he was struggling, and that's what took him from losing his card to receiving the 2010 Byron Nelson Award for lowest scoring average on the PGA Tour.

As part of my doctoral program I took a course in human achievement. For one assignment my advisor gave me the task of exploring the underlying patterns of excellence, not just in athletics but across achievement domains. "Research the best of the best, Gio," my advisor said, "and look for the patterns. What do they all have in common?" That question has been the cornerstone of my work for the past 15 years.

At a general level, the patterns are common and well known: discipline, work ethic, practice, intelligence, composure, and commitment. You can peruse the self-help section of any bookstore and find no shortage of advice on living a better life. But there are also intangible variables such as interest, engagement, enthusiasm, and love for what you're doing! It is well documented that people generally fall into flow when doing their favorite activities, so keeping alive the passion for the game helps fertilize the field for flow.

KEEPING IT REAL

To illustrate, in his 2009 book *Born to Run*, author Christopher McDougall chronicles the modern phenomenon of distance runners who make traditional 26-mile (42 km) marathons seem like wind sprints. These ultramarathoners tend to think of 42 miles (68 km) as their normal distance, and sometimes run more than 75 miles (120 km) at a clip. While exploring this unique subset of the population, McDougall uncovered the life of a native tribe who live in the Sierra Madre Mountains of Mexico called the *Tarahumara*, a people who are widely recognized as the leading distance runners on the planet. The Tarahumara not only run superhuman distances but do it on a diet based largely on corn meal and beer and while wearing simple leather wraps on their feet in lieu of pricey running shoes. Even more amazing is that the Tarahumara rarely report fatigue, illness, or injury.

Many explanations have been offered for the high-performance running capabilities of this tribe, but none are more compelling than their psychological traits, which contrast strikingly with those of American runners. While the Tarahumara were increasing their distances and lowering their times, America's best distance runners were doing the exact opposite. The people running in leather straps and drinking beer were improving, whereas those eating energy bars and running in the most technologically advanced running shoes ever created were getting worse. According to McDougall,

> By the early '80s, the Greater Boston Track Club had half a dozen guys who could run a 2:12 marathon. That's six guys in one club in one city. Twenty years later you couldn't find a single 2:12 marathoner anywhere in the country. . . . So what happened? How did we go from leader of the pack to lost and left behind?

> The American approach . . . was too artificial and grabby. Too much about getting stuff and getting it now. It wasn't art; it

was business, a hard-nosed quid pro quo. No wonder so many people hated running; if you thought it was only a means to an end, then why stick with it if you weren't getting enough quo for your quid?

McDougall explores the decline of American running in more depth and in doing so asks a number of provocative questions that could be applied to the game of golf:

How is it that all the research and technology of modern science has reduced the progress in running?

How do the Tarahumara incur fewer injuries without access to modern shoes?

How does cornmeal fuel them better than our modern-day energy bars and protein shakes?

McDougal's simple and direct conclusion accurately elucidates the reason that Matt Kuchar has been able to rise quietly to the top of the golfing world. "The real secret of the Tarahumara: They'd never forgotten what it felt like to love running" (p. 92).

The point that McDougall makes is consistent with research in psychology. His argument that the introduction of rewards into running undermined the sport and delayed progress of American runners is nothing new. Recall our discussion of the difference between intrinsic and extrinsic motivation and the effect that motivation has on a golfer's experience and ability to get into flow (chapter 6).

Psychological researchers have shown that differences in motivation have a profound effect on performance. For example, students who read because they enjoy reading (i.e., those who have intrinsic motivation) tend to remember more of what they read, read more often, and do better on reading tests than students who read because they will receive rewards. Kids who read because they "have to" may be able to pass an exam, but research shows that when reading is no longer required they choose to do something other than reading. On the other hand, kids who are encouraged to love reading do as well or better on standardized tests of achievement and are more likely to pick up books spontaneously of their own free will. Like the Tarahumara and intrinsically motivated golfers, these kids will continue to hone their skills throughout the trajectory of their lives because they enjoy doing so.

Similarly, research on students in the United States reveals a sharp decline in students' interest in their schoolwork and their enjoyment of learning after third grade. In other words, U.S. students generally like learning and attending school up until the third grade. At that point, their motivation and enjoyment begin to decline. Researchers note that this shift in motivation occurs as grades are introduced into the curriculum. Initially, the focus is on learning for the sake of learning, socialization, and cooperation. Later, the focus shifts to earning grades, impressing teachers, and competing against peers.

Perhaps the most confounding thing to researchers is that curiosity, the desire to learn, is an inborn, intrinsic trait. Many theorists argue that schools, with all their programs and extrinsic rewards, interrupt that natural curiosity and undermine the very learning that they are charged with promoting.

The message from all this research for golfers is that in addition to being self-reinforcing, good golf brings rewards that can be distracting and disruptive. Whether those rewards take the form of attention, money, status with the in social group, or just personal best scores, extrinsic rewards exist at all levels of golf. Golfers who allow those rewards to interfere with their mind-sets are also inviting static and clutter into their minds—the type of static that penetrates their ability to focus and keep quiet. Golfers can certainly enjoy these rewards, so long as they are careful not to let the rewards supplant their intrinsic interest in, and passion for, the game of golf. Enjoying the rewards that come with the game and simultaneously enjoying the game on its own terms is entirely possible; the key is to maintain perspective with regard to motivation.

Ultimately, the lesson to learn from the Tarahumara, the psychological studies, and Matt Kuchar is to keep falling in love with golf. You will continue to grow, develop, and change as a person, and as you do, your golf will evolve. By enjoying each stage of development for what it is, you'll see the solutions to your game more quickly and effectively, keep better perspective, manage stress better, and maybe, just maybe, win the Byron Nelson Award someday! In Matt's case, his love for golf allowed him to view that disappointing Sunday as a learning experience rather than a negative experience. He channeled his energy into answering a simple question that all fearless golfers ask: "What can I learn from this experience?" From that question came Matt's realization that he tended to play too conservatively on Sundays if he was near the lead. He learned his lesson, refined his process, and took a more aggressive mind-set into his very next Sunday. The result was a final round 69 at Turning Stone, and a win.

CHAPTER 11

Justin Rose

Understanding Your Motivation

Mike Anzaldi/Colorsport/Icon SMI

was walking across the driving range on Tuesday at the 2010 Players Championship in Ponte Vedra, Florida, when I heard a call from my friend and colleague, the noted swing instructor Sean Foley. With a stable of golfers that included 4 of the top 50 in the world (Sean O'Hair, Justin Rose, Hunter Mahan, Stephen Ames, and soon Tiger Woods), Sean was one of the most sought-after swing coaches on the PGA Tour. He is also one of the most well-read, knowledgeable, and dynamic coaches I've ever met. He has a tremendous understanding of both the golf swing and its role within the larger context of golf.

"Gio," he said, "I may have a project for you." As it turned out, the project he was referring to was his client Justin Rose, with whom Sean had been working for about a year. By the time the 2010 Players Championship rolled around, Justin's mechanics and technique were superb; he was swinging the club exactly as Sean wanted him to swing it.

> **SEAN:** The warm-ups are incredible, Gio. Flawless! I've never seen better!
>
> **GIO:** *And yet?*
>
> **SEAN:** And yet, we're not getting results. I think it's between his ears because his practice sessions are a thing of beauty.
>
> **GIO:** *I've heard this story before—great mechanics, bad results. Keep me posted and let me know if you'd like me to step in and offer some assistance.*

Over the next few days, Rose's pattern of good warm-ups followed by poor results repeated itself, albeit with a slight difference. Rather than just having good warm-ups, Justin had an awe-inspiring series of prodigiously good warm-ups. "As good as he's ever hit it in his life," coach Foley told me. Every shot that Justin was hitting on the driving range was flush: wedges, long irons, and driver.

Like amateur golfers, professionals who have great warm-ups tend to have high expectations for good play. They meet these expectations much of the time, but not always. Golf is too fickle and complex to allow such direct correlations. I've been studying golf closely for the better part of 20 years, and I've observed bad warm-ups that lead to great rounds and great warm-ups that lead to bad rounds.

Great warm-ups do lead to great rounds—and to rounds of every other type, which I guess is why Jack Nicklaus astutely observed, "Practice rounds and warm-ups are meaningless beyond what they may do for your confidence." Acceptance of this fact is an effective way to keep expectations in check, which probably helped Nicklaus win 73 PGA Tour events and 18 majors.

In Justin's case, the result of his exceptional warm-up the week of the Players Championships was a disappointing 72, 72, which was poor enough for a missed cut. Thus, the frustrating pattern of under-achievement for someone of Justin's pedigree, talent, coaching, and technique continued.

The week following his missed cut, Justin and I had the first of what would be many breakfasts together. I started by asking him some simple questions regarding his thoughts and beliefs about competition, golf, what it takes to play outstanding golf, and other fundamental questions that would help get me closer to how he understands the game. His reaction to one question in particular stood out.

When I asked him why he played golf, he didn't have a clear answer. He'd never thought to ask himself that question. Because he'd been playing from a young age, golf was simply what he did. In some respects, golf was just his habit. I probed further. "You've gotten out of bed every day for the past 10 years to practice the game of golf and in that time you've never considered asking yourself why you actually do it?" He found this observation as humorous as I did. "That," I told him, "might be a good place to begin understanding those missed cuts."

CHANGE YOUR MIND, CHANGE YOUR GAME

One of the interesting things about working on the psychological side of things is that you are able to see qualitative changes in people before you ever see changes in performance. The person changes, and then the game follows. Altering the thought patterns and belief systems of people is a unique and rewarding undertaking, and one that should never be taken lightly or attempted with anything less than 100 percent buy-in by the golfer.

The process unfolds rather predictably:

1. It begins with teaching simple ideas and psychological con-structs.

2. The person then internalizes the ideas and holds them up to his or her own experiences.

3. The golfer tests the ideas against present and future experi-ences and during this phase has an "aha" moment when the ideas crystallize.

4. Finally, after considering the ideas for some time, the golfer integrates them into his or her belief system. The ideas then

serve as the new lens through which the golfer sees the world, interprets experiences, and engages the game.

The endeavor proceeded that way with Justin. As he began to explore the whys of his golf, I introduced him to the concept of achievement goals. Through the lens of achievement golf theory, he began to see his own mastery and ego tendencies. Consequently, he began to understand his underlying motivations and intentions and thus put some structure on his mind-set and belief system. By working toward becoming a mastery-oriented golfer, he began to untangle the conflict and confusion in his mind. Why? Because after golfers becomes clear about their purpose for playing, then their reactions, focus, and mental clarity fall in line with that motivation.

I find that few people understand the relationship between their motivations and their thoughts, feelings, and performances. When I explain to athletes the differences between mastery and ego orientations, these relationships often come into better focus. Review the following examples:

If the reason that you are playing is

to be liked by the people you're paired with, you'll be at the mercy of how you think you're being perceived.

to impress people with your golf game, then you'll be at the mercy of your score.

to beat a specific golfer, then your mental clarity is likely to fluctuate depending on how you're playing relative to how they're playing (talk about uncertainty!).

to make money, then you're mental focus and intensity will vary relative to how much money you perceive you are or are not making.

to shield yourself from threats to your ego (e.g., self-image), then you run the risk of becoming nervous or angry when your ego is threatened or questioned.

If, however, your motivation is

curiosity, then you'll be perpetually engaged in the task.

to grow and evolve as a player, then your experiences will be fully accepted and you'll remain free.

to enjoy yourself throughout the round and day, then you'll seek the type of enjoyment on the golf course that makes you mentally free.

So, you see, a golfer's motivation is often at the core of his or her mind-set. But it is not just the amount of motivation that is important; it is the quality of motivation as well. Answering the basic question, "Why do you play golf?" can, as with Justin, set in motion the type of belief change required for transformational golf. From there, you can begin a constructive dialogue that quiets your mind or, more accurately, allows your mind to quiet itself and function in a harmonious manner that allows for flow.

The following week, our second together, as a newly minted mastery golfer, Justin finished 10th at the BMW Championship in Wentworth, England. The next week at historical Colonial Country Club, we began to work toward the mastery golf routine that I teach my players. By doing the preshot and postshot routine, Justin evolved from simply thinking like a mastery golfer to thinking and behaving like one on the golf course. This moment is critical in my process with golfers. Most important for Justin was the ability to accept poorly executed shots and move on with a clear mind as he began to view golf as both a performance with a score and a continual learning process. As he stayed focused on his process that week, he finished next to last in the field for those players who made the cut (T71).

As with Matt Kuchar's experience in 2009, Justin's relatively poor result at the BMW Championship was a key turning point, because it provided him an opportunity to avoid letting himself be defined by his results and instead to practice the habit of mastery golf, that is, to immerse himself in learning from an experience rather than reacting to it.

The choice that you face following a poor performance is clear: Do you focus on the result and get disappointed, or do you learn your lesson and apply that lesson with a focus on long-term improvement? As Doc Rivers says about basketball, "You've got to go through something to get something." Justin had said that he wanted to play mastery golf, and he had gone through the experience of performing poorly. Was he ready to reap the benefit?

Mastery golf requires handling both good and poor outcomes a certain way. I told Justin, "The game is testing whether you really mean what you say. It is testing whether you've actually learned your lessons and the degree to which you've internalized them."

And then something remarkable happened. For the first time since he was a teenager, Justin reacted to a poor finish with the mind-set of a mastery golfer rather than an ego golfer. Rather than being embarrassed, angry, or frustrated by a poor result, he approached the following week at the Memorial energized, excited, and eager to play with a mastery mind-set. Justin explained why he was so composed:

I've been thinking. The reality is, I just want to know how good I can become at this game. I want an answer to that question: How good can I become? That question isn't going to be answered in one week, or even two. So I am not going to get flustered over one week. It's a long process.

Going into the week, Justin employed some key principles. We took a page right out of Nicklaus' book of wisdom in emphasizing to him, "You won't win a golf tournament on Thursdays. But you can lose it on Thursdays. Therefore, the first three holes are not about score. They are about establishing the rhythm of your routine with a conservative strategy." By employing that strategy for the first two days, Justin was able to put himself into contention going into the weekend, a situation that he hadn't historically handled very well. In fact, he had a history of building nice leads in tournaments only to lose those leads on the weekend.

True to form, Justin shot a lackluster (by Tour standards) 70 on Saturday. He dropped several spots on the leaderboard and went into Sunday trailing by 4 shots. Rather than wallow in disappointment, Justin focused on the fact that he was only 4 shots off the lead and that his game was in good shape. He recommitted to his process and adopted the strategies of mastery golf. This commitment to process over performance outcomes, this shift from ego to mastery, is part of what sets up golfers for flow.

GREAT EXPECTATIONS

To understand the sense of urgency Justin felt at the Memorial, you have to understand his past. When Justin Rose came on to the PGA Tour in 2001, massive expectations had already been placed on him. In 1998 at the age of 17, he almost won the British Open, finishing fourth. In the years that followed, he went through a significant slump, missing 21 cuts in a row at one point. He eventually recovered his game but spent the better part of nine years on the PGA Tour as an also-ran, coming close several times but never closing the deal.

The pressure of extremely high expectations can be suffocating, and the more time that passes without a win, the more pressure that golfers can feel, both chronically and acutely. During competition, these expectations can leap to the forefront of the brain and interrupt the flow of their thinking just as they're trying to execute a shot. This phenomenon is not unique to tour players, but the bigger the stakes are, the heavier the weight is of the expectations that golfers feel as pressure and nerves.

In the face of all that pressure, golfers frequently try to force the win or the result that they want. This approach usually fails miserably. If you try to force an outcome, you get the opposite result. If you try to force a low score, you often score higher. If you try to force a win, it is unlikely to happen. Strategic golfers know that you play the percentages by playing the appropriate shot.

As it happens for many golfers, Justin's instinct told him to go into Sunday and to be aggressive right from the get-go. The details vary from golfer to golfer, but the philosophy is a cowboy version of golf that goes something like this: "Fire at every flag, go for par fives in two, be aggressive on every putt, and throw all strategy, patience, and ball placement to the wind."

I asked Justin to do the opposite and let patience and discipline define the round by using the first few holes to establish the rhythm of his routine. I advised him to play the golf course rather than the leaderboard. "Do not chase the leader," I urged. "Play your own game relative to what the golf course offers. Once you know how you're hitting the ball after three holes, you can adjust how aggressive you want to be." This advice is golf's version of cyclists' drafting—hang around until you see what the leader is doing but always focus on your own game plan. This is a wise strategy for most golfers most of the time. Counterintuitively, I often advise golfers to wait for opportunities, not to force opportunities, even if they are trailing—especially if they are trailing!

By waiting for, and capitalizing on, opportunities Justin found that by the 9th hole, he had closed the gap from four shots to two. In other words, he had chased down the leader by ignoring him, focusing on his own game, and playing the appropriate shot on every hole. By the 15th hole, Justin was tied for the lead. Coming up on the 18th hole, he had a two-shot lead. He ended up winning that tournament for his first PGA Tour win, and he did it by playing smart, strategic golf in which he never broke his routine or took a risk. After the final-round 66, Justin talked about the calm, patient approach that led to his victory.

I wasn't really focused on the number. I was just very much into my game plan. I think I talked to you guys about this on Thursday, just really trying to play one shot at a time, stay focused, not get ahead of myself. I've obviously been in this situation with you guys a long time, in and around the league. Obviously, this is the first win. That's probably because it's a week where I really stayed the most patient, the most within myself, and the most calm.

SUCCESS IS RELATIVE, AND FAILURE IS A LEARNING OPPORTUNITY

The lessons Justin Rose took from his win at the Memorial mirror several of the principles outlined in this book. First, a golfer always has a best way to play a golf course relative to his or her game. That fact does not change whether the golfer is in the lead or trailing by several strokes. It does not change because 1, or 100, or 1,000 people are watching. It does not change whether the stakes are $5, $500, $5,000, or $5,000,000. And it does not change whether the golfer is paired with Winnie the Pooh, Rory McIlroy, or the president of the United States. Golf is always a game that is best played when golfers evaluate their game relative to a particular golf course. They must come up with a game plan and execute that game plan regardless of the situation.

For golfers on the PGA Tour, failure has a unique role. Most experts in and around the PGA Tour see failure as being central to the game of golf. In many ways, golf is a game of failure in the sense that most golfers can go several years without a win. One win out of 40 tournaments would be considered a strong year, and three wins in a season might garner someone Player of the Year honors. Consider that the collective record for the top 21 players in the world in 2005 was 22 wins against 516 events that they did not win. This statistic becomes more pronounced when we realize that the top two golfers accounted for 10 of those 22 wins, thus leaving numbers 3 through 21 to divide 12 wins among them.

In a sport set up to be so stingy with winning, success becomes a relative enterprise. Additionally, because of the precise nature of the game, fractional lapses in any of its facets—mechanical, motivational, strategic, or physical—often mark the difference between winning and not winning, or having a job and losing a job. Consider that the difference in stroke average between the 7th-ranked player in the world and the 126th-ranked player was a single stroke. In 2005 the 7th ranked player in the world averaged 70.7 strokes per round, earned over $3.5 million, and kept his playing privileges for the following year. The 126th-ranked player (the level at which a PGA Tour golfer loses his playing privileges for the following year) averaged 71.73. The 126th-ranked player earned $3 million less and lost his playing privileges over the difference of a single stroke per round. In a game in which arbitrary bounces and breaks interact with sudden gusts of wind that can take a ball out of flight, what constitutes success?

Because of the unique nature of golf, trying to get as much mileage out of every win and learn as many lessons as possible is important. Although I find all golf tournaments interesting, the next two are especially interesting because they elucidate the direct relationship between good thinking and winning golf. Going into the Travelers Championship in Hartford, Connecticut, Justin was just coming off his win at the Memorial. By sticking to his routine, Justin was able to play the type of golf that most people only dream of. His first three rounds of 64, 62, and 68 were definitely flow states and were the highlights of a stretch of golf that would have him leading 14 of 16 tournament rounds in a row during 2010.

Whenever a golfer wins something of significance, a good deal of attention comes with the win. Whether it's status at your local club, respect among friends, or, as is the case with the PGA Tour, world-wide attention, this audience effect, as it is called by psychologists, can be hard to cope with. Even a newly minted mastery golfer can have trouble blocking out a sudden burst of attention.

Now that Justin was back in the public eye, the spotlight proved a little too bright for him to hide in his mastery mind-set and fearless routine. As the Sunday unfolded, Justin was visibly nervous and edgy on the golf course. Shot after shot was slightly off the mark; putts that the week before seemed to have eyes for the bottom of the cup were now sliding by the hole. By the time he made the turn, he'd already lost the lead. He shot a final-round 75 for a ninth-place finish.

I was excited about his performance and told him so. I think he thought that I was nuts. How could anyone be excited about blow-ing a lead? I quickly sent out a message to the entire team: "This is not a funeral, nor a reason to sulk. It's an opportunity to learn. You will learn and you will be better." The point of my message was this: There is no way to improve without making mistakes! In other words, we couldn't learn unless we had the experience to learn from! That's why I was insistent that his Sunday 75 was exactly what we needed to happen and that he would be a better golfer if he interpreted his 75 as a learning experience.

That Monday we had a longer than normal conversation, and rather than following our typical process, I was direct about expressing my ideas. I made him a "Sunday Guide for Closing," which he took into the next week at AT&T, a guide that explained the key mental aspects of closing out a golf tournament.

A key principle to effective functioning in any competitive domain is the principle of kaizen, which we talked about in chapter 6.

Although kaizen translates literally from its original Japanese simply as "improvement," it has come to embody an entire belief system whereby people see themselves as dynamic creatures, capable of endless improvement. This belief that we are always capable of getting better requires us to immerse ourselves in a process of continual challenge, growth, and learning. And learning is what golf is all about.

I end my weekly conversations with my golfers by asking them to tell me something that they learned from the previous week. I ask them to put aside their emotional reactions from the week before—no sulking, no overreacting, no getting lost in the psychological devastation that comes with relentlessly reminding yourself of how close you were, what could have been, or how much money you've lost—and instead immediately get into a mastery mind-set of identifying what lessons can be learned.

Justin went into the AT&T Classic in Philadelphia. The legendary golf course was set up to be difficult, and Justin had been saying that he was treating it as the U.S. Open. The other thing that was exceptional about the week was how Justin was handling his media days leading up to the tournament. After "choking" at Hartford (media term, not mine), Justin sat in front of the media and patiently answered questions. But he answered questions from the mind-set of a mastery golfer rather than from the mind-set of an ego golfer. He wasn't embarrassed by his performance. Rather, he was encouraged because he had learned valuable lessons. "I am sure that last week's tournament has made me a better golfer," he said. In private Justin had said to me, "You know what? I would rather learn my lesson about rhythm and tension and tempo now, rather than having to blow a major to learn it. I see this as a good thing. A learning experience."

I smiled. Those are the words of a mastery golfer.

The following excerpt from his Friday at AT&T is a little long, but it perfectly illustrates how mastery golf plays out in real life. It explains how golfers can become better through adversity if they transform failures into learning experiences and then apply those experiences. Think of this as a golfer mentally flushing away the negativity.

> **QUESTION:** *Can you put into words what you learn out of an experience like Sunday?*
>
> **JUSTIN ROSE:** Yeah, this is the way I see it: Closing out a golf tournament is difficult. You do learn things, and it depends how long it takes until you give yourself another situation whether you really—when you learn something, you've got to practice

it for it to become natural, right? So if you're not in contention that much, it's very difficult to learn the lessons or to put into play the lessons that you learned.

So this week I'm very happy to have the opportunity to go out there, test myself and put into play what I learned last week. On Sunday I really thought that I went out there thinking very well. Everything from that perspective was the same. My game plan didn't change, my strategy didn't change, and my commitment didn't change. I just felt a little bit tighter, which is, I think, that's the human body. Do you know what I mean?

But obviously today where—there were just some obvious things that didn't work out for me there at Travelers, which is easy when—nothing happened for me at Travelers. It was just a day where if I hit one or two good shots and got a little bit of rhythm going, I think the day would have been so different. But that was the thing that I struggled with—my rhythm. I think everything got a little quick. Like I said, that's the natural thing to happen under pressure.

QUESTION: *Did winning at Memorial make it easier to bounce back mentally from last week?*

JUSTIN ROSE: Yeah, definitely. I turned up here Monday morning feeling like I was a better player than I was Sunday because you learn. My game doesn't go away overnight. You have an experience like that, and if you ask yourself the right questions and if you deal with it in the right way, you become better. That's what learning is all about, and that's what growing and improving is all about.

QUESTION: *You sort of half answered this, but how quickly did it take you or how long did it take you to get over what happened at Hartford, and secondly, what did you learn—how do you prevent something like that from happening again if you're in that position?*

JUSTIN ROSE: You can never prevent it from happening again. I think that's the first thing to accept. You can't be scared of it happening again. You've just got to put yourself in that position, dig in, do your best. You know what I mean? But with all the right tools, golf happens. I didn't do a lot wrong at the Travelers to shoot five-over—I didn't do a lot wrong. It's just golf.

First, if you accept that, it's a lot easier to go out there and play, but there are things you can put in place. And experience: Tiger, Phil, these guys, they get into contention a lot, and therefore it becomes more normal, and those feelings that they face become easier to deal with. So it'll be easier this weekend than it was last weekend, and obviously the more and more I put myself in contention, the easier it will be going forward.

A number of key principles are embedded in this statement. Justin talks about learning, about leaving the past behind, about digging in and doing your best, and most important about recognizing that the nature of golf is such that you can have a poor result without doing a lot wrong. This is effective thinking perfected. Justin did not brood or overthink or panic. He simply accepted the inherent variability and randomness of the game and determined to keep pressing forward with freedom and enthusiasm. By staying out of his own way Justin let his good play continue. As fate would have it, he again played his way into contention and went into Sunday with the final-round lead, which he closed for his second win in three weeks.

After the round of golf and the win, Justin observed,

This was an important day for me. Obviously, I was in here Friday talking about how I wanted to be getting better as a player and that is ultimately the truth, but I knew having not closed out last week, it was important for me just for myself to do it today. I felt like I really did put into play the lessons I learned at Hartford. I played much slower and I really felt calm. I didn't feel like the nerves got the better of me at all the whole weekend, so I was much better at that. It was good fun. I felt very much in control of my emotions and it's been a long week, but I'm very glad we've got to this point with a win.

Stuart Appleby

Developing Appreciation

The study of professional athletes' career paths yields interesting findings regarding skill, ability, and motivation. Perhaps most remarkable is the frequency with which professional athletes run into, and must deal with, unplanned, unpredictable, unforeseen circumstances. Injuries, slumps, marriage and relationship issues, personal crises, family chaos, and illnesses often disrupt pro athletes' lives and impede their improvement.

Developmental psychology is the branch of psychology that studies the life path of people from birth to death and has the aim of detecting patterns and changes that happen throughout the course of life. Developmental psychologists investigate such things as the unique features of adolescent behavior, the shaping of individual identity, the factors at work in the midlife crisis, the ways in which happiness and depression change over the life course, and even changes in memory and cognition with age. Developmental psychology clearly has applications for the world of sport. Athletes face the same challenges that the general population faces, and then some. For instance, after playing for many years, every athlete invariably faces the question, "How long do I want to play? Is the sacrifice worth it? What would I do next in life?" Fortunately, empirical and historical evidence have yielded techniques and strategies that can assist athletes at all levels in dealing with the challenges that they face.

By the time he'd turned 39 years old in May 2010, Stuart Appleby had tasted tragedy and experienced deeper levels of unforeseen adversity than most people will have to experience in their lifetime. The crushing force of blindsiding experiences like the sudden death of a loved one can inflict deep wounds and impair the ability to function, but they can also be transformational events that strengthen people and propel them forward. In Stuart's case, the latter happened.

For the better part of a decade, from 1997 to 2007, Stuart Appleby was one of the most consistent, competitive golfers on the planet. During that stretch he qualified for all 40 majors that were played. He won eight times on the PGA Tour, including three consecutive wins at the Mercedes Championship in Kapalua, Hawaii. He played on five consecutive Presidents Cup teams, and was a staple inside the world rankings top 20. By any objective standard, Stuart Appleby had a great decade. Given the challenges that he faced before and during that period, his performance was outstanding.

Developmental psychology would say that, when attempting to make sense of a slumping or skyrocketing golfer, putting the performance into context against the backdrop of previous patterns of behavior is always important. Thus, we need to look not only at what is happening with a golfer at any given moment but also at his or her recent experiences within the larger scope of an entire career. Being familiar with the person's history is important because when something changes in a golfer, a causal element, a reason, is always present. Doctors use the same problem-solving process when they explore a patient's medical history.

A GOLFER'S TWO BEST FRIENDS

The game of golf tends to test two fundamental psychological properties of a golfer: confidence and motivation. I can say that every golfer I have ever spoken with has faced the danger of losing his or her confidence or motivation, and commonly both at the same time because confidence and motivation travel hand in hand. As the game beats golfers down, they are typically less motivated to practice and invest time in getting better. This lack of practice results in worse play, which chips away at their confidence. The lower confidence negatively affects performance, which in turn reduces their motivation to practice, and the cycle continues until something eventually gives way or breaks the cycle. An important thing to know is this: On the eternal timeline, every golfer goes through this process.

For whatever reason, by the time 2008 rolled around, Stuart Appleby couldn't quite see the game as clearly as he had when he was younger. Although he had a good year, internally he was feeling uninspired. What followed from this motivational lull was the worst season in his professional career in 2009.

You may have noticed that two strong themes are inherent in this book. The first theme is that golf is a mirror in that it gives golfers a clear reflection of their strengths and weaknesses. The second theme is that many of the most vital lessons that enable golfers to improve are lessons that they learn during times of adversity and bad golf. This second theme is not meant to be an inspirational homily, or to make golfers feel better about their bad golf; it is a fact, and spending a lifetime close to the game has taught me to appreciate how true it is. The bottom line is that, in the game of golf, if you learn the right lessons and correct the flaws effectively, then you will improve.

Beginning in late 2008 and rolling into 2009, Stuart's explicit goal was to become more mentally free as a golfer. A decade of great results had gotten him too attached to those results, and as a result he was tightening up a bit. A decade of world rankings had gotten him hypersensitive to those rankings. He had moved in a direction more toward outcomes and out of his processes.

Just as people can recognize the need to work out without taking steps toward their goal, golfers sometimes recognize the need to change their mind-sets, but they don't necessarily know exactly how to do it. Just as people sometimes need personal trainers to get them into the gym doing the right exercises, golfers often need some help developing strategies and staying on the path toward their goals. Stuart needed some guidance in understanding his situation and in turning it around.

As with other golfers, my first priority with Stuart was to determine why he played and to examine the essence of his golf psychology. Was it mastery or ego? In other words, did he play for passion or for accolades, two qualitatively different types of motivation that yield different psychological, and ultimately, performance patterns.

PERILS OF SUCCESS

Recall the decline in the marathon times that McDougall wrote about in *Born to Run*, a decline that he attributed to the introduction of extrinsic rewards like money and contracts into the sport of running. Like those runners, golfers who've worked hard to achieve great success can be distracted and put off course by that success. The process often begins in high school with uniforms and free golf balls; expands in college with scholarships, bags, and the prestige and perks that come with being a student–athlete; and becomes full blown on the PGA Tour where the perks include equipment, money, cars, and sponsorships. That is not to say that money was the reason behind Stuart's poor performance in 2009. Many golfers, during the course of their careers, become overattached to outcomes. They expect to perform at a certain level, and for 10 years Stuart was able to generate good outcomes without too much difficulty.

In pro golf, winning represents something larger than simple greenbacks. It represents the type of expectation that can afflict any golfer who has been on a good run. Good results tend to raise the expectation of more good runs. Although high expectations can be a good thing at times, the expectations that accompany a string of successes can also often lead a person to develop a sense of entitlement. In other words, because they have been able to show up and win golf tournaments, on some level they come to believe that showing up is all they have to do to win. Golf, alas, is too demanding a game for that.

I've said it before in these pages, and any golfer who has ever spent time with me has undoubtedly heard me say it more than once: The game is giving you exactly the experience that you need to get better. I don't mean that in a general or vague sense, the way that parents may tell a child that adversity builds character (although it frequently does). I mean it in a literal and precise way. The game of golf is always giving you exactly the experience that you need to improve.

For example, if you are a golfer who consistently blocks your driver, the game is telling you that you need to figure out something to improve that part of your game. If you consistently miss pressure putts, then you need to figure out what is happening to improve that part of your game. If you are stuck in a prolonged slump, as unpleasant as it may be, then the game is giving you a clear message that you either have the wrong equipment or are doing something in your technical or mental game that is consistently bad. By delivering you sliced balls, missed putts, blocked drives, and poor scores, the game is saying, "You need to improve this or that particular thing." The same is true when you are playing well. The game is giving you exact and accurate feedback, saying, "You are doing many things well." The experience is exactly what you need at the time.

Morgan Freeman's lines from the 2007 film *Evan Almighty* serve as a perfect analogy:

Let me ask you something. If someone prays for patience, you think God gives them patience? Or does he give them the opportunity to be patient? If he prayed for courage, does God give him courage, or does he give him opportunities to be courageous? If someone prayed for the family to be closer, do you think God zaps them with warm fuzzy feelings, or does he give them opportunities to love each other?

This is precisely the way that the game of golf communicates with golfers. When they need to build patience, golf often gives them the double bogey that will enable that very trait to develop. Interestingly enough, when golfers learn patience, they have fewer double bogeys.

REBUILDING FROM WITHIN AND WITHOUT

In the case of Stuart Appleby, the game was giving him a lot of frustration and poor results. As unpleasant as it was for a brief spell, the experience was exactly what Stuart needed. To rebuild his golf swing, Stuart began to explore his motivation and purpose and to revisit his determination to the game. It was during this period of poor scoring when Stuart underwent his greatest growth as a golfer. As I do with many of my golfers, I simply asked Stuart to avoid the obvious, impulsive reactions such as disappointment and instead to look for the larger lessons that the game might be inviting him to learn.

During this difficult time, he had to explore why he was scoring so badly. One of the conclusions he came to was that he had no control over his tension levels. The type of stress that comes with bad golf increases tension in the body. This tension was preventing him from effectively executing the golf swing that he and Steve Bann had relentlessly crafted into one of the finest on the PGA Tour. Tense, stressful, angry golf has physiological and chemical effects that all but make it impossible to play golf in flow. Psychologically, the negativity deteriorates the seamless transition of our thoughts. Physically, the stress hormones prevent the smooth, rhythmic movements that characterize golfers in flow. Before Stuart could transform his golf game, he had to transcend his base emotions.

So a couple of weeks before the Greenbrier, Stuart began to dial down his tension levels. Rather than think about his swing, he simply focused on his rhythm and tension levels. Suddenly, he began finding it easier to get into the proper positions in his backswing. His performance began to improve. He tied for 29th at the U.S. Open, tied for 27th at the Travelers Championship, tied for 18th in Reno, and then it all came together for a record-breaking Sunday 59 to win the Greenbrier.

What, specifically, allowed the 59? The exact lesson that he learned while he was slumping: "Monitor your tension levels. Soften your grip pressure." Coming down the stretch on Sunday, his hands and forearms remained soft, which allowed his swing to behave correctly. He posted the lowest score in the history of the PGA Tour.

This turn of events illustrates what psychologists call reciprocal causation. In golf, flow states generate a quiet mind, simple thoughts, low tension, and smooth rhythm. But when a golfer has been slumping for a while, thinking that a simple attitude change can necessarily lead to flow is unreasonable. So we focus on the symptoms, and what happens is that embracing simple thoughts, low tension, and smooth rhythm helps lead to flow states.

Additionally, Stuart had to examine the factors that led to the poor play and the tension in the first place. In reviewing the fallout from his long string of successes, Stuart realized that he sometimes felt as if he had to go play. Indeed, this type of attitude develops when we take golf (or anything else in life) for granted.

The slump Stuart went through served to shift his perspective from *having* to play somewhere to *getting* to play somewhere. His slump gave him so much gratitude that he played every chance he got! When getting into tournaments was no longer a guarantee, he began to love golf again and to feel appreciative for the opportunity. After 7 weeks in a row, he appreciated the chance to play 8 weeks. After 8 weeks in a row, he appreciated the chance to play 9. After 9 he appreciated the chance to play 10 (most golfers fret after playing 3 in a row!). After 10 weeks in a row, he appreciated the chance to play 11. And in the 11th week, he won!

You would think that after shooting 59 and winning for the first time in three years, Stuart Appleby would have wanted to take a break from the game, that he would have felt a sense of relief, as if a burden had been lifted from his shoulders. But his new perspective took root, and he wasn't just talking different. He *was* different. So what did he do after shooting 59? He played the next two weeks in a row.

He finally relearned the lesson from legendary teacher Harvey Penick: You never *have* to play golf. Golf is a privilege. You *get* to play golf. Stuart would not have learned this lesson had he not gone through his prolonged struggles. After he began to regain perspective, he developed appreciation. After he developed appreciation, the game let him back in. There are lessons in there for all of us.

CHAPTER 13

Camilo Villegas

Maintaining Perspective During the Highs and Lows

Bill Streicher/Icon SMI

Bobby Jones famously said, "I never learned a thing from a tournament I won." He was, of course, referring to a theme I've repeated throughout this book, namely that although bad golf can leave a very sour taste in your mouth, the implicit lessons are invaluable in the process of getting better. In the words of author Daniel Coyle, accelerating the learning velocity of skill development requires that we accept failure as part of the learning process: "Struggle is not optional—it's neurologically required: in order to get your skill circuit to fire optimally, you must by definition fire the circuit suboptimally; you must make mistakes and pay attention to those mistakes" (Coyle 2009, p. 43).

From this perspective it can be very instructive to study the career of my client and friend Camilo Villegas. By doing so, you will be able to understand the process that top golfers employ to keep their games razor sharp, appreciate the difficulty of keeping your game functioning at high levels over long periods, and learn perspectives that I believe will be helpful as you seek to increase your own learning velocity and improve your game.

Anyone who has studied the career trajectories of golfers knows that golf is a game that has built-in highs and lows. Over the course of a 20- or 30-year career, every golfer can expect to go through various stages. Even Major champions such as Jack Nicklaus, Mark O'Meara, Ernie Els, Vijay Singh, and Retief Goosen experience fluctuations in performance. The reasons for these ebbs and flows in a career are often complicated. They can be motivational, technical, injury related, equipment related, or just a function of the natural variability that comes with refining the craft for a very long time. Regardless of the specific cause, the career trajectory of a golfer inevitably rises and falls.

Fluctuations in performance are not isolated to golf. As documented in his film *Letting Go*, 11-time surfing world champion Kelly Slater went through several peaks and valleys in his heralded career. From 1992 through 1997, his wins rose year after year: 28 wins in 6 years, averaging 4.7 wins per year. His peak year was 1996, when he won 9 times. What followed was a 5-year stretch (1998 through 2002) in which he won a total of 3 times. Think about that: 9 wins in 1996, 7 wins in 1997, 0 wins in 1998 and 2000, and only 1 win each in 1999, 2001, and 2002. But was his career over? Hardly. After absorbing his 5-year slump, Slater began winning regularly again in 2003 and in 2008 won 6 times. If you graph Slater's wins, the pattern is

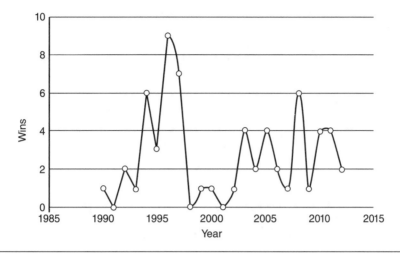

Figure 13.1 Surfer Kelly Slater's highs and lows from 1992 through 2012.

similar to what you'd expect from most great athletes, especially golfers (figure 13.1).

In the words of world champion skier Bode Miller, professional sports entail "building years" and "performance years" (Miller 2005). Building years are when athletes work out the kinks in their game so that they can have performance years when all that work shows up on the scoreboard. Thus, rather than trying to avoid minor slumps, setbacks, and building years, it is typically smarter for athletes to prepare their minds to go through these ups and downs and keep their confidence intact.

If there is one feature of golf at the highest level that most amateurs are unaware of, it is how infrequently golfers actually have their A-games and how much time they spend searching for the key to unlocking their potential. These searching phases often become turning points in a golfer's development.

As with most great golfers (Matt Kuchar, Justin Rose, Bryce Molder, Hunter Mahan, Ben Hogan), Camilo's career has been marked by long periods of solid play interspersed with growth or building phases that have functioned as turning points to propel his game up a notch. Reviewing a few of these will help you understand the nature of his difficult 2011-2012 stretch of play.

For his first five years on tour, Camilo was on a roll. The numbers provide a pretty accurate picture that, as he matured and improved as a golfer, he progressed up the money list and entrenched himself as one of the game's top talents (table 13.1).

Table 13.1   Camilo Villegas Tour Performance From 2006 Through 2010

Year	Cuts made/missed	PGA Tour $-list
2006	18/11	38
2007	17/7	41
2008	19/3	7
2009	18/2	46
2010	17/3	17

LESSONS ON PUTTING AND PERFECTION

One of the early shifts in Camilo's thinking came in March of 2006 at the Doral tournament in Miami. It was in his rookie year, when he finished second to Tiger Woods (who had won 8 out of the 14 PGA Tour events in which he played that year), that Camilo learned two powerful lessons:

1. Great putters miss putts.
2. Winning golf tournaments doesn't require you to play perfectly. It requires that you react well, stay free, and have fun.

These may seem like obvious statements to many golfers, but by the time you've mastered the game at the level that Camilo has, sometimes the obvious things are not quite as obvious as they once were. When you have been great at golf since age 7, as Camilo has, it is natural that your expectations get and stay high. But Camilo's particular set of gifts had created a situation that was bound to land him in a pickle. The situation is a simple, common, but often-overlooked aspect of the game: For many great ball strikers, putting confidence takes more of a hit over time than it does for worse ball strikers simply because great strikers (Ben Hogan, Fred Couples, Chad Campbell, Vijay Singh) have more opportunities to miss. The poor ball striker usually misses 7 greens per round, chips it to 3 feet, and thus faces fewer long putts. As a result, he has more short putts and makes more putts in a given day. That is why you often see the poor ball strikers on tour leading the putting statistics (Brad Faxon did so for the better part of 10 years). Conversely, great ball strikers like Camilo hit about 15 or 16 greens per round, and their putts are usually farther away than those by golfers who chip the ball close to the hole. Think of the average distance a 5-iron ends up from the hole as opposed to the average chip from off the green.

Camilo is in the category of a great ball striker and has been since he was young. As a result, Camilo missed more putts than the average golfer, even the average PGA Tour player, because he historically gets the chance to putt more often from a greater distance. And missing putts has a way of chipping at your confidence, no matter who you are.

But watching Tiger softened the way Camilo interpreted missed putts, and the effect on his confidence became less severe. You see, in 2006, Tiger was 137th in putting average *because* he was 1st in greens in regulation! Tiger won 8 times, and he did it while *missing a lot of putts* . . . but he missed a lot of putts because he had so many chances! Witnessing this firsthand allowed for the type of mental shift that can really open up the floodgates of a golfer's potential. Though he didn't win, the lessons Camilo learned were part of what propelled an exceptional five-year run from 2006 to 2010 and is a lesson that I think every golfer should have handy at all times.

ACCEPTING OUTCOMES

Camilo had begun the 2010 season on a hot streak, with good finishes overseas and a record-breaking scoring average the first half of the PGA Tour season (through six tournaments, he had established the lowest scoring average *ever*). While playing great, he hadn't secured a victory. Something he said in February rang a familiar tone: "I should be winning these tournaments. I am hitting the ball so good!" After a couple of PGA Tour wins and consistently good play, Camilo quite reasonably began expecting good play literally every time he teed it up. Although high expectations can be a good thing, they also have a down side: They don't allow golfers to accept outcomes that conflict with their expectations.

Remember, golf requires that your game evolve as you evolve as a person. This is true for everyone and is another reason why a mastery approach that focuses on learning and growth is so effective. It allows you to learn new lessons, to remember previous lessons, and to continually reinterpret lessons to improve your future effectiveness.

Over the past 15 years as I've watched golfers' careers ebb and flow, I've noticed that many of their turning points come in the form of a simple lesson or eternal truth about the game that they may have learned when they were junior golfers: "Keep your head still when you putt." "Soft hands." "Don't slide off the ball on your backswing." And that, in many ways, reveals something fundamental about the nature of golf. Success isn't only about doing the simple things well; it's also about doing the simple things well *consistently over time.*

As in 2006, in 2010 Camilo's high expectations had gotten the better of him. To help recalibrate his thinking, I did a drill with him that ended up serving as a powerful lesson. I pulled out a sleeve of silver coins along with a Canadian eagle gold coin. We played a game with the following rules:

From 7 feet, Camilo would get a silver coin for every putt he made. I laid the silver coins on one side of the hole so that he could see them as he was putting. Every time he made a putt, I would move a coin to the other side of the hole so he could see his stack of "winnings" grow. If he made 5 in a row from 7 feet, he would get the valuable gold coin.

"What happens if I miss?" he asked before we began. "Nothing," I said. "You get coins only if you *make* them." He chuckled, set his eyes onto the hole, shifted them back to the ball, and smoothly rolled in his first putt. His stroke was free, fluid, and smooth. His release was pure, and the ball rolled beautifully. It wasn't long until he had my entire stack of silver coins, as well as my coveted gold coin. He made almost all of his putts, going 16 for 20 from 7 feet.

I then moved him to phase 2 of the game. After he had accumulated a stack of precious metal (worth the value of a small car), I changed the rules: Camilo would still putt from 7 feet, but he would lose a coin for every putt he missed. I had no more coins to give, so he had nothing to gain, only to lose. If he missed two in a row, then he had to give back the gold coin. As in the first trial, he had to attempt 20 putts.

After a few makes, his stroke quickened a little bit, and his release shortened and looked a little more indecisive and just a bit more desperate. He was trying harder. Pressing. As such, the ball came off a little less pure, and it wasn't long until I had many of my silver coins back. After a while, with nothing to gain and valuable coins to lose, he stopped enjoying the game. It was no longer fun.

It didn't take long for Camilo, who graduated from the University of Florida as an academic All-American with a 3.9 GPA, to pick up the lesson I was trying to give him. Having made it into the top 10 of the world golf rankings, Camilo fell into the same trap he had fallen into his rookie year, the same trap lots of good golfers fall into: He began trying to play perfectly and to be unforgiving of mistakes. He felt every bad shot, every missed putt, every less-than-perfect chip deeper and more acutely and more negatively than he had when he was a rookie playing with nothing to lose and everything to gain. Why? Because having climbed that high on the world rankings list, every miss felt like he was losing control of his grip on the world rankings, and so he tried extra hard on each one, only to find that the harder he tried and the less control he was willing to give up, the less accepting he could be. Soon he was no longer free and flowing in the rhythm of his game.

The ultimate lesson for Camilo was the same as for most golfers: He putts best when he isn't thinking about outcomes, results, or the consequences of a made or a missed putt. It came down to excitement and passion on the front end of a putt and full acceptance on the back end of a putt—which means not trying to control too much! I wasn't advocating reckless golf to my friend as much as I was advocating fearless golf to him. I wanted him to be free again—free to enjoy putting without being a prisoner to outcomes.

LEADING WITH ATTITUDE

With his new attitude firmly entrenched, Camilo left the next day, and what followed was one of the most explosive months of golf I'd seen from any golfer in a long time. He went to the Accenture Match Play Championships, which pits the top 64 golfers in the world head to head. In short order he disposed of Dustin Johnson, two-time match play champion Geoff Ogilvy, Ben Crane, and Retief Goosen. Before he knew it, he was in the quarterfinals against one of the world's hottest players, Paul Casey. The two played a wonderful match against one another, with neither one giving in. It was a record-setting, 23-hole, 6.5-hour endurance contest! With just a couple holes left, Camilo had a chance to close out the match on 17 if he made a straight 3-foot putt—but he missed the 3-foot putt. Had he made the putt, he would have closed out Paul Casey and made it to the finals against eventual winter Ian Poulter. Three measly feet had stood between Camilo and the win. Boy, oh, boy, was this going to test his newfound attitude!

Camilo walked off the green and immediately had a microphone in his face. When asked how tough it was to miss that putt, he replied:

A couple of mixed feelings, I would say. You say, you know what, I missed that putt on 14, but look at the shot I hit on 13. I mean that's—to me, that bunker shot can be one of the best—it's probably the best shot I have ever hit. And I put it under one of the best shots in golf, under the circumstances. That's fine. Again, I was 1 down going to 18. I won the hole, gave myself a chance. Like I said, there was mixed feelings last night. But I took it very good. I took the loss very good, we played 24 holes, and anyone could have won. You can say, oh, you know what, don't think about that three-footer. You know what, it's okay. I've got no problem with it. I wish I would have made it, yes, but you know what, it ain't going to change me as a person. If I keep this attitude the rest of the year, I think it's going to be a good year because I'm having fun.

Camilo went out the next day and beat Sergio Garcia in the second bracket. But I made a mental note of just how great he handled the missed putt and how perfect his response to the situation was. He accepted it fully, and I knew that he would remain free going forward.

The next week he went out to the desert for the FBR Phoenix Open, where he opened the tournament with a 9-under-par 62. His attitude, once again, was excellent. It is no surprise, then, that he needed only 25 putts on the day. And it's important to understand that Camilo's attitude was not great because he was making putts. Remember, before his attitude switch, he had been putting badly. Rather, Camilo was making putts because he had a great attitude:

The way I'm approaching it is just, again, have fun. Just go out there and I've got nothing to lose. You go, you hit a putt, if it goes in, great; if it doesn't, you just give a little smile and go to the next one. It seemed to work last week. I obviously played good today, and we'll continue that good attitude and see what happens.

He played nicely the next two days, finished with a top 10, but just as in 2006, he didn't win the tournament. Rather than focus on the outcomes he could not control, he simply focused on his processes and what he called his "attitude of gratitude." The following week the Tour headed to South Florida for the Honda Classic. Camilo kept telling people of his attitude of gratitude and his passion for the game. As a result of his great attitude, he finished the week second in putts per green in regulation. On March 5, 2010—exactly 4 years after his first epiphany in South Florida that even great putters miss putts—Camilo once again was in South Florida speaking of having fun, of gratitude, and of being mentally free. Only this time, he was holding a trophy as the champion of the 2010 Honda Classic!

MAKING SENSE OF THE DETAILS

An achievement domain is defined as anything that has a measurable outcome. Sports such as golf, basketball, and football have a scoreboard. In the business world, there are bottom-line sales and profits. In the educational arena, students and schools are often measured by grades or test scores. As a performance consultant, I've worked with them all: professional billiards players, surgeons, chess players, abstract painters, financial traders who sleep 4 hours per night, performance musicians, students, golfers, and fighter pilots.

Working across a variety of domains has given me a pretty good understanding of the unique nature of various arenas. It has taught me that psychological freedom means something different to pianists and pilots, that discipline has different meanings to golfers and financial traders, and that being fearless means totally different things to wakeboarders and scientists.

Based on this multifarious experience, I can say with all honesty that golf at the highest level is the most challenging endeavor I've ever come across, and it therefore requires the most advanced, nuanced, and fundamentally sound psychological understanding. Not to diminish the difficulty and complexity of other sports and endeavors, but nothing requires such exacting mental fortitude as playing the game of golf consistently well. The reason has to do with the unique differentials between the quality of a golfer's play and his ultimate score.

As I was reviewing the leader board from the 2012 HSBC World Golf Championship tournament in China, I was reminded of the unique challenges that accompany golf. Here are some of the massive score differentials that individual players experienced that week:

Brandt Snedeker: 60-72, 12-shot differential

Jason Dufner: 71-64, 7-shot differential

Ernie Els: 63-70, 7-shot differential

Louis Oosthuizen: 63-72, 9-shot differential

Lee Westwood: 61-72, 11-shot differential

Nick Watney: 62-72, 10-shot differential

If you talk to players on the Tour, as I have done for the past 15 years, and ask them what the difference was between their high and low rounds, they are likely to say, "Not much." They probably prepared the same way, had equally good warm-ups, and hit a number of high-quality shots. They likely didn't feel especially different from round to round, and they didn't try harder or less hard.

So you may wonder, *What sense do you make of a game that can deliver such radical differences in outcomes when the processes feel exactly the same?* It is in this respect that golf can be maddening: Golfers are judged on outcomes rather than processes in a game where the same processes can produce radically different outcomes!

In most areas of life there is a pretty direct correspondence between process and outcomes. If I put 10 gallons of gas in my car, I can drive 300 miles. With the exception of a couple of miles either way, it is fairly predictable. The same is the case with caloric intake and weight, study hours and learning, weekly hours running and resting heart rate, and other activities where processes and outcomes correspond.

Among all activities, golf stands alone in five respects:

1. The game's sensitivity to internal psychological changes
2. The way small changes in something like a golf ball or driver can correspond to massive differences in scoring
3. The amount of variability a golfer can experience in a single round
4. The amount of variability a golfer can experience over a career
5. The discrepancy between processes and outcomes

It is from this perspective that golf is a game of beauty and difficulty that I interpret the most recent segment of Camilo's professional journey. Just as with Kelly Slater's low periods, a common reaction to Camilo's difficult 2011-2012 phase is to ask, "What's wrong with Camilo?" This type of reaction happens at all levels of competitive golf. Even when junior players are having challenging scoring years, I frequently see parents or junior coaches make the assumption that something is wrong. Often, there *is* something wrong. But just as frequently, small details contribute to vast discrepancies in scoring. Consider these statistics from Camilo's performance in 2012, a year in which he finished 144th on the PGA Tour Money List:

Greens in regulation: 4th

Scoring average before cut: 24th

Overall scoring average: 73rd

Ball striking: 23rd

Bounceback: 7th

Both his driving distance and accuracy were in the top two-thirds for players on the Tour. In addition, Camilo made 7 of his last 8 cuts, and in his last four tournaments he ranked 2nd, 15th, 10th, and 1st for greens in regulation. In those tournaments, he finished 30th, 29th, 20th, and 28th.

Based on these numbers, it seems reasonable to think that Camilo should have had a very strong, or at least a very solid, year. Being that golf is a game where accurate thinking is at a premium, what sense does one make of these numbers?

Before answering that question, let me clarify my point. I am not saying that Camilo had bad luck, that golf isn't fair, or that he played great all season. None of those would be particularly accurate statements. What I am saying, and trying to emphasize, is just how difficult it can be to get a realistic picture of a golfer and how difficult it can be to make sense of golf.

Sometimes the game can be so elusive that you are left without a clear direction on what to fix. In fact, at the highest levels of competitive golf, what holds golfers back is not that they can't swing the club properly but that they cannot make any clear sense about the state of their games because what they experience on the course does not always agree with what the objective numbers say. These golfers have access to the best instruction and technology on the planet, yet they still struggle with the multifaceted nature of the game. They may feel like they are playing well, but the money suggests that they are not. They may have confidence in their putting until they realize that they rank near the bottom. They may view themselves as great wedge players until they learn that their average proximity to the hold with a wedge in their hands is not quite as high as they would have thought. Compounding the problem is that the real answer may lie in composite statistics like overall driving or strokes gained in putting, which, while helpful on a general level, do not help isolate a solution.

In Camilo's case, it took a long time to make sense of things. From February 2011 to June 2012 we couldn't quite figure out why he was playing well but couldn't squeeze a good finish out of a tournament. As usual, the numbers guided us. Accompanying all those great statistics in 2012 were some score-crushing statistics, including these three:

1. Total putting: 142nd
2. Sand saves: 151st
3. Final-round scoring average: 154th

So which numbers are more indicative of the overall state of a golfer's game? Even the poor statistics just listed, when combined with statistics such as 4th in greens in regulation for the season and 24th scoring average before cut, can lull you into thinking that there is nothing wrong.

But as we began to reflect on the previous several years, we realized that while he was doing many things well on the course, he was having the occasional lapse in concentration that, at just the wrong time, might cost important strokes. Another partial cause was that his posture and setup had shifted slightly over the years so that he was now standing more upright. This change rerouted the club and his angle of attack. Camilo has such gifted hands that he can hit shots, even from poor posture. However, occasionally when he didn't rescue the shot midswing, he would hit foul balls that were much worse than his historical misses. These rogue shots happened only occasionally, but they were definitely costing strokes and spots on the money list.

That may sound like an easy progression of puzzle solving, but that's my point about why good psychology is so important to golf: These things are not always obvious. Golf's elusive nature sometimes means it takes an entire summer, or sometimes an entire season or two, in order to make the right sense of this game. In Camilo's case, it took combing through a year's worth of data to finally see the pattern. Performance dips are common, even for history's greatest players, for the same reason recreational golfers go through slumps: The game requires that golfers go through times with poor results and still maintain confidence. It is something that every golfer has to learn.

By midsummer 2012, when Camilo began to improve his posture and work on a new routine to focus his concentration, his performance numbers began to look like the numbers of old. Many of his important metrics began to reappear (greens in regulation) and his putting stats improved dramatically as well. And that is when he was able to make 7 of his 8 cuts and begin moving things back in a positive direction.

While things are still not perfect for Camilo, his experiences present a realistic picture of the ebbs and flows of competitive golf and how being just a little bit off can have a measurable impact on performance statistics. It is this elusive and often frustrating feature of the game that prompted Jack Nicklaus to write, "And that, friends, is the nature of this game, and all you can do about it is lick your wounds and go on and wait for another day, hopefully with at least a wry smile on your face" (Nicklaus 1997, p. 266).

More often than not, the best thing to do when you're playing badly is to simply remain very patient, accept that the downturn is a natural part of your development, and trust that if you stick to your process, things will eventually correct themselves. When Justin Rose had a bad Sunday, rather than abandon his process, he trusted it and won the very next week. After Sean O'Hair missed a cut in the British Open, he doubled down on his confidence and won the next week in Canada.

Golfers who want to play at a high level for a long time cannot afford to abandon processes that have historically served them well. They cannot afford to get bullied by the game. Great players must have the ability to capitalize when the stars are aligned, but they also need the ability to absorb the often-unpredictable nature of achievement domains and the parallel ability to believe in themselves even when the results provide reason to doubt.

In Camilo's case, rather than make a swing change, he made a small adjustment in his setup and has begun making progress. While Camilo's journey is a story that is still being written, I believe it provides deep insight into the difficulty and importance of accurate thinking in golf. It illustrates why it is so important to focus on learning rather than ego and, above all else, to remain patient in this game of ups and downs.

CHAPTER 14

Sean O'Hair

Being in the Present

The modern word *tantalize* comes from the fable surrounding Tantalus, a character from Greek mythology. According to legend, the gods saw to it that Tantalus, who had committed acts of treachery, would spend eternity standing in a pond of water. Each time he bent down for a drink of water, the pond would recede and stay just beyond the reach of his cupped hands. Similarly, fruit trees hung over his head, yet when he would reach for a piece of fruit, the branches would rise and remain just beyond the reach of his hands. His story is one of temptation without satisfaction, of eternal deprivation.

Tantalus occupies many domains. Racecar driver Dale Earnhardt Jr.'s quest for victory in 2011 was chockfull of near misses, close calls, and what-ifs. Despite racing at a consistently high level, contending regularly, and achieving 12 finishes in the top 10, his ultimate goal of winning eluded him. In a parallel fashion, research scientists are familiar with the feeling. Many academic researchers spend a lifetime trying to solve a single proof or seeking to prove or disprove the smallest of details from a particular theory. When it seems like they are getting closer to a finding, the research trail often goes cold. Einstein, while being celebrated as the most successful physicist of modern times, spent 30 years of his life in a failed attempt to create his grand unified theory. Of his quest, Einstein wrote,

The years of anxious searching in the dark, with their intense longing, their alternations of confidence and exhaustion and the final emergence into the light—only those who have experienced it can understand it.

Golfers can certainly relate to Earnhardt's frustration and Einstein's words. The parallels are clear: extreme dedication and longing in a lengthy quest for excellence.

In a manner similar to Tantalus' punishment, golf has a way of teasing the mind and keeping the prizes just out of reach, at least for a while.

A common phrase among golfers of all levels is, "I am so much better than my scores are showing." It's another way of saying, "I am so much better than I am playing." Most golfers spend the bulk of their playing lives in some version of purgatory—not quite hell, not quite heaven. They play OK, but not quite at the level of their potential. They know that they can do better but only rarely get into flow and play as if inspired

Golfers feel most like Tantalus during the often-cruel moments when they are extremely close to a sought-after achievement, be it a personal best score or an elusive first victory. They get right up next to it only to watch it recede.

Finishing way down the leaderboard sometimes seems easier, or at least less anguishing. If you are never really in the tournament, you are less invested, so your emotions emerge relatively unscathed. But the close calls and the dashed hopes can be damning. The belief that they are on the verge of the win, that they are so close they can almost taste it, lives on in their minds and keeps golfers awake at night.

TANTALUS PLAYS GOLF

Anyone who watched the 2007 British Open understands that Tantalus plays golf. Sergio Garcia, who led the first three rounds of the tournament and began the day with a three-shot lead, couldn't will a putt into the hole. Needing to make a par for his first major championship victory, Garcia had a 10-foot (3 m) left to righter for his first major title. As he had been doing all day, he hit a perfect putt. The high-definition coverage captured every moment of the ball's journey as it came off the putter face perfectly and rolled on a direct line to the hole. The ball rolled closer and closer to the hole and began to disappear. It seemed certain that Sergio had won his first major championship! But then the ball that was halfway into the hole hopped back out. Again, golf allowed Sergio to taste the thing that he wanted most, a major championship, but then kept the full satisfaction of the win just beyond him.

Great careers in golf are characterized by close calls and near misses. The game's greatest, Jack Nicklaus, is known for winning 18 major championships. More interesting from a psychological point of view is that he was able to cope with many near wins. The numbers are telling; over the course of a 45-year career, Nicklaus played in 163 major championships. He finished top 10 in 73 of them. Although he did win 18 of those, he also came close to winning 55 other times. Of those 55 top 10s without a win, 19 were second-place finishes. It is the coming close, the Tantalus, that so often causes golfers to drink too much, get divorced, change their swings, fire their coaches, or quit the game altogether. I've seen my share of all those reactions.

Arnold Palmer lost three playoffs in the U.S. Open alone! One of those was when he took a seven-shot lead into the 1966 U.S. Open and lost. Forty years later, Palmer recalled how that tournament still kept him up at night. Ninety-four professional wins. Seven major championships. Thirty-eight top 10s, 19 of which were top 3s. And yet the thing that stays on his mind? "It hurts so much to come close and not win," he said.

Greg Norman's career was defined by its own version of Tantalus' punishment. Norman finished in the top 10 in 30 major championships, more than 30 percent of those that he entered. Despite his two major wins, historians of the game universally see his dramatic failures as being the distinguishing features of his career.

In 1986 Norman went into the final round of every major championship with the lead, a feat now often called the Norman Slam or the Saturday Slam. At the Masters that year, needing only a par to secure a playoff spot, he made a bogey. He shot a final-round 75 at the U.S. Open and a final-round 76 at the PGA Championship to fall out of contention in both tournaments. Even more characteristic is Norman's record at the Masters. In 1987 in a playoff, Larry Mize chipped in from 45 yards (40 m) away to snatch a victory from Norman. In 1989, coming into the 72nd hole Norman again needed a birdie to win and a par to get into a playoff. He teed off with a 1-iron, made bogey, and again fell a shot short. The epic, and most memorable failure in his career (and some would argue in the history of golf) came at the 1996 Masters. He opened with a course record 63 that propelled him to the top of the leaderboard, where he remained for three days. With five previous top-five finishes at Augusta and a six-shot lead, Norman seemed like a sure thing. The media were convinced that even someone with luck as bad as Norman's could not lose a six-shot lead. Norman's long-awaited Masters victory was about to materialize.

Rather than take you through every cruel moment of that round of golf, I'll let you consult the history books. I will leave you with a paragraph from the *Sports Illustrated* column, April 1996, written by Rick Reilly:

> *Golf is the cruelest game, because eventually it will drag you out in front of the whole school, take your lunch money and slap you around. Golf can make a man look more helpless than any other sporting endeavor, except perhaps basketball when you air-ball a free throw in the clutch, and nobody we know has air-balled free throws for an afternoon on national TV. Norman shot 78. He had taken his glorious victory parade and driven it off a pier.*

Thirty top-10 finishes in majors: 2 wins, 28 near misses. Nine top-10 finishes at Augusta: no wins. Temptation without satisfaction.

REMOVING THE STRAIGHTJACKET

Long before I knew Sean O'Hair personally, I had formed an impression of him. Every time he was paired with one of my clients, he displayed the quiet confidence of a champion. Every time his name came up in conversation among other Tour players, it was always in the context of how gifted he was at being able to shape golf shots.

But the quality of his putting stroke, which I had watched on the practice green for years, did not correspond to his putting statistics. He had a perfect stroke, but his putting statistics were consistently outside the top 100 on Tour.

One other thing intrigued me. Coming down the stretch at the 2007 Players Championship at famed Sawgrass Country Club with a chance to win, Sean tried making birdie on the par-three island hole and dumped his ball in the water. Sean had met Tantalus.

But it's what Sean had to say afterward that I found particularly interesting. Rather than apologizing for such an aggressive play, I heard him tell reporters at the media center, "I'll make plenty of money in my career. I wanted the crystal." I smiled. I didn't know Sean O'Hair, but I could tell that he was something special. Sean O'Hair wanted to win golf tournaments. He was fearless.

At the age of 28, Sean had been a professional golfer for over a decade. He had been chasing his dream for quite a while, and since a great 2009 season, the dream had been slipping away from him. Flashes of excellence were followed by poor play, so that playing at the level of his potential seemed perpetually out of reach.

"Playing in a straightjacket" is how many golfers describe the way that the game feels when their minds are not letting them play freely. Indeed, forces were acting on Sean, and they were working against him—forces that he didn't know how to identify or influence. All he knew was that when he played golf he felt like a cyclist pedaling into a perpetual headwind.

By the time he reached out to me in July 2011, he had missed 8 of his 10 previous cuts. Compounding the problem was the fact that Sean was well out of the top 125 on the PGA Tour and in real danger of losing his playing card at the end of the season. The pressure was on. Sean would have to come off missing all those cuts and find a way to play well enough in the eight remaining tournaments against the best players in the world to earn enough money to keep his card. Sean was hardly in an ideal situation.

We had work to do to rebuild the confidence that enabled him to stand over that shot and fearlessly pull the trigger. As you can imagine, this task is difficult when a person's livelihood is on the line. On that day, July 9, 2011, Sean and I spent about seven hours talking about the mind— how it interprets pressures in golf, how those pressures influence perception and physiology, and how all those factors compromise the golf swing.

Ultimately, I asked Sean to change his perspective. Rather than take the view of eight tournaments left, I asked him to look at the next 20 rounds of golf: "There is no Thursday, there is no Sunday. For the next 20 competitive rounds, I would like you to focus on the process we are going to implement." He agreed that he would commit to our work for 20 rounds of competitive golf.

Although a lot goes into great golf, some of the keys that Sean and I discussed are keys that you've seen throughout this book:

The game attacks rhythm and tension.	Key: Have soft hands and play in rhythm.
Reactions matter.	Key: Reacting with anger breeds fear. Reacting with acceptance breeds freedom.
Situations change the value that we place on a shot.	Key: Treat every shot the same.
Golf bullies people into over-thinking.	Key: Dumb it down.

His first tournament, the following week, was the British Open. Sean played nicely on Thursday, shooting a 74 on a day when scores were generally difficult. On Friday Sean stayed patient and birdied his 13th, 14th, and 15th holes to move inside the cut line by a full shot. If he parred the 18th hole, he would make the cut by two shots. If he bogeyed the 18th hole, he would make the cut by a single shot. Barring a disaster, Sean would be playing on the weekend in the British Open. He stood on 18 and striped his drive. Shot 1. As often happens in links golf, the ball caught a ridge and funneled into the rough. From there Sean made the correct decision and simply tried to run the ball up near the green. Shot 2. The ball came out hot and plugged into the lip of a bunker, forcing him to play out sideways. Shot 3. He then chipped on to the green. Shot 4. His bogey putt slid to the left. Shot 5. He tapped in from 2 feet (60 cm). Shot 6. Double bogey. He missed the cut.

In 1920 psychologist Sigmund Freud famously observed that sometimes a cigar is just a cigar. The golf equivalent is that sometimes a missed cut is just a missed cut.

As I've mentioned in previous chapters, research shows that confidence (self-efficacy) shapes the way that people interpret their experiences.

The mind of a confident golfer interprets a missed cut as something benign: "No biggie. Water off a duck's back. Everyone misses cuts. I'll be fine. Just have to work out a few things on the range."

The mind of a golfer who has lost his confidence interprets a missed cut in an entirely different manner. Missing a putt like that at the British Open has the power to make a golfer's mind go down into a spiral:

> *Double bogey. Missed cut. What if I lose my card? What if I lose my livelihood? How will I make a living? Panic. PANIC! PANIC!!!*

As anticipated, that double bogey felt like it meant a great deal to Sean. That viewpoint is clearly understandable, especially in the high pressure of the PGA Tour.

As I always do with my golfers, I tried to steer him out of emotional reactions and into mastery golf.

> **GIO:** *I know this is hard for you to hear right now, but the game is trying to teach you something. What is the lesson? You need to measure progress by things other than short-term results. I know this is bad-tasting medicine, but I also know that double bogey, just like the double bogey yesterday, are exactly the two things that were meant to happen this week. Find the lesson in those two holes, and you'll have made great progress. This is round 2 of 20.*

It took more than 24 hours, but then I received my next message from Sean:

> **SEAN:** The lesson from yesterday is to be in the present moment. I've been thinking about the 18th hole since it happened. I'm not in the present. I am in the past. I've got to accept and get into the present.

DISPATCHING THE DEMONS

Sean's next tournament, the following week, was the Canadian Open. He had a long flight from England to Vancouver and a lot of time to think and face the internal demons that all golfers have to deal with. He was 143rd on the money list, coming off a missed cut, but he could feel that something inside him was changing. Internal change was preceding external change.

Shaughnessy Country Club in Vancouver, British Columbia, was set up like a major championship. The players marveled not only at the beauty of the golf course but also at the shapes of the holes and the difficulty of the setup. On Thursday Sean played a solid round of golf. It was a day, as golfers say, when he played great but got nothing out of it. "3 of 20." I reminded him. I told him that his score was irrelevant to me so long as he stayed aware of what was happening inside him: "For now you have one mission: Make every shot about the shot itself, not about the score, rankings, your career, your past, your future, your family." We set the goal to make every round a little freer and a little less cluttered than the round before. By doing that, Sean had a great Friday (4 of 20) and Saturday (5 of 20). He'd made it into the final group on Sunday.

Playing with a lead undoes many golfers. It is the lights and music that make them quick, tight, and out of sync. In Sean's case, it would have been easy for him to revisit the moment the week before when he panicked. He could have been thinking, "One good round and I save my card. One good round and I take care of my family. One good round and all this pressure and these troubles disappear." Fortunately, he wasn't thinking any of those things. On Sunday morning he called before heading to the golf course. The tone of his voice was calmer and more peaceful. He said to me, "I am ready for the challenge today," and then recited a few keys:

This is round 6 of 20. My job is to be free.

Dumb it down.

Have soft hands on the putter.

I reminded him of one final key: "Make today about rhythm. The game will try to bully you into being quick. No matter what happens with your score, stay in rhythm. This is round 6 of 20." He thanked me and then before hanging up he added, "Whatever happens today, I am OK with it."

Acceptance.

Sure enough, five hours later after a calm, composed round of 2-under-par 68, Sean was again a PGA Tour winner. In his victory speech he mentioned the word *humbling* several times.

When I called to congratulate him on his win, there was a long pause at the other end of the line. Then I finally heard a statement that showed me he was still in the process of becoming a mastery golfer: "6 of 20."

CHAPTER
15

Bryce Molder

Playing Your Own Game

David Allio/Icon SMI

Bryce Molder is, statistically speaking, the greatest golfer in the history of college golf. During his four years at Georgia Tech, Bryce set records for the most number of rounds in the 60s, the lowest single-season scoring average, and the lowest four-year scoring average. He joined David Duval and Phil Mickelson as being one of only four golfers ever to be named a first-team All-American four times. Several players from his college team were sent to the PGA Tour, including Matt Kuchar, Matt Weibring, and Troy Matteson.

As you can imagine, the expectations that people had for Bryce as he made his way to the PGA Tour were extremely high. Right out of the gate, Bryce was named one of the young guns of his generation, considered ready to challenge the established golf hierarchy, and expected to win right away. Bryce is so talented that he almost met those expectations, finishing second at New Orleans in one of his first starts on the PGA Tour.

As that first year progressed, Bryce began hearing the whispers of swing instructors and commentators, who pointed out perceived flaws in his golf swing: "Your fundamentals are poor. Your swing was good for college golf, but it won't hold up on the PGA Tour." Imagine that! A golf swing that was good enough to break all those college records was not good enough.

To an impressionable young golfer, those voices are difficult to ignore. And susceptible golfers who hear them enough begin to doubt themselves. The self-doubt creeps in incrementally. A missed fairway that used to be accepted now becomes an indictment of the golf swing. Every less-than-perfect shot becomes evidence of being too tall, too flat, laid off, stuck, supinated, or pronated. Rather than a bad shot being seen simply as a part of playing golf, it is seen as a fundamental flaw. Late into his first season on tour, Bryce became convinced that he needed to overhaul his golf swing from the bottom up.

This occurrence is all too common on the Tour. Most of the time golfers overhaul their way into obscurity and are never heard from again. For example, Craig Perks, after winning the Players Championship in 2002, decided to use his two-year exemption to make serious changes to his golf swing. He proceeded to miss 40 of 50 cuts over the next three seasons and abruptly retired from the game. Isn't it strange that a player who had such success—who had beaten the best golfers in the world on TPC Sawgrass, one of the most demanding courses in the world—would find it necessary to overhaul a swing after a few bad tournaments? Craig Perks is one of many to make that decision. During an era in which everyone seems to be in love with the golf swing, people forget that great golf has many features other than the full swing and that golf is not a game of perfect.

As a junior at Oklahoma State University, Scott Verplank won the Western Open back when it was played at the difficult Butler National Golf Course in Oak Brook, Illinois, a Chicago suburb. Take a moment to think about that: A college player showed up and beat 139 of the best professional golfers in the world.

Then, during his rookie season, Verplank became convinced that he needed to hit the ball higher to compete on tour. The message that Scott received was the same as Bryce's: A swing that was good enough to earn All-American honors three times and win a PGA Tour event was not good enough. This sort of logic leaves me in disbelief. As a result of changing his swing to hit the ball higher, Verplank spent the next several years battling the yips with his driver and fading into obscurity. Only after he took control and played his game (low, penetrating ball flight) was he able to fight back and become one of the most consistent golfers between 1995 and 2011. Fortunately, Scott Verplank bounced back, but many golfers do not fare as well.

The lesson is clear: A golf swing that is good enough to win at high levels should be changed only after a lot of careful consideration and deliberation. Far too frequently great golfers amplify the flaws in their swing and come to believe that it's not good enough to compete with. What happens is that after they convince themselves that their swing is bad, that belief manifests itself as reality.

REJECTING THE EXPERT OVERHAUL

Because he's a dedicated student, Bryce stuck with the process of attempting to rework his swing for four years. During that period he was so lost that he was routinely missing cuts on the smaller developmental tours that dot the United States. I received a phone call while working with some of my players in Hilton Head. Bryce said that he'd finally had enough, that he was looking for a new direction, and that he wanted to start seeing the game differently. I was excited. "Let's get to work!" I said.

With the help of his old college coach, Bruce Heppler, and a new teacher, Mike LeBauve, Bryce began to simplify the game again. Rather than think about every position in the golf swing, Bryce began focusing on fundamentals: setup, ball position, and alignment. Slowly but surely, the natural ability that earned him all those college accolades began to reemerge. The result was a good 2007 season on the

Nationwide Tour in which he finished in the top 25 to earn his way back on to the PGA Tour.

A turning point in Bryce's mental development came in 2009 when he remarked,

> *You know what? I don't have what's considered the "perfect" golf swing. But you know something? I don't think I want the perfect golf swing. Perhaps having the perfect golf swing prevents you from being able to hit different shots. So all I'm looking for is the ability to know my misses and be able to correct them.*

This statement was the sign of a golfer who was evolving from someone who plays "golf swing" to someone who likes to use his ability to work the ball, to shape shots, and to use his creativity to score. By accepting who he was and what his game was, Bryce began to show steady improvement. He played his way into contention regularly in 2008 and 2009, and in 2010 he even contended in the PGA Championship. As his steady play continued, his confidence began to grow.

But as it happens in golf, a new challenge emerged. Although he put himself into contention regularly, Bryce wasn't closing the deal, so questions emerged about whether he had what it takes to win on the PGA Tour. This phase is natural in the development of any golfer. The best high school players are questioned about whether they can compete in college. Great college players are questioned about whether they can be successful pros. Even after players win on the PGA Tour, they may be dubbed "the best not to have won a major." Because Bryce was new to contending on Sundays, he was expectedly uncomfortable while leading on Sundays.

Specifically, as the pressure increased, what happened with Bryce is what happens with most golfers. Their rhythm quickens a bit, their mind races a little bit, and, most important, with every bad shot they feel as if they are letting the tournament slip away. Golf has a way of doing that to the mind, of amplifying the negatives. The more they try to hold on to a lead, the more they hold on to the golf club and try to steer the ball around the golf course, resulting in the very thing that they are trying to prevent: bad shots.

ACCEPTING IMPERFECTION

I saw Bryce's progression as a natural progression. Winning is a process, and golfers sometimes have to stumble a few times before they learn to win. Note that I use the word *learn* deliberately, because winning regularly on the PGA Tour requires learning many lessons along the way.

Over time our conversations centered on the idea of acceptance, and I advised Bryce the way I advise all golfers:

When you hit a bad shot, you need to simply accept it. You don't have to like it, but you do have to accept it and move on. You didn't close out this tournament? Learn from it, accept it, and move on. Don't dwell or sulk. It does no good. Most great golfers—including Nicklaus, Hogan, Palmer, and Woods—spend years not closing before they spend years regularly closing. You feel nervous in contention? Don't fight it; simply accept it and make fearless swings at your next target. You can't keep expecting perfection from an inherently imperfect game.

Many golfers get lost in this game because they want Sundays in contention to feel perfect. They believe that to win a golf tournament, things need to be perfect. But that is almost never the case. True winners know how to accept when things are less than perfect so that they can then be free. Because they are free, they eventually start hitting more quality golf shots.

This message of accepting bad results was not a message that Bryce initially liked hearing. He's not alone. Most golfers don't like hearing from me that the road to excellence has to pass first through acceptance of poor shots and bad feelings. These supercompetitive people spend most of their lives fine-tuning habits to prevent themselves from hitting bad shots. Selling them on the idea that they need to accept the very thing—bad shots—that they strive to prevent isn't easy!

When I try to convince golfers of the virtue of acceptance, my argument isn't for acceptance for its own sake, but because acceptance often leads to the physiological and mechanical patterns that set the stage for great golf. Think about the other possible reactions—anger, embarrassment, frustration, rage. What path do those emotions typically lead a golfer down? Typically they take the golfer on a path of bad physiology, poor focus, negative thoughts, and terrible rhythm. Conversely, acceptance, humor, curiosity, and other positive emotions allow the mind and body to stay in relative composure. Physiologically, your tension levels, blood pressure, and heart rate don't spike when you are walking around a golf course practicing acceptance, feeling free, and staying in touch with your sense of humor. Research shows that humor releases the adaptive chemicals beta-endorphins and HGH while reducing the stress hormones cortisol, epinephrine, and DOPAC. Essentially, how we react to our golf shots can make our bodies either toxic or healthy.

When I explain it that way, golfers are typically more likely to buy in to the power of positive reactions.

Bryce went forward and began actively accepting that golf is a flawed game and that we are flawed beings. Rather than resist mistakes, he learned from them. His humor on the course improved, as did his freedom, relaxation, and ultimately his scores.

Bryce was soon tested by being in contention on a Sunday. He went into Sunday's round playing in the final group. All his acceptance had made him mentally and physically free, and going into the Sunday round he felt ready to get the job done. But the game gave him exactly what he needed, if not what he wanted. As free and fearless as he was, he simply didn't win the tournament. But rather than be depressed or fuel his self-doubt, he simply acknowledged that he controlled everything he could, that he played well enough to win, and that it simply wasn't his day. No sulking, no funerals, no self-defeating remarks. Just good, healthy acceptance and a rededication to maintain a positive attitude and keep learning.

Going forward, Bryce had an up-and-down season during which he faced times when he hit the ball well but didn't make putts, or made putts but didn't hit the ball well; hit the ball poorly but got a lot out of his rounds, and hit the ball well but didn't score. Virtually all the experiences the game *can* deliver it *did* deliver. Through it all, Bryce kept accepting and focusing on using each week to (1) learn a simple lesson and (2) be more mentally free. What I found inspiring was that he didn't let results cloud his clarity. He began making clear, accurate attributions, and he always seemed upbeat and optimistic that the path he was on would lead to good things.

Bryce was so clear about this point that negativity didn't even enter the equation anymore. He was setting the stage for flow.

SCRIPTING THE PROCESS

Those who study football know that some football coaches often predetermine the first 10 plays of the game, even before the game begins. Known in sport as scripting, the point is to take control of processes, evaluate what is happening, and then make adjustments. One of the upsides of scripting plays is that it buffers people from changes or swings in momentum. In golf the purpose of scripting is to ignore the score and get into the process over the course of four days. Although we do not script the actual shots that we will hit (because those choices are affected by, among other things, weather), we do script routines, reactions, and process goals. A common script that helps us ignore the score is to lay down the goal of kaizen, incremental improvement, throughout a tournament. When we do this, we aim to ignore the score and be a little better each day—a little more disciplined in our routines, a little more committed to our shots, a little more in rhythm so that our best swings should happen on the final nine holes of a tournament.

For the week of the Frys.com open, Bryce's scorecards read like an ideal script. His scores perfectly mirrored his increasing freedom: 71, 67, 65, 64. He birdied his final hole to force a playoff and then birdied four out of his six playoff holes for his first PGA Tour win.

In working with golfers for over 20 years, I had never seen a golfer go from so high on the mountaintop as the elite player in college, to so low when he was slumping, and to the heights again during that final round when he was in flow. During his 5-year slump, it seemed reasonable at times for Bryce to stop chasing his dream of winning on tour and leave golf. It seemed as if he might never get it back, especially when he was shooting in the 80s on smaller tours and getting beat by amateur golfers. But Bryce kept rolling with the game, learning, and growing. His story is a story of dreams and resilience, of humility and talent, of growth, and ultimately of acceptance and freedom.

TEN KEYS
TO FLOW
ON THE COURSE

If there is one fundamental rule of success that is almost universally acknowledged by successful people I've studied, it is the importance of learning what to do with failure. To quote my friend, author Daniel Coyle, the brain requires failure to improve: "Struggle is not optional; it's neurologically required." You will read more about this theme going forward in this book, but now is a good time for you to consider how you've handled your failures so far, and how you may handle them in your future. If you thoroughly embrace all the material in this book, you will still struggle. But ultimately, you will improve, and you will increase your chances of getting into flow more frequently.

A mastery orientation, sufficient self-efficacy, the proper challenge–skill balance, and the ability to channel setbacks into learning opportunities to create an environment for continual growth and improvement will help you achieve the calm state of mind that can lead to flow. The stories from the PGA golfers and the lessons that they learned will inspire you. But in addition to all that, I have found that golfers benefit from specific keys and exercises that they can return to repeatedly.

In this section I offer specific measures that you can take to increase the likelihood of getting into flow and thus the frequency with which that happens in a given round or tournament. Depending on your personal style, your current state of mind, the aspects of the game that you struggle with most, and the particular situation that you find yourself in, some chapters may prove more or less helpful than others at any given moment. I offer this particular group of keys because I have found that successful high-level golfers who get into flow with regularity exhibit them. Whether you implement them all in order or select and perfect the ones that speak most directly to you and your game first, these keys will help you experience flow.

Study Success

There is an adage to the effect that success is not accidental. Although most golfers believe that the bulk of their work begins and ends with the development of their golf swing, for the competitive golfer a sound golf swing is a launching point rather than a destination. To many golfers, working hard means going out there and beating balls, when, in fact, working hard should mean working to learn everything it takes to be a complete golfer: developing effective swing mechanics, improving fitness, getting the right equipment, and fashioning the mind toward winning. When you watch a PGA Tour professional on television, what you don't see is all the work that happens behind the scenes. Every one of them is working on his body, mechanics, and mental sharpness.

Jack Nicklaus observed, "Once a golfer has developed and ingrained a fundamentally sound method, by far the biggest mountain left to climb is learning how to win."

Note that he says "learning" to win. Winning is not necessarily the natural result of effort and practice. To win (a lot in Jack's case), you have to understand the art of winning. While Jack Nicklaus spent his youth studying the mind and manners of the great Bobby Jones, an entire subsequent generation of golfers studied Jack. This group includes the likes of K.J. Choi, Nick Price, Tiger Woods, Geoff Ogilvy, and Ernie Els. Greg Norman studied Nicklaus' game while he was an up-and-coming pro in Australia. He ends his book *The Way of the Shark* (Norman 2006) by reflecting,

And then there was the incomparable Jack Nicklaus—my childhood hero, a man who was already a legend in the world of golf. Jack sat down with me in the locker room of my first Australian Open and encouraged me. When I was anxious at my first Masters, he put his arm around me, and mentioned that he was nervous too. When I was leading the 1986 British Open going into the final day, he pulled up a chair at dinner the night before and offered me some advice. The next day, when I won, he went out of his way to congratulate me. And I'll never forget standing together in his driveway in the rain talking about golf.

As did Nicklaus and Norman, Tiger routinely surrounds himself with people who are the best at their craft, and he picks their brains. Not coincidentally, his close friends include Peyton Manning, Michael Jordan, and Wayne Gretzky, some of the best winners in their respective sports of our generation.

Although trial and error is a large part of learning in golf, some lessons about being a winner are more efficiently learned vicariously. If you study successful people in any area of life, including sport, you will find, as I have, that rather than guarding their secrets, they tend to be remarkably candid about how they reached the top.

Leo Mason/Action Plus/Icon SMI

Emulate the habits of legendary golfers like Jack Nicklaus and those who have achieved great success in other walks of life.

I'm often bewildered when competitive golfers come to me proclaiming that they love the game, that they want to become great, and that they are working hard to accomplish the goal of being great. Then in the next breath they tell me that they've never read Jack Nicklaus' autobiographical book *My Story* (Nicklaus 1997). Here is a book in which Jack Nicklaus takes you through his preparation, thinking, experiences, and strategies as he won the bulk of his major championships. The book offers an opportunity to learn from one of the best to play the game. Would you ignore him if he were to sit next to you and start offering tips? Of course not—he's Jack Nicklaus!

Even a laid-back player like Bubba Watson spent his rookie year on tour arriving at the golf course at 5 a.m. on Tuesdays on the off chance that Tiger Woods might ask to play a practice round with him. "Hey, he's the best player in the world," Watson said. "If I can learn from him, why shouldn't I try to play with him?" Two years later, he and Tiger had become good friends. They regularly play practice rounds together, and Bubba has indeed learned a lot from the world number 1. Bubba is a student of success. Similarly, Rory McIlroy and Jack Nicklaus have fashioned a friendship, and each time they talk it's about how to win majors, according to Rory.

IMPROVING YOUR SKILLS

Because being great is a process rather than an isolated event, you should think of your development as a winner as a process. Among the many ways that you are actively pursuing to become a winner, seek out role models of success and study them. Specifically, study their beliefs and attitudes, their strategy, their motivation, and their thoughts on winning.

First, expand your personal network. Bring as many successful people into your own life as possible and find out what you can learn from them. Observe them. Listen to them. Ask questions. Think about their actions and their words. Greg Norman spent 331 weeks as the number one player in the world and garnered 88 professional wins. Perhaps just as impressive is the business career that he has developed since his days as a competitive golfer (CNBC reported that his net worth is in excess of $250 million). Of the keys to his success, he advised, "And when I reflect on it in later years, I realize how important it is to surround yourself with intelligent, decent people" (Norman 2006, p. 28).

Second, read books about winning written by and about winners. Those who have been successful in their field are bound to have had a lot of material written about them.

As a student of competitive excellence and winning, I've always enjoyed autobiographies. I believe that we have much to learn from the voices of the champions. Toward that end, I suggest that you either develop a library of your own or develop an organized system of keeping important ideas easily accessible (not a terribly difficult task in this era of digital devices). The fact that you are reading this book tells me that you have some interest in learning how to be successful, at least at golf, but don't limit your journey to this book or this topic. Read widely and learn great lessons.

I've compiled a short list of books that might start you on your journey to understanding winning in golf. Note that many of the books have nothing to do with golf per se, but the lessons therein cross over well to the game of golf.

Fearless Golf—Gio Valiante

They Call Me Coach—John Wooden

The Sweet Science—A.J. Liebling

My Story—Jack Nicklaus

How I Play Golf—Tiger Woods

Extraordinary Minds—Howard Gardner

Hogan—Curt Sampson

Driven From Within—Michael Jordan

Every Shot Must Have a Purpose—Lynn Marriot and Pia Nilsson

Sacred Hoops: Spiritual Lessons of a Hardwood Warrior—Phil Jackson

Turning the Thing Around: Pulling America's Team out of the Dumps— and Myself out of the Doghouse—Jimmy Johnson

Golf Is Not a Game of Perfect; Golf Is a Game of Confidence—Bob Rotella

Harvey Penick's Little Red Book: Lessons and Teachings From a Lifetime of Golf—Harvey Penick

Winning—Jack and Suzie Welch

The Talent Code—Daniel Coyle

The Way of the Shark—Greg Norman

A winning state of mind results from observing, listening to, and reading about winners and then finding a way to match their habits and strategies to your own set of assets, skills, habits, and beliefs. Studying their proven methods and then adapting their approach to suit your particular situation is an effective way to expedite the process of learning to think and behave like a winner.

Reflect on where you are in your game and get a clear picture of where you want your game to go. Identify successful models who have been able to craft a game that resembles your ideal and do everything you can do to learn from them. Additionally, identify people in your own life who either detract or contribute to that vision. For those who detract from that vision, try to limit the effect that they can have on your game. For those who contribute to that vision, treat them like the assets that they are and invite them along on the journey to great golf.

CHAPTER 17

Manage Time Effectively

You may be tempted only to glance at this chapter and move past it in haste, figuring either that you are just fine at time management or that it has little to do with golfing performance. Let me assure you that this topic deserves serious consideration. The platform for many of the turnarounds that I am credited with has been time management. Simply put, when golfers come to me in a slump, I change the direction of their games by changing the way that they spend their time.

Ask competitive golfers whether their golfing performance changes when they are put on the clock at a tournament, and they will answer that it does. With the exception of the elite, one of the most common challenges that golfers need help with has to do with being put on the clock.

Why does time matter? Because we play golf in time, and time is the invisible factor that affects every single part of the game, both on and off the golf course.

Within the arena of performance psychology and kinesiology, it is generally agreed that all biological and metabolic activities vary rhythmically in a manner that corresponds with chronological time. Golf is no exception. As I write these words, I have just finished speaking with a PGA Tour golfer whose playing partner had shot 63 on Friday and then posted a Saturday score in the 80s! This inconsistency is one of the most maddening things about the game. You can tune up your technical and mental games perfectly, but if your circadian rhythms are thrown off and you are biologically unbalanced, your body will shift into survival mode!

Heart rate, body temperature, cardiovascular pressure, inflammation, bloating, and subjective perceptions all ebb and flow according to reasonably predictable time tables. The best way to create a sustainable model of performance in the face of those tumultuous variables is to keep as many things consistent in your life as possible. Not surprisingly, the best golfers tend to be great managers of time. Former world number 1 Nick Faldo was obsessive about tending to the details of his practice schedules. On more than one occasion when he was younger, Tiger Woods mentioned that no matter what time he went to bed, he woke up at 5 a.m. "sharp!" He often starts his day with a workout before heading to the golf course for his morning practice session.

Those of you trying to become great golfers who are sleeping in until 9 a.m. should know that you've already spotted Tiger four hours of work! I tell my golfers to own their mornings and not squander them.

No one would expect you to put in the hours on the course that are required to be an elite PGA Tour player. But it is worthwhile to consider the pattern of behavior that makes dedicated golfers successful. Throughout history the best in all walks of life have factored time management into the equation. Ben Franklin might have said it best: "Dost thou love life? Then do not squander time, for that is the stuff life is made of."

As a college professor, I strive to help my students develop time management skills, because I have seen what a huge difference having such skills can make not only in their academic careers but also in their professional success. As a practicing mental game consultant, I bring these same lessons to my work with golfers because the fact is that it is difficult enough to master anything without also feeling rushed or pressed for time. In fact, trying to master anything while being pressed for time is explicitly counterproductive. It is the nature of habit development that the habits we are working on are often accompanied by other habits that are unintended and undesirable. Imagine that I am trying to habituate an effective preshot routine. Day after day I show up late to the golf course as daylight begins to fade. I am forced to rush through my preshot routine. As a result I have ingrained the habit of a preshot routine, but I have also habituated the habits of being late and rushing through my practice. Consequently, on the golf course my routine feels anxious and rushed—all the result of careless practice and the mismanagement of time.

The more you come to understand the philosophy of what I teach, the more you will understand the critical importance of time and time management because they have a direct effect on one of the single greatest psychological fundamentals in golf—rhythm. As you've previously read, the "lights and music" that surround golfers affect both tension levels and the rhythm at which they play golf. We talk more about this in detail in other chapters, so for now I'll just say that rhythm is part of flow. The golfer who is chronically late for practice and late to the golf course is habituating a mind-set that is rushed and that interferes with developing a good rhythm. This habit is therefore antithetical to generating flow.

Rushing to the first tee is the quickest way to ensure that your round will begin badly, send you sideways, and kill any chance of flow. I've repeatedly seen golfers arrive late to the course and have to rush through their warm-up. The rushing tampers with their rhythm, their timing, and their confidence. Their thoughts become scattered and fragmented, and they spiral into an unproductive, cluttered mind-set. Many of them ingrain the habit on the driving range and bring the rushing mind-set with them onto the golf course. Even at the PGA Tour level, hurrying can make a golf swing come apart. If mismanagement of time can undo the golf swings of men who spend a lifetime crafting those swings, imagine what it can do to the golf swing of an amateur!

Do you want to know how important time management is to great golf? Just ask Justin Rose. One of the first skills that Justin and I tried to implement into his processes was that of time management. After Justin came to understand the significance of time management and the way in which it can bleed into his golf game, he began to take it more seriously. I can't say that this was the main factor in his going from zero wins in 9 years to three wins in 18 months on the PGA Tour, but I can say that after he began to emphasize this habit, his body of work improved and the wins followed.

Arriving early and being punctual set the pace and internal rhythm that pervades all aspects of a golfer's life and game. The process of changing someone's time management is predicated on the fact that most people are not accurate when it comes to understanding time. "I'll be there in 5 minutes" typically means that the person will arrive in 15 minutes. People who think that it takes a half hour to drive to the golf course are surprised that when they include unanticipated factors (buy gas, stop signs, heavy traffic, parking), it usually looks more like 45 minutes. So beginning with this fundamental assumption, I try to recalibrate people to becoming good at managing time.

1. Rule 1: Always assume that something will take longer than you anticipate. As I explain to my golfers, adopting this approach means that if you are right and it does take longer, then you are usually right on time. If you are wrong, then the worst thing that happens is that you arrive early somewhere and can take advantage of that free time.

2. Rule 2: Time management is a habit to cultivate on and off the course: When trying to improve golfers' time management, I also spend time with their friends and families because being chronically late is seldom isolated to golf. People who are late to practice or late to the golf course are typically late in other areas of their lives. Thus, we try to enlist friends and families to bring in accountability.

3. Rule 3: Don't just talk about it; do it. Getting golfers to show up early is more important than talking to them about showing up early. I often spend the first week with a golfer going to tournaments, going to practices, and sometimes even going to dinner to make sure that the person is doing time management rather than simply discussing time management.

4. Rule 4: Notice and appreciate when others are on time. Because I am often part of a golfer's inner circle—those people whom the golfer chooses to surround him- or herself with—I make it a point to excel at time management in my own life. I work hard to be a good model of time management and punctuality, and I go out of my way to point out when one of my golfers is doing a good job of time management.

Having worked with Hall of Fame golfer Vijay Singh, I was able to see firsthand what an effective manager of time Vijay is. During my 15 years of traveling with PGA Tour golfers, I have never seen Vijay late for a practice session, late for a tee time, or in a rush to get anywhere. Vijay has a slow, casual shuffle around golf tournaments, and he always seems to play the game at a steady, even, relaxed pace. Time management is one of the habits that have enabled Vijay to capture the number-one world ranking for 32 weeks and achieve 58 professional wins, including 3 major championships. Note that an astonishing 23 of those wins came when he was in his 40s.

Jake Drake/Icon SMI

Let Vijay Singh's exemplary time management skills and extraordinary work ethic inspire you to step up your own efforts in these areas.

After winning the 2002 Tour Championship, Vijay explained his training schedule:

> *You know, I work out twice a day, once in the morning and once in the evening. That should tell you how hard I work. On a regular Tour event, I work like 40 minutes with my warm-up in the morning and probably an hour in the evening, four times a week in the evenings. But every morning, I work out. When I go home, like tomorrow, I have another program set up. It's an ongoing thing. A long time ago, a guy said to me, "Once you reach 35, 36, that's when you kind of start going downwards." So you've got to work twice as hard to keep that one step up. And I've been doing it.*

Imagine the type of time management and discipline required to maintain that regimen for the better part of 30 years. I will be the first to admit that time management can be a detail that is easy to overlook. After all, it is more fun to hit golf balls or practice putting. But make no mistake about it, your ability to manage time will eventually show up on your scorecard, so take it seriously.

IMPROVING YOUR SKILLS

Although not everyone can be a morning person, I do suggest that mornings are typically the best time to work effectively. The chances of your being interrupted between the hours of 5 a.m. and 8 a.m. are dramatically less than the chances of your being interrupted between the hours of 8 a.m. and 11 a.m. That quiet, undistracted time is essential for being able to focus on the skill development necessary for golf.

Although one of my keys for success is to own your mornings, I have to allow for the fact that not everyone is a morning person. Some people have early morning commitments or have children whose mornings also begin early, so they can't dedicate their mornings to themselves or their golf game. On this note, recognize that the definition of being an effective manager of time can vary from person to person. Depending on individual responsibilities, time management is more a state of mind than an unbending schedule. Let me ask you this: When you have a free 20 or 30 minutes, do you find yourself surfing the Internet or doing something productive? During days when your responsibilities ease up, do you fill in your spare time by being lazy or working toward your goals? Indeed, when you really dial in to how to use time effectively, you realize that each moment of each day counts and that you can keep moving in the direction of your goals even when you can only steal little windows of time throughout the day. Sleep habits, diet, goal setting, and the company that you keep all contribute to the quality of your life, to the quality of the time that you use, and to the degree to which you can experience flow both on and off the golf course.

If you want to pattern yourself after most PGA Tour professionals, then get to the golf course an hour and a half before your tee time. Get in a good stretch or even a light workout. Be sure that your strategy is sound and that you have checked and double-checked your equipment. Spend a few minutes getting your game face on before you head to the driving range for your warm-up. You will likely find your warm-up more productive, your rhythm more fluid, and your overall performance better. Most important, you'll improve your chances for generating flow.

Practice With a Purpose

Traveling with the PGA Tour for the past 15 years has allowed me the privilege to engage in conversations with some of the best minds in the game. I have spent time with great swing instructors and coaches like Sean Foley, Mark Blackburn, Butch Harmon, David Leadbetter, Mike LeBauve, Jeff Paton, and the unparalleled Buddy Alexander. I've chatted with historically great players, including Toms, Els, Nicklaus, Palmer, Price, Love, and Couples in addition to the stars of this generation. Through my work I've also had the chance to exchange ideas with the top psychologists, scientists, and researchers from a variety of domains including neuroscience, medicine, kinesiology, physiology, and, of course, psychology. One of the beautiful things about golf is that many of the greatest minds converge in this one arena—trying to figure out this wonderful game that Sean Foley calls "the beautiful struggle" and that Jack Nicklaus calls "the mystifying, aggravating, wonderful game that had become my life's work" (Nicklaus 1997, p. 127).

Perhaps the most interesting and hotly debated topic has to do with efficient practice. Ultimately, the questions have to do with whether there is a right way to practice, whether practice can be a formula, and how much individuality exists across practice. For instance, it is commonly believe that more practice leads to sharper and better skills. Certainly, scientific and colloquial evidence supports this belief. Generally, better golfers tend to be those who work hard and who practice more. But then there are the exceptions to that rule, and some golfers believe that there is such a thing as too much practice. When asked the question about working on his short game, Hall of Famer Fred Couples argued that if he practiced as much as other people, he would get worse. Nicklaus agreed that many golfers weaken their game by hanging around the practice tee too long. During my personal interview with Jack, he quipped, "I see these guys hitting it great and they just stay out there until the sun sets. What are they doing, waiting till they hit a bad one?"

These opposing views were illustrated during the 2011–2012 season as Rory McIlroy and Luke Donald battled back and forth for the number 1 slot in the world golf rankings. Those who were able to watch it up close could see that they have different approaches to golf and to practice. Rory's warm-ups are admittedly pretty short. After arriving late to the golf course before his tee time on Sunday of the 2012 Ryder Cup, Rory commented,

My warmup sessions aren't—if I warm up for 40 minutes, it's a long time anyway. I warmed up for like 25 minutes before I won the PGA this year, and it doesn't really—just to get loose, but I'm pretty loose anyway. It was probably a really good thing I didn't have to think about it too much.

One could never imagine Luke Donald saying such a thing, and Luke made this observation about the difference in practice habits between them:

Well, I've said in the past, I think Rory is one of the most naturally gifted players there is. He just has that look about him—free flowing, hits the ball far, just seems really effortless. I don't really watch myself play that much, so it's hard to talk about myself in those terms. I feel like personally, if I don't work hard and grind it out, I'm not going to be that successful. It's just not that easy for me. I can't take weeks off, come back, and expect to hit it well. I'm just not one of those players that is able to just pick up a club and start where I left off. It takes a lot of work, a lot of effort, and that's kind of how I've been able to be successful.

So the question remains for golfers and coaches alike, What is the best way for a golfer to practice? Although a great deal of individuality is involved, some guiding principles can certainly be helpful.

THE PSYCHOLOGY BEHIND PRACTICE

At the root of practice is the psychology of habit development. Many of the greatest observers of human behavior have landed on habit as the ultimate factor in human behavior and performance, and numerous axioms have been created to help reinforce that lesson. Aristotle observed, "We are what we do every day. Excellence, therefore, is not an act but a habit." William James was perhaps the first psychologist to flush out the rules that guide habit development. He once wrote, "Ninety-nine hundredths or, possibly, nine hundred and ninety-nine thousandths of our activity is purely automatic and habitual, from our rising in the morning to our lying down each night." His laws of habit are still the guiding principles used today.

Warren Wimmer/Icon SMI

Maximize your time on the course and the range by making the purposeful practice Luke Donald regulary performs a habit.

The Great Ones Talk About Practice

While I am practicing I am also trying to develop my powers of concentration. I never just walk up and hit the ball. I am practicing and adopting habits of concentration which pay off when I play. . . . Adopt a habit of concentration to the exclusion of everything else around you on the practice tee and you will find that you are automatically following the same routine while playing a round in competition. Play each shot as if it were part of an actual round.

Ben Hogan

All my life I've tried to hit practice shots with great care. I try to have a clear-cut purpose in mind on every swing. I always practice as I intend to play. And I learned long ago that there is a limit to the number of shots you can hit effectively before losing your concentration on your basic objectives. I have to believe that some of the guys who virtually live on the practice tee are there because they don't have anything better to do with their time. And I have to believe they often weaken their games by letting their practice become pointless through sheer monotony or fatigue.

Jack Nicklaus

At a tournament, I don't really spend a whole lot of time there on the range, or even on the putting green or anything like that. When I get to a tournament site, I feel like my game should be ready. That's one of the reasons why I don't play as many weeks as a lot of these guys do, because I spend a lot of time practicing at home. I do most of my preparation at home. Once I'm at a tournament site, I'm there just to find my rhythm, tune up a little bit, and get myself ready to go play the next day.

Tiger Woods

Hogan, Nicklaus, and Woods all practiced with purpose. Hogan didn't simply hit balls. He hit balls while developing his powers of concentration. Hogan knew that those two things—the physical movement of the golf ball and the mental act of concentration—become associated through repetition and time. Indeed, the meaningful elements of practice will group together into a cohesive framework when you are practicing the right way in a process known to cognitive psychologists as chunking.

Nicklaus was also working to habituate high levels of concentration while also attending to the third principle of skill acquisition outlined by Anders Ericsson: limited, focused practice sessions that had clear purpose. In reading his comment that "my game should be ready," you can interpret that as "my habits should be ready." If you practice effectively—purposefully with high levels of concentration—then you will not have to think about those habits on the golf course. They will already be there.

Habit development has transited into the world of sport with the term *practice*. A few landmark works of science help define the rules by which athletes practice their craft. Perhaps the most famous paper is titled "The Role of Deliberate Practice in the Acquisition of Expert Performance" by Anders Ericsson and colleagues. In this paper Ericsson outlines his formula for expert development, the now-famous 10 years by 10,000 hours rule, touched on in chapter 3. "We have shown that expert performance is acquired slowly over a very long time as a result of practice and that the highest levels of performance and achievement appear to require at least around 10 years of intense preparation" (Ericsson, Krampe, and Tesch-Romer 1993, p. 366). I have paraphrased their framework for the three key steps in the acquisition of expert performance:

1. Deliberate practice requires available time and energy for the individual as well as access to teachers, training facilities, and materials.
2. Motivation is important during practice.
3. Deliberate practice is effortful and can be sustained only for limited periods to maximize gains.

On this final point about limited, efficient practice, note that the trajectory of Luke Donald's career improved after he had children. Many reasons might be at play here, but the strongest case I can think of would be that he had less time to waste and so had to engage in shorter, more focused practice sessions. At the 2012 Memorial, Luke was asked whether it was tough to find time with his children. He replied,

Well, I think it's made me a better practicer. I do feel like I want to spend more time with my kids, but it makes me every time I go to the range, I have a bit more of a plan now. I still work hard, but I can be a little bit more efficient with my practice.

The key thing to understand about habit development as relates to practice is this: Everything registers. Habits group with other habits in a process known as association. For example, while you are hitting balls, you are practicing not only the physical action but also the habits of mind, mood, tension, rhythm, and attention. For that reason, motivation is a key component of skill acquisition. Merely going through the motion of hitting a thousand golf balls may certainly habituate your golf swing, but if other things distract your attention, then you are also habituating distraction. If you are sloppy in your practice, then you are habituating sloppiness. The great ones certainly invest time, but they do so with motivation and intense attention to the proper details.

HABIT AND FLOW

By now, I am sure that you have made the connection between practice habits and flow. Flow is a state of mind characterized by effortless effort and a quiet mind. Almost every golfer I spoke to about their flow states attested to the fact that they have few, if any, technical thoughts while they are in flow. All they have to do is think about the target or the shot that they want to hit, and they can execute the shot with ease.

Regular, deliberate practice develops habits by wrapping myelin around neurons that make circuits fire with more efficiency. When it comes to practice, there is no substitute for careful, focused, repetition. As Daniel Coyle wrote in *The Talent Code*, "Nothing you can do—talking, thinking, reading, imagining—is more effective in building skill than executing the action, firing the impulse down the nerve fiber, fixing errors, honing the circuit" (Coyle 2009, p. 87). The more you practice, the more your habits follow the rules of automaticity. That is to say, the more you repeat an action, over time the less you have to think about that action. Actions become automated in the brain. And characteristics of automaticity share many characteristics with flow: unthinking, automated habits that emerge when we are not consciously thinking about them.

IMPROVING YOUR SKILLS

All this research leads us to some practical applications as they relate to effective practice in golf. Practice in golf consists primarily of two types: practice to ingrain the mechanics of a swing, short-game shot, or putting stroke and practice to compete. Time on the range practicing your golf swing is undoubtedly time well spent. But while you are paying attention to your take-away or your position at the top, that process is becoming a habit. In other words, the more times that you repeat a move while putting your attention on that move, the more habituated both the move and the focus become. And that process is what is required to ingrain a sound habit. The problem is that if you were to go out and try to play on the golf course, you would likely find it difficult to hit many good shots because your focus would automatically go to where your hands are at the top of the backswing, which means you would not be focused on either impact or target. Therefore, you need to designate the purpose of your practice.

If you have a lot of time before you have to play another competitive round of golf, then it is fine to focus your attention on particular aspects of your golf swing. This approach is helpful in crafting the habit that you need.

If, however, you need to ingrain habits while also playing competitively, then your practice sessions should look very different. Many of my players use the three–four rule. They hit three balls while putting their focus on the technical skill that they are trying to habituate. They then hit four balls simply thinking about their target. They rest for a few moments and again hit three balls focusing on the technical skill and hit four balls simply thinking about their target.

Regardless of whether you are practicing exclusively to ingrain a skill or trying to develop a skill while still trying to play, you may want to end every practice session with the six-shot drill. The six-shot drill consists of trying to hit the following shots while visualizing nothing but the shape of the shot:

Low draw

High draw

Low straight

High straight

Low fade

High fade

The six-shot drill is effective because it habituates all the skills required not only for technical excellence but also for effective playing. It remains the most effective drill I have ever come across for helping golfers play better. (At the highest level of excellence, this becomes a nine-shot drill by adding a midlevel shot of each kind to the repertoire.)

Practicing in rhythm is important. Indeed, developing the habit of rhythm in practice is the best way to ensure that you will keep your rhythm on the golf course, which, in essence, increases your probability for engaging the mechanisms that lead to flow.

The implications of what we know about practice require that you

1. have a clear purpose for your practice session,
2. make sure that you are motivated enough to pay attention to what you are doing,
3. break your practice sessions into short segments by taking a break at least every 45 minutes, and
4. make sure that you practice with the right rhythm, tempo, and grip pressure because those skills will group together with the other skills that you are habituating.

Driving Range Versus Golf Course

I have saved an important topic for the end of this section—practicing on the driving range versus practicing on the golf course. Ultimately, the honing of the precise skills that are required for excellent golf requires a balance of both. The reality is that there is no determining factor that is best for you! Golfers like Matt Kuchar, Chris DiMarco, and Phil Mickelson love to work on their game as they are playing matches with friends. Phil Mickelson always plays in a tournament the week before a major championship because it helps sharpen his competitive focus. Other golfers like Tiger Woods and Justin Rose also like to habituate their skills on the golf course, but they value intense, focused sessions on the range with their instructor Sean Foley to help myelinate the moves in their golf swings.

Time is an issue for many people, and having enough time for both the range and the course is not always easy. When golfers can choose between spending time on the range or on the golf course, I always encourage them to default to the golf course. Being on the golf course habituates the skills that lead to flow. They are practicing concentration, preshot routines, and shaping shots to targets. Additionally, all facets of the game are being touched: driving, irons, pitches, short game, and putting.

Practice sessions that are competitive or have measureable outcomes are always a good idea because they heighten the habit of concentration. One of the key challenges for golfers who move from college golf to professional golf is loneliness. College golfers have teammates to practice with, coaches to structure their schedules, and competitive qualifying rounds to play against one another. Pros, on the other hand, tend to spend countless hours traveling and practicing alone. This routine often translates to purposeless, sloppy practices. For that reason you should find a place where you can practice and play at a club where it is relatively easy to find a game with other players so that you can continue to sharpen your habit of competitive focus.

Besides playing competitive matches on the golf course, drills with measurable outcomes help heighten your focus during practice. I suggest a drill to all my golfers, particularly my junior golfers, to help them be purposeful during their short-game sessions. The drill is called the Tucker Short Game Test (TSGT). Developed by master teacher Jerry Tucker, the TSGT helps students quantify their skills, measure their progress, compare their skills against professionals, and track their improvement. I have included it at the end of this chapter (with Jerry's permission) so that you can see how it works. I have seen this tool improve the short game of many players. Most important, it gets them practicing with a purpose and myelinates the skills that translate to the golf course.

Included in the version of the TSGT presented here are the results from a highly successful PGA golfer's test at Jerry's top-notch short game facility in Stuart, Florida.

Your initial step toward practicing with purpose will focus on the part of the game that really matters: the short game. Specifically, visit www.jerrytuckergolf.com and download the test. Run through the exercises and drills and begin keeping a log of your progress. Make sure that you carve out time to record your scores and identify where you fall relative to other golfers who have taken the test. Use this tool regularly, and keep tracking your progress. Your ultimate goal is to beat the scores shown in figure 18.1!

DATE: *11/11/08*

NAME: (signature)

HDDP: *PGA Tour*

Skill	Distance	Pro Pt.	Results	Score	Total	Avg. putt	Skill hdcp
Short putts	3'	Holed		4-4			
	4'	Holed		4-4			
	5'	Holed		3-4			
	6'	Holed		4-4			
	9'	Holed		2-4	17-20		+4
Long putts	20'	Safe zone	①-②-①-②-③	5-5			
	40'	Club length	4-②-②-in-①	4-5			
	60'	Club length	③-③-②-②-①	5-5	14-15	1'11"	+5
Chips	40'	4'	①-5-5-①-①	3-5			
	60'	6'	9-in-①-④-①	4-5	7-10	2'10"	0
Pitches	50'	5'	7-in-①-④-④	4-5			
	75'	7½'	18-9-⑥-⑤-⑦	3-5	7-10	6'1"	+1
Trouble assortment	Within 20%		⑥-18-⑦-③-⑦	4-5	4-5	8'2"	+2
Sand	20'	4'	②-③-③-①-③	5-5			
	40'	6'	7-9-10-⑤-④	2-5			
	60'	8'	⑥-④-②-④-13	4-5	11-15	5'2"	+2
Wedges	30 yards	6'	②-④-③-④-③	5-5			
	45 yards	6'	9-9-7-④-9	1-5			
	60 yards	9'	②-⑤-15-④-10	3-5			
	75 yards	9'	③-⑦-④-18-12	3-5			
	90 yards	9'	⑦-⑨-⑥-③-12	4-5	16-25	6'10"	+3
Total score				76-100	5'10"		

Improvement priority

1. *Chipping*

2. *40' sand*

3. *40 yd. wedge sand*

Short game handicap = 45

Figure 18.1 Tucker Short Game Test results.

Courtesy of Jerry Tucker.

CHAPTER 19

Achieve a Mastery Mind-Set

What are the first two questions you are typically asked after you complete a round of golf? Think about it for a moment. You are walking off a golf course or perhaps standing near the clubhouse when someone engages you in friendly conversation. I do this exercise with people who come through my golf academies, and I always get a chuckle when, moments after they've guessed the two questions, they appear on the screen in front of them. So what are they? What two questions are you typically asked after you play golf?

Almost certainly, the first question is "How did you play?" And, more than likely, the second is "What did you shoot?"

Do you see the potential problem here? Both questions are clearly ego oriented. They equate playing well with scoring well. Having read this far into the book you know that a good round of golf cannot be evaluated on score alone. In a game of endless growth many barometers of improvement are available. Also, as other athletes have observed, golfers experience scoring periods and growing periods. As such, golf requires an approach that is both creative and accurately reflective of the nature of the game itself.

Perhaps even more troubling, the prevalence of these questions and the mind-set that spawns them can rub off on a player. Players routinely hear these questions not only from golfers who are nearby as they finish but also from friends, family, colleagues, and acquaintances. So it's not surprising that the longer people play golf, the less they tend to focus on learning and enjoyment and the more they tend to focus on the social or ego-building aspect of the game.

Let's say, for instance, that you begin playing for love of the game (as most of us do) at age 10. You get wrapped up in the sheer joy of continual challenge, discovery, growth, and improvement. You find golf inherently and intrinsically fun. But those around you can't resist inquiring, "What did you shoot?" So, if you average 75 rounds of golf a year up to the age of 40, you will have had to answer that question 2,250 times, and that's if only one person asks about your score or performance after each round.

In a sense, the entire social network surrounding the game encourages, if not conditions, us to be ego golfers. And in doing so, it undermines our ability to immerse ourselves in the process of playing and improving.

Conversely, imagine how good you could become if you were encouraged and conditioned to be a mastery golfer? This approach is precisely what I take with many of my clients. We see dramatic improvement when they free their minds from the paralyzing pressures that accompany playing to impress others with their short-term performance and shift to a mind-set of playing as a means of learning and improving.

IMPROVING YOUR SKILLS

Although I might not be there to coach you personally, you can create your own buffer zone against ego-oriented thinking after each round. Instead of obsessing on your score, do what the world's best golfers have been taught to do. After a round of golf, focus instead on these two questions: "What did I learn from today's round of golf?" and "How can I continue to get better?" By putting the right questions in your mind immediately after a round of golf, you can condition yourself to become a mastery golfer and immerse yourself in the process of continual improvement known as kaizen.

Maintaining the mind-set of a mastery golfer isn't easy, because the more popular ego-oriented thinking is difficult to escape. So prepare yourself for the inevitable—the "How did you play?" and

"What did you shoot?" questions and the scorecard comparisons from those you encounter at the course. Rather than falling into that trap of following their line of thinking, be ready to respond with an answer reflecting your mastery mind-set and the mastery questions that you've already asked yourself. Without ego or embarrassment, add something like this to your response: "Just as important as what I scored was that I learned a lot, and I had fun doing it. I think my game is heading in the right direction."

In addition, start keeping a golf journal. In that journal, besides noting the mundane details of the round, include a section in which you describe the things that you learn from each round. Describe in detail what brought you to each lesson and how that lesson relates to your long-term goals in the game.

Here's an example of something worth noting about the journal. A golfer I worked with who was working to diminish his ego habits while sharpening his mastery habits wrote about a conversation that he had with a friend. His friend was describing his round of golf in textbook ego terminology. My golfer realized that his friend's account was exactly how *he* used to describe his rounds, and he further realized that he did not want to act like his friend or to focus on the numbers. This experience was a vivid example of mastery versus ego golf, and my golfer recorded it in his journal. This experience served as a turning point in his development and sent him on a path to greater emotional freedom in the game that led to a pattern of much better golf over time. The fact that he wrote about it allows us to revisit this experience regularly during our conversations. This kind of touchstone experience can craft a golfer's psyche.

After you've accumulated several journal entries, review them from time to time to make sure that the lessons become ingrained and become your habits of mind. The golfer who focuses on the process more than the number of strokes taken has a better chance for long-term improvement that will lead to what he or she seeks: fewer strokes taken.

To mastery golfers such as Jack Nicklaus, Ben Hogan, and Justin Rose, golf is a game of continual learning and improvement. Innate talent is only half the battle. The other half is layering the proper lessons on top of that talent. The great Bobby Jones once said that he never learned anything from a tournament that he won. We can guess that he spent far more time looking for lessons when he lost.

Jones' comments aside, you can learn something from every round of golf that you play, regardless of the score. Bad scores or

Bobby Jones understood that the value of any performance lies in its ability to further your mastery of the game.

challenging rounds can certainly uncover areas that need improvement; good rounds can provide the platform for taking your game to even higher levels. The lessons are always present in this game, so long as you are diligent about finding them. Ultimately, chronicling your growth and development as a mastery golfer is valuable. Before you know it, mastery golf will become second nature, and you will find yourself impervious to the outcome-based orientations and comments of others.

Discern Between Real and Perceived Limitations

The whole subject of mastery orientation begs the question, Just what are your limits? Philosophers long ago and human performance specialists in more recent times have pondered the limits of human capability. During the Enlightenment, a sect of free thinkers known as the Illuminati explored the concept of *perfectibilism*—the idea that human potential has no limitations and that most limitations that people run into are self-imposed. This idea, while seemingly extreme, has been gaining acceptance within the scientific community. I'll explain the psychology behind this momentarily, but first, a story.

When I was 17 years old, I was a lifeguard, and on weekends I gave swim lessons to some of the kids who frequented the beach. I recall a 7-year-old swimmer, Benjamin, who got me interested in psychology by giving me a raw and visible demonstration of self-imposed limitations and the way in which the brain acts on us to subdue our capabilities.

Because he was a beginning swimmer, our goals that summer were modest. Ben's parents wanted him to be able to submerge his face underwater and to be able to swim a full length of their family swimming pool by himself. Although achieving this goal sounds like an easy task—the type of thing that many kids learn in an hour—it wasn't easy for Ben. He was so terrified of the water that even putting his feet in the water was, for him, a monumental accomplishment.

You could see the panic on his face build as he got closer to the pool. He would try all sorts of things to distract me from the task at hand. Part of the problem was that Ben was 100 percent convinced that he could not put his face in the water or swim on his own. When I asked him to put his face underwater, he simply couldn't. He wasn't being defiant. I watched him try for several days, and his brain would no sooner let him submerge his face as it would let me walk into oncoming traffic. His survival instinct kicked into gear, and I would watch him battle himself as he tried to submerge, get his nose wet, and then spring to the surface, looking at me hopefully. "Did I do it, Mr. Gio?" he would ask. "Not yet, Ben. Still have a ways to go," I'd say.

Similarly, when he got more than a body's length away from the edge of the pool, he turned and swam straight back to his point of departure. Again, he wasn't being defiant. When he got to a certain point, something in his brain would just click and send him back to safer ground. In a way, he reminded me of the actor Jim Carey in the movie *Liar Liar*, a man whose unconscious mind would not allow him to do what his conscious mind was ordering. Even at this early age, Ben's brain was not allowing him to do what he was clearly capable of.

Theories of the brain abound, but most scientists in the area of evolutionary psychology agree that the adaptations that have evolved in the brain serve the singular purpose of keeping us alive. Even the dreaded fear response that golfers experience is in place because fear, in a variety of capacities, leads to greater survival rates. This functionality of the brain and body reveals itself in many ways. When the temperature gets too cold on the skin, the brain send signals down the spinal cord for the muscles to contract and retract rapidly, to shiver, as a mechanism to warm up the muscles. In other words, the nervous system has a built-in threshold for cold. After the skin hits a certain temperature, the brain interprets that by saying, "OK, skin, you're going beyond this certain point. Let me bring you back to a comfortable level."

The same thing happens when we get too hot. Again, receptors on the skin send signals up the spinal cord to the brain. The brain processes the information and signals back down the spinal cord to the eccrine and apocrine glands to produce the sweat that, as it evaporates, lowers the temperature of the skin. For that reason, patients with certain spinal cord injuries have difficulty regulating their body temperature. Similarly, when the brain misinterprets messages from the skin, some people sweat chronically or not at all.

The brain's action as the central regulator to keep the body safe and comfortable is well documented, but what does that mean for elite athletes or those looking to push beyond the realm of comfort? When distance runners push themselves too close to their limits, they experience fatigue and exhaustion, which signals to the brain to slow down, stop, and rest. Although athletes sometimes choose to ignore the fact that the brain is signaling that it's time to stop, rarely if ever does the brain let people push themselves too far. Of the millions of people who run marathons every year, remarkably few ever die, even when pushing themselves to their limits. Runners usually collapse or vomit before they die. When the cognitive, conscious brain tries to push us past the limit, the unconscious brain fights back, saying, "You are in dangerous territory. My job is to protect you at all costs, even if it means shutting down your digestion. You're tapped!"

The brain and central nervous system have all sorts of survival mechanisms that process information unconsciously and snap a person back into balance and comfort. But here's an interesting proposition put forth by Dr. Thomas Rowland (Rowland 2011):

The internal, unconscious mechanisms that help regulate heart rate, body temperature, and digestion are the very mechanisms that place limits on individuals who are trying to break through their own personal thresholds.

Psychologists have long known that people often self-sabotage when they get out of their comfort zone. As William James observed,

Most people live, whether physically, intellectually or morally, in a very restricted circle of their potential being. They make use of a very small portion of their possible consciousness, and of their soul's resources in general, much like a man who, out of his whole bodily organism, should get into a habit of using and moving only his little finger. Great emergencies and crises show us how much greater our vital resources are than we had supposed.

Through his astute observations of human behavior, James was able to detect this restricted circle in which people live. What James did not have access to a hundred years ago was the scientific research on brain anatomy that we currently have. Today researchers are concerned with where the extra resources reside and how to tap into them to push past personal barriers. One of the key findings from recent brain research has to do with the unconscious governors that instigate that perceived threshold. According to Rowland, humans have a central governor that acts like a subconscious protective brake and limits how hard our unconscious brain will allow us to push ourselves. Rowland puts forth convincing evidence that even the world's best endurance athletes actually have more to give, if only their brains would let them.

> *The point of the central governor is to ensure that there is always a reserve so in a sense, it always promotes underperformance. Even in the world's best performances, there is still a reserve—the athletes could have gone faster. That is why they don't die at the finish. (Rowland 2011, p. 16)*

Rowland's central governor hypothesis provides insight for the type of self-handicapping and self-sabotage that William James and other psychologists have witnessed for years. Just as the brain keeps nutrients, glucose, and oxygen stores to make sure that we have a comfortable reserve, it keeps us feeling comfortable when we stay within our perceived limitations but often pushes back when we seek to break through performance thresholds. As a result, most people tend to fall back to their average. What promotes the discomfort that golfers feel when they get out of their comfort zone? The answer is that exceptional performance is abnormal, uncomfortable, and by definition unknown, and the brain is designed to keep us in a comfortable realm full of familiar experiences.

Going back to the example of my young swimmer Benjamin, the resistance that he felt when he put his face underwater came from a place deep inside him that told him, "That's dangerous." But his central governor was preventing him from doing something that he was clearly capable of doing. His brain was, in Rowland's terminology, promoting underperformance from a deep, internal place that was precognition. Ben was afraid before he knew what he was afraid of.

What was the path to getting him swimming like a fish and breaking through those barriers? My approach was much like the work I do with golfers; I redirected his focus and played games with him. I turned his thoughts away from the fear and toward games that promoted retrieving the ball from underwater and swimming lengthy distances. At one point, as he was propelling his body away from the edge of the pool and toward me, he kept saying, "I can't, Mr. Gio. I can't, Mr. Gio." As he got closer, I took tiny steps back to make him swim a little farther. He traversed the length of the pool, saying, "I can't," even as he was swimming! When he finally made it to the other side, he looked back with alarm at what he had done. But the mental block was cleared, and from that point forward he was able to swim the length of the pool easily.

Similar things happen to golfers. I've known Matt Kuchar for more than a decade now. Coming out of college, he had no real sense of how good he was capable of becoming. But as he stayed out on tour longer, Matt kept breaking through more performance thresholds. One of them came at the Memorial when, over the course of the weekend, he made something like 20 birdies in 36 holes. Although he had sprinkled in some bogeys, Matt thought that it was cool to learn that he could make that many birdies. As such, he expanded his personal threshold and no longer experienced any resistance to making tons of birdies.

Many people who don't live in a competitive realm as I do think that exceedingly high achievers break through their limitations in moments of divine inspiration. Nothing could be further from the truth. Breaking through limitations is generally the result of the

Jeff Robinson/Icon SMI

Recognize your self-imposed limitations, and then adjust your mind-set and behavior to overcome them. Although Brandt Snedeker played well as a junior golfer, he has truly come into his own as a pro.

consistent application of better processes that are often ordinary, common, or mundane.

In a landmark article titled "The Mundanity of Excellence," Daniel Chambliss (1989) makes a compelling argument that the difference between the elite and everyone else is not that the elite make quantitative changes in their work but that they make qualitative changes that alter the character or nature of the thing itself.

In explaining the difference between club swimmers and Olympic champion swimmers, he says,

> Instead, they do things differently. Their strokes are different, their attitudes are different, their groups of friends are different; their parents treat the sport differently, the swimmers prepare differently for their races, and they enter different kinds of meets and events. (Chambliss 1989, 73)

Chambliss concludes,

> "Excellence is accomplished through the doing of actions, ordinary in themselves, performed consistently and carefully, habitualized, compounded together, added up over time" (Chambliss 1989, 85).

This approach can be successful in any area of life. For example, a golfer I work with wanted to lose 20 pounds (9 kg) during the off-season. We didn't attack the weight loss in one massive action. Instead, we changed one small thing. Each morning when he awoke, rather than put his feet into his slippers, he put them into his sneakers. That's all I asked him to do: Each day when he woke up, make his first move be to put his feet into sneakers (which lead to the gym) rather than slippers (which lead to the breakfast nook). Then, each morning he walked down the hall to his in-house gym and got in a morning workout. By applying this rather mundane behavior regularly, the weight melted off, and he went on to have a terrific season the next year.

IMPROVING YOUR SKILLS

French philosopher Teilhard de Chardin once wrote, "It is our duty as human beings to proceed as though the limits of our capabilities do not exist." Note that this quote relates directly to flow, because flow represents a state of mind in which we actualize our potential and move beyond our perceived limitations.

Although beliefs are not something that we can touch or feel, mountains of research in psychology show that beliefs have a measureable and direct influence on human attainment. Because beliefs powerfully determine how we interpret experiences, when we act in a manner that is inconsistent with our beliefs, they cause us to self-sabotages our skills.

To break through your performance barriers, begin by auditing your belief system with an eye toward identifying any self-limiting beliefs that you have about your capabilities in golf. Ask yourself directly whether you are placing self-imposed restrictions on yourself.

Next, adopt the type of limitless growth mind-set that I have put forth in this book. Give yourself the benefit of the doubt and assume that the William James quotation presented earlier in this chapter applies to you and that you are living within a restricted realm of your potential.

Finally, although a shift in perspective and beliefs is an important first step toward high achievement, breaking through your limitations also requires that you change your behavior.

Although implementing changes in behavior is a long-term process, you can get started immediately. Follow these steps:

1. Identify the behaviors that relate to your golf game. Specifically, identify the manner in which you practice your technical skills, the regularity and discipline with which you apply your best habits, and the good and bad features of your attitude.

2. Remember that breaking through perceived limitations results from the accumulation of consistently applied behaviors, so your goal is to begin making qualitative changes in your practice sessions.

3. After you have identified qualitative improvements that you can make, commit to doing the little things regularly every day. You may find it helpful to enlist the automatic reminder feature on your cell phone to remind you to do those things every day.

4. Get honest with yourself about your attitude. Identify the good and bad aspects of your attitude and look to apply the best parts of yourself consistently. Don't just think the right things; also say and do the right things.

By making small, qualitative changes over time, I am confident that you will be able to push your talent to levels that you may have previously thought unattainable. More relevant to this book, because flow is the amalgamation of various psychological mechanisms coming together, you will be habituating the technical, psychological, and behavioral habits that lead you to playing golf in flow!

CHAPTER 21

Craft Your Environment

F ar too often I see golfers on the golf course dressed sloppily and eating hot dogs with one hand while they talk on their cell phones with the other. They rummage through their bags trying to figure out which pocket holds their tees, their ball markers, or their golf gloves. In simple terms, they are disorganized, and they create an environment around them that is reminiscent of Pig Pen from the old *Peanuts* comic strips. These conditions are not likely to produce flow. On the contrary, cell phones and other disruptions are the antiflow.

The concept that environmental changes influence behavior changes is well known and widely accepted, and you've no doubt experienced and witnessed how gloomy, rainy days tend to dampen people's moods whereas bright, sunny skies help to boost spirits. Such responses are hard-wired, or innate, evoked by processes similar to those that help us feel sleepy at night and more alert during the day. Research has verified that the amount of pollution in the air not only harms cardiovascular and respiratory health but also has an influence on mental well-being and even the ability of the brain to process information (Weir, 2012). This kind of wiring has led some people to embrace feng shui designing, which promotes the creation of a set of environmental conditions that are said to be conducive to better health and overall well-being. As a natural result of all the research showing the importance of environmental factors on performance, I caution my golfers to be aware of all aspects of their environment, including their ventilation and air filters, their home gyms, the hotels that they stay in, the food that they keep in their cupboards, and the people whom they keep in their inner circle. Ultimately, crafting a healthy environment that is conducive to high achievement will have an effect on the scorecard.

If you are skeptical about the influence that the environment can have on behavior, the following story may change your mind. A restaurant owner once faced a tricky problem. His restaurant provided such an enjoyable atmosphere and such good food that customers were in no rush to finish their meals and leave. People liked sitting at their tables and taking their time dining. As a result the restaurant had a huge waiting list every night. He had created an environment in which people wanted to eat, but the waiting lists were often so long that many customers grew weary of waiting and left to dine elsewhere.

Looking for help, the owner consulted a team of psychologists from a local university to find a way to get people to finish their meals quicker and make room for waiting customers without compromising the quality of the customers' dining experience. In the restaurant business this action is called turning tables. After a month of observing customers' behavior and timing the average time that people spent eating, the psychologists made a recommendation that they thought should solve the problem. Before reading further, take a guess what the researchers proposed.

They suggested that the owner install dimmers on the light switches so that every time the restaurant started getting full, the owner could make the lights marginally, almost imperceptibly brighter. With nothing to lose, the owner tried this approach and found that people ate significantly faster.

When questioned after they ate about why they ate quickly, customers were unaware that the lights had been brightened. Surveys showed no dip in satisfaction. Turning over tables more quickly increased the number of customers coming through the restaurant, which increased profit for the owner.

On some nights, however, the restaurant's waiting list was still problematically high. The owner again consulted with the team of psychologists. After watching for another few days, the consultants suggested a change in the music that was playing. Although the classical music that the owner was playing was soothing and conducive to the dining experience, it was slow in cadence. The psychologists suggested playing classical music with a quicker tempo. The subtle change of playing faster music, like the brightening of the lights, resulted in customers' eating more quickly without decreasing their enjoyment.

The suggestions made by the team of psychologists are consistent with research findings across psychology showing that what people think, how they behave, how they feel, and, obviously, the speed with which they do things can all be altered by subtle shifts in the environment. What's more, these behaviors can be altered without people even being aware of it.

Psychologically speaking, neural circuitry connects the eyes to the thinking part of the brain called the cortex (where thoughts register). Other circuitry bypasses the cortex and connects the eyes directly to the limbic system (where unconscious processes register). Dubbed the high road and the low road of mental processing, second-by-second processing of information includes both types of information going into the brain; some we're aware of, but most we're not.

The lesson here, and the key fact about human behavior, is that subtle fluctuations in the environment can unconsciously trigger psychological fluctuations in the individual. Many of our changes in mood, arousal levels, and feelings are triggered below the level of our awareness. The implications for golfers are tremendously important.

Although golfers do not face fluctuating lights and music, they nonetheless face all sorts of subtle fluctuations in their environment, including the people around them.

Have you ever wondered why star athletes and successful people travel with an entourage? In many cases the entourage is that person's way of trying to take charge of the immediate surroundings. Think about it. Do you have certain people in your life who put you in a good mood? Do you have certain people in your life who make you feel good about yourself? Do you have certain people in your life who build your confidence? If you lived your life, as do most professional athletes, in an achievement domain in which positive feelings and confidence are of paramount importance, you'd understand why they want to surround themselves with such supporters.

One of the most consistent findings from social psychology is how various traits tend to travel through our social networks. In a study reported in the *New England Journal of Medicine*, even obesity travels through social networks. Researchers who conducted a study of over 12,000 participants concluded that a person's chances of becoming obese increased by 57 percent if he or she had a friend who became obese in a given period. Similarly, if a person's spouse became obese, the chances that he or she would also become obese increased by 37 percent (Christakis & Fowler 2007).

If obesity can travel through and across social networks, so can optimism, confidence, discipline, and work ethic. In fact, researchers who studied the lounges where schoolteachers take their breaks reported that teachers who spent time around other teachers who were critical of students became more critical themselves. Similarly, students who hang around with kids who do drugs are more likely to begin using drugs.

Now I know that in some situations you cannot select whom you partner with or whom you are paired with. Such circumstances are especially common as you climb the ladder of golfing success. PGA Tour players have their parings selected for them. The same holds true for most high-level amateur events and even high school and junior golf tournaments. But whenever you can determine the setting and company that you keep, opt for those who will nurture your best qualities, buttress your confidence, and push you sufficiently to maximize your abilities.

ENVIRONMENTAL VARIABLES ON THE COURSE

The features that frequently change in golfers' environments include whom they're playing with, how others are playing, the prestige of the tournament, and their own score or standing relative to other golfers. It is well known that golfers begin to feel different when they are playing with the boss or with an important client; it is just as well known that golfers begin to feel nervous as they start approaching their personal best scores.

I knew a golfer who could shoot 67 at a golf course, but when he saw a banner announcing that a particular match was an official tournament, his 67 invariably turned into 76. The golf course, the clubs, and the golfer did not change. But one subtle cue—the banner announcement—changed everything. This trigger altered his behavior on the course, just as the lights and music were triggers for diners in the restaurant.

In golf, allowing subtle cues to alter the speed with which we do things or to disrupt the positive thoughts that allow us to play our best is a recipe for disaster.

Earlier in this book we established that a key characteristic of mastery golfers is that they view golf as a game in which they compete against two things—themselves and the golf course—rather than against a score, an opponent, or another golfer.

Conceptually, that sounds great. The real difficulty, as most golfers quickly understand, is actually doing it. "How do I play the golf course? How do I ignore distractions?" Most rounds of golf have plenty of distractions that can take our focus off the golf course. For the amateur golfer, those distractions may come in the form of playing with a boss or colleague; for the professional, they may come in the form of cameras and leaderboards.

Golfers who want to shift from an ego to a mastery mind-set must make the decision to change their behavior.

What can a golfer do to defend against environmental cues and distractions, especially those that occur at a level beyond his or her awareness? The bulk of the answer can be summed up in a single word: routine.

Competing in golf requires that golfers develop and stick to a routine as well as they can on every shot. On the PGA Tour, what appears to the gallery as one golfer playing against another is actually one golfer getting into his routine on a golf course as well as he can while another golfer gets into his routine on a golf course as well as *he* can.

On the scoreboard of the 2007 British Open, the final holes appeared to be a contest between Sergio Garcia and Padraig Harrington. In fact, the real contest was between Sergio's ability to

Accomplished pros like Padraig Harrington develop and use a great routine to tune out distractions and help generate flow.

immerse himself in his routine at Carnoustie and Padraig's ability to immerse himself in *his* routine.

I always teach people that golf is not a horse race as much as it is a dart game. You can't influence your opponent as you can in football, and you're not trying to play against someone else as you do in basketball. You pick targets and commit to those targets. The event is self-contained and isolated, just like darts.

If you watched the 2007 British Open closely, and especially if you watched it through a psychological lens as I do, you would no doubt have noticed that part of the reason that Sergio's uneven Sunday round differed so much from his first three flawless rounds was that his routine had changed. It had become quicker and tighter than it had been on the previous three days. On the other hand, Padraig Harrington spent time before the playoff working with his sport psychologist Bob Rotella on his routine to ensure that it was in sync and would be able to withstand the pressure of the moment.

Certainly, both Nicklaus and Woods worked on their routines throughout their entire careers. Jack has said that he never went into a competition thinking that he had to beat another golfer. Rather, he prepared himself and his game for a particular golf course. Tiger learned that from Jack, as he said after winning the 1996 U.S. Amateur championship:

> *All I do is stay in my same routine. Even though I have certain putts that are bigger than others, you never see me out of rhythm. I always stay the same pace, do everything the same. So what I did the first hole today and the last hole today is exactly the same. There's no change. I think that's probably one of the biggest keys. That's what Nicklaus was good at. You could time him. Every routine he had was exactly the same.*

Whether they talk about it publicly or not, every coach and every athlete at the elite level knows the importance of establishing pre-performance routines. Zach Johnson puts it this way:

> *I have little things that I tell myself about my round, about my day. Really, nothing changes from week to week. It could be a Thursday at a random tournament; it could be a Sunday obviously at Augusta. I say the same things to myself, just how to approach each shot, how to approach each hole.*

IMPROVING YOUR SKILLS

The development of routines is an extremely effective means of manipulating the environment, and it is entirely within your control.

Routines not only lock you into a pattern of behavior that is resilient to all kinds of situational stimuli but also protect you from thinking too much. The more that we can turn over the details of any task to automatism, the freer we are to concentrate on the task itself.

Golfers tend to get quick and tight when they are under the gun, or they tend to camp out over a shot longer than usual. Either way, the situation tends to get them out of the normal, comfortable rhythm at which they play their best.

The purpose of a preshot routine is to automate the process and help you achieve your best rhythm. To develop an effective routine, you must do the same thing every single time. Furthermore, you must do the same thing at the same rhythm every time. Automating your actions and rhythm increases your ability to get into flow.

Routine is the essence of excellence in competitive domains. Great golf routines have three parts:

1. select shot,
2. make fearless swings at precise targets, and
3. accept results.

It's just like a wash cycle at home: wash, rinse, repeat.

A great preshot routine begins with standing behind the ball and seeing the shot that you want to hit. Some golfers like to visualize the shot, whereas others, including Tiger Woods, would rather let their bodies feel the shot that they want to hit. Of utmost importance is to be perfectly clear about the shot that you want to hit. At this stage of the routine, you want to be decisive before going to the next phase of the routine. Going into a shot being indecisive about the shot that you want to hit creates mental clutter and often prevents you from hitting a good shot. If you can't get that clarity, then exercise the discipline to begin the routine over. You must be decisive about the shot you want to hit!

When you are clear about the exact shot you want to play, have a trigger that gets you ready to address the ball. Experiment to determine what type of trigger works best for you. Chad Campbell likes to lift his left sleeve. Camilo Villegas lets the club slide down his hands as he approaches the ball.

After you are aligned, you should be on autopilot from there on out. Give the same number of looks, the same number of waggles, and make a committed, fearless swing to the target. After the shot is over, accept the outcome and prepare for the most important shot in any round of golf, the next one.

No golfer—professional, amateur, or recreational—can hope to master the game without having worked hard to develop an effective preshot routine. And after you have developed that routine, you must work hard to master and maintain the self-discipline required to implement that routine before every shot.

Your preperformance routine is important because it buffers you from the fluctuation and randomness of changing situations. More to the aims of this book, however, a good routine also fosters the quiet mind that is essential to generating flow.

CHAPTER 22

Respond Positively to Negativity

Playing consistently good golf is difficult, and golfers cannot control some features of the game. You may find this statement obvious, but it becomes more profound and meaningful as you progress through the game of golf and become a better player.

Rather than brush past that statement, I would like you to take a moment to digest it and let it sink in. And after you've done that, consider that even Tiger Woods, who for a time had mastered the game at a level never previously seen, wrote, "Sometimes the game seems so difficult you wonder whether the effort is worth it" (Woods 2001, pp. 8–9). And finally consider that Nicklaus began a book about all his wins by stating, "I did come along fast in golf, and did not fully learn how difficult the game is until after I turned professional" (Nicklaus 1997).

I don't begin this chapter by asking you to consider the difficulty of the game to intimidate you or because I want you to think negatively. Quite the opposite is true. My point in arming you with this understanding is that after you truly understand how difficult it is to play consistently at a high level, you are more likely to be nice to yourself when the going gets tough. I want you to let yourself off the hook when things are not going your way. I have watched golfers really berate themselves and beat themselves up in this game. I have witnessed tantrums and torrents, seen flying putters and fisticuffs, and watched this game make grown men cry. More often than not, golfers blame themselves for things that are not under their control at all, but rather are part of the curious makeup of a complex game. Rather than berate themselves, they should let themselves off the hook and chalk it up to the fact that playing consistently good golf is difficult and some features of the game cannot be controlled.

Now that we've established that golf can be difficult, we must decide on the best approach to take to a game that has such a fickle, complex, unpredictable nature. One thing that many of the great golfers throughout history have done is precisely what I allude to in the title of this chapter: They respond positively to negativity. As Gary Player observed during an interview with *Forbes* magazine (Burke 2010),

Colorsport/Icon SMI

Make Gary Player your role model for using mental discipline and psychological strategies to deal with difficult situations. These techniques helped him rack up 134 world-wide wins.

Letting negative thoughts enter your mind will guarantee failure. I remember when the weather was rough I'd hear others in the locker room say how horrible it was and how they hated playing in the rain and wind. Right then and there they had lost the tournament, because they set themselves up for failure. I told myself that I loved playing in the wind and rain and went out and played with a positive mind-set.

Player offers a clear example of responding positively to negativity, but having a positive attitude in bad weather is just the tip of the iceberg. More commonly, the negative whispers come not from Mother Nature, but from our internal dialogue. Reflecting on your career to date, have you ever found yourself on the course thinking thoughts such as "I can't believe I blew that last shot—I am so stupid," "I'm terrible at this kind of shot," or "I'm never going to catch him now!" Alternatively, have you ever had positive thoughts such as "I nailed this one—I am back on track," "I'm getting better at this type of shot," and "I can do this!"

The empowering message of this chapter and one of the great things about golf is that we do have control over one important thing—we have total choice over how we react to situations. Every round of golf provides many opportunities to respond positively to negative whispers.

Matt Kuchar is a modern-day example of a golfer who responds positively to negative whispers. At the 2007 AT&T National, he told reporters,

On the golf course, it's easy to beat yourself up. You just have so many more bad things happen than good things happen it seems. Just to get a win, win every 100 tournaments, would be great. Your winning percentage, you just don't get that much success out here. It's hard; it beats you up. But if you do stay positive, good things do happen.

As I spent time with Matt recently, his commitment to staying positive was evident on the golf course. During a stretch of golf where he couldn't get anything going, he felt himself becoming impatient. Then, as his impatience was whispering to him, the game did what it often does to golfers: It gave him a bad break in the form of a perfectly struck shot that kicked off the green and into a hazard. Matt was able to recognize what was happening inside him, so he told himself, "You have a great short game, and this is why you practice it, for moments like this." He hit a fantastic shot and saved par. He then recognized that he was still a little off-kilter, so he coached himself, "Settle down, Matt. Stay patient. You are playing well, and if you stay patient, good things will happen." And so they did. Matt went on to make several birdies and keep the momentum of his good golf going.

The psychology behind Matt's internal dialogue can be traced back to the psychologist William Purkey, who posited the idea that each of us has a *whispering self*—an inner voice that guides us and helps direct our behavior (Beach 2001). The problem, according to Purkey, is that most people give more weight to negative whispers than to positive ones. Purkey's approach to success revolves around getting people to replace the negative, self-destructive dialogue with positive, reasonable, encouraging dialogue. The core of Purkey's philosophy is what he calls invitational education—a practice of communicating messages that summon forth human potential while identifying and changing forces that defeat potential.

All golfers have a whispering self that accompanies them as they strive to perfect their game. If you take the advice from chapter 16 seriously and begin to study success, then you will see that on his march through the majors, Jack Nicklaus was engaged in a constant internal dialogue. And that dialogue had countless moments in which he tried to become negative with himself. Sometimes the negative self won, but not often. By his own admission, Jack always favored the positive over the negative.

As someone who studies the game closely, I can tell you that the response to mishaps in the game is often the difference between winning and losing tournaments. The 2012 Masters provided perhaps the best example of how to respond positively to a tough situation. Bubba Watson had never won a major, he had surrendered a Sunday lead earlier in the year, and he had missed a makeable birdie putt on the 18th hole that put him into a playoff with major champion Louis Oosthuizen. On their first hole, Watson drove the ball deep into the right trees. A tower and trees were located between him and the green. The only way he could have possibly put the ball on the green would have been to play a 30-yard (27 m) hook that, to most golfers (even professionals), would be so improbable that they wouldn't even attempt it. Bubba's self-talk, and the talk of his caddie, illustrates the point of this chapter with clarity:

> *The first time I ever worked with my caddie, Boston, six years ago, I told him, I said, "If I have a swing, I've got a shot." So I'm used to the woods. I'm used to the rough. And we were walking down here and I said, "We were here already. We hit it close here already today," because I was in those trees. I got there. I saw it was a perfect draw, a perfect hook. We were walking down the fairway going, "We've been here before. You're*

good out of the trees." And he said, "If you've got a swing, you've got a shot." I get down there, saw it was a perfect draw. Even though the tower was in my way, I didn't want to ask if I get relief or anything, because it just set up for a perfect draw—well, hook. That's what we did. We just kept talking about, you never know what's going to happen out here. Anything can happen. You know, so that's what we did walking down the fairway.

In this case, Bubba perfectly framed a situation. He had the choice to criticize himself after both the missed birdie on the 18th hole and the poor drive. But he didn't. Instead, he responded to the negatives (missed putt, bad drive) with the perfect attitude: "If you've got a swing, you've got a shot." The resulting shot enabled his first major championship. His response to adversity offers a great lesson to everyone interested in cultivating a winning attitude in golf.

Golfers have repeatedly recalled for me times when positive self-talk served as the turning point in a round, a season, or a career. They've also recalled times when negative self-talk skewed their perceptions and led to periods of poor play.

IMPROVING YOUR SKILLS

Self-talk is a powerful tool to effect change within yourself. So here is your assignment: Reflect back on some of the harsher or more critical things that you've said to yourself or called yourself because of golf. Make a list of them. When I've done this exercise in the past with golfers, I've heard some pretty cruel comments. Golfers have told themselves how much they stink, how worthless they are, how they'll never be any good, and how they should quit and give up the game. I've had golfers talk about how they are unworthy of being loved and valued because they believe themselves to be such failures at the game of golf. In the interest of good taste, I will avoid including the many creative but harsh expletives that I have heard golfers use in criticizing themselves and their game.

After you have made a list of 10 or so negative statements, pull out a photograph of a loved one. Lay the photograph next to the list and imagine what it would do to his or her feelings of confidence, self-worth, motivation, and value to hear those things. Would those statements lead your loved one to being his or her best or to becoming fragile and tentative? You should abandon the exercise if it becomes too difficult or painful to get through. Know that you are not alone. None of the golfers I know has ever been able to get through even the second statement. But the point of the exercise is not completion so much as it is to learn the valuable lesson that words matter. I ask my clients, "If these words would have an effect on your loved one, and you wouldn't say them to him or her, what makes you think they don't have the same effect on you?"

They immediately get the lesson.

The next thing that I do with my golfers is to reframe the experience by having them make a list of positive statements. That is what I want you to do next. Develop a list of energizing, positive, enhancing statements that you can use as go-to touchstones during times of adversity. Rehearse them regularly so that you develop the habit of using positive self-talk in responding to negative whispers.

As a child, my dad frequently recited the following quotation, which was framed on the wall of our garage:

> Watch your thoughts, for they become words. Watch your words, for they become actions. Watch your actions, for they become habits. Watch your habits, for they become character. Watch your character, for it becomes your destiny.

The original source of that famous quote is uncertain, but it speaks to the power that words and language have in shaping our perceptions that ultimately become the lens through which we view the world.

If you play golf, you will be faced with situations that can reasonably be interpreted as unfortunate. You will sometimes have lapses in concentration, miss the occasional short putt, and have your weaknesses revealed. The way you react in these situations and the things you tell yourself will largely determine how you experience the game going forward.

CHAPTER 23

Control
Your Body

Regardless of how effectively you might shape your environment on and off the course, you can't anticipate or control everything that happens around you. And when you are exposed to these sometimes-unpleasant situations, your emotional response and corresponding body reaction can be as significant as or more significant than your cognitions. As far back as 1898, researchers documented that children ran significantly faster when in pairs than when they were alone because of a hypothesized increase in energy that occurs with the presence of others (termed *dynamogism*). Later research has documented that, independent of mastery or ego orientation, the mere presence of an audience, called the audience effect, can change such physiological factors as electrical conductance of the skin, the sharpness of motor skills, muscle tension, and coordination (Jowett and Lavallee 2007). Because many physiological changes are automated, golfers need to learn to manage their bodies in a way that gives them maximum control at all times.

Research in behavioral laboratories across the nation suggests that the pairing of any stimuli—for example, the presence of a harmless mouse—with something alarming like a siren or a shock of electricity serves to connect the two stimuli. If it happens enough times, simply seeing a mouse is enough to produce the rapid heart rate, elevated blood pressure, and rapid breathing associated with pain and fear.

What we experience as the emotion of fear is often the aggregate of various chemicals located in particular brain regions that combine with other factors such as heart rate, tension levels, and rapid breathing. At this point distinguishing between physiological arousal and somatic anxiety is important. Arousal refers to the objective changes in the body's physiology; somatic anxiety has to do with a person's interpretation of those physiological changes.

My main point in this chapter is that performing at an elite level requires that you develop the tools to manage both. As we discussed in our section on self-efficacy, it is important to be able to interpret that arousal as adaptive; it is always better to interpret that energy as excited and eager rather than scared or frightened. With that said, you also need to manage the physiology itself by learning to read yourself and by engaging the right tools to stay in the proper state of body and mind. Nicklaus captured these two, the arousal and the soma, nicely when he observed,

> I have always gotten nervous at golf. I have played 90 percent of my rounds in major championships with a touch of tremor. There has always been some floppiness in my stomach. Moreover, I have always welcomed those feelings in that, so long as I am playing well enough to have genuine confidence in my game, they will get me up, keep me alert, and prime me for maximum effort (Nicklaus 1997, p. 268).

In what is famously known as the James-Lange theory of emotions, William James suggested over a century ago that emotions follow, rather than precede, physiological reactions to events. James provided the example of a man walking through the woods and seeing a grizzly bear. His physiological reaction is to tremble at the sight. His heart races, and he begins to sweat. The man then interprets these physiological reactions and concludes that he is afraid.

Modern brain research validates the direct relationship, through neural circuitry, between specific brain regions and certain parts of the face. For example, asking a stroke victim to smile often produces a lopsided grin such that the muscles in only half of the face are actually firing. Telling the same person a funny joke produces a full-faced smile. The reason for the different reactions is that trying to smile registers in the thinking part of the brain, the cortex, whereas finding something funny registers in the limbic area. The part of the brain that is engaged determines which part of the face responds.

The opposite is also true—the physical action can stimulate the brain and the emotions. Studies show that holding a smile on one's face produces feelings of happiness. Conversely, holding a frown can change a person's affect to sadness.

We know now that a reciprocal relationship exists, such that thinking can change our behavior, and changing behavior can change how we think and feel.

What this means to you is that the time-honored admonition to "act like a champion" is well-founded, because it is likely that doing so will help you look and feel, and therefore perform, like one.

Sport psychologist Bob Rotella once observed that confident golf consists of "playing with your eyes," alluding to the fact that when athletes are confident most are simply zeroing in on their objective

Adopt the body language and physical habits that accompany flow. Note Rickie Fowler's relaxed, confident demeanor as he plays off the fairway.

and letting their bodies react without thinking too much about the mechanics of their action. Similarly, people who are in flow have a determined, focused look on their faces and a quiet look in their eyes. When you study athletes in flow, as I have for years, you see clearly that flow does indeed have a distinctive look.

I've personally seen athletes transform before my very eyes and go from casual conversation to total concentration in a flash. Ben Hogan once said that his round of golf began the moment that he put his hand on the locker room door. When he gripped the handle or knob, he found his focus, fell into rhythm and concentration, and kept it until the final putt dropped on the 18th green.

You can't control everything in your environment, but you can do things to mitigate its influence. Although we will focus on controlling your body, you need to be able to control what features of your environment you focus on. As I've indicated previously, because scores in a golf tournament are erratic, they tend to bring about an erratic state of mind and an erratic nervous system. In 1957, while still a young man striving to develop his ability to regulate his internal constitution, Jack Nicklaus qualified for the U.S. Open. After starting 3-under through three holes, he saw his name on the leaderboard, and he proceeded to shoot 80-80 to miss the cut. This is an example of a golfer who couldn't control his environment but could have controlled which features of the environment he paid attention to. Fortunately, Jack learned this valuable lesson and henceforth focused not on the score or the field, but on the golf course itself.

The ability to maintain composure under intense pressure is the hallmark of a champion. Maintaining composure has both cognitive and physiological benefits. In the heat of battle, even the most comforting thoughts are of little help when they are paired with a heart rate in excess of 100 beats per minute and a breathing count that is triple the normal rate.

Being a fearless mastery golfer and developing the ability to generate flow with regularity require the joining of great thinking with a measure of control over the physiological processes that change under pressure.

IMPROVING YOUR SKILLS

As with most things golf related, controlling the body begins with self-knowledge. This aspect will be a little different for each golfer. Specifically, people tend to fall into one of two categories. High-arousal people tend to be excitable, and they work themselves into a frenzy that is counterproductive to golf. Low-arousal people do the opposite. They are so laid back that they overlook important details, are often sloppy in their habits, and can even be lazy with their golf swing on the course. Knowing your tendencies is important. Most people have it in them to be either high or low arousal, depending on the situation (e.g., environment!). Thus, you need to be able to read the signs in your body and mindset and determine whether you need to ramp things up or settle yourself down.

Although many sport psychology professionals default to the inverted-U model (figure 23.1) for understanding the relationship between physiological arousal and performance, I have found that Hanin's zone of optimal functioning (ZOF) model (figure 23.2), which states that athletes perform better when their anxiety falls within their ZOF, captures the dynamic of golfers more accurately. Invariably, after you've played enough golf, you are able to identify the approximate level of arousal that is associated with your best golf. Using the ZOF to track those changes is a good way to become more in tune with your body and the way in which it relates to your golfing performance.

The processes for learning to tweak your body range from the obvious and common to the more extreme. Athletes,

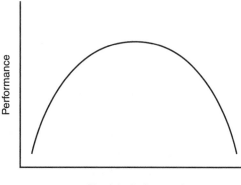

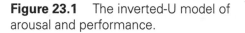

Figure 23.1 The inverted-U model of arousal and performance.

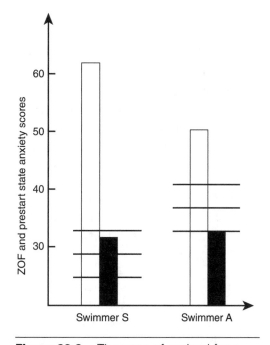

Figure 23.2 The zone of optimal functioning model. The white bars represent anxiety levels during unsuccessful performances, the black bars represent anxiety during successful ones, and the horizontal lines mark the ZOF.

Reprinted from Y.L. Hanin, 1986, State-trait anxiety research on sports in the USSR. In *Cross-cultural anxiety, vol. 3,* edited by C.D. Spielberger and R. Diaz-Guerrero (Washington, DC: Hemisphere Publishing Corp.), 54, with permission of Taylor & Francis Group. Permission conveyed through Copyright Clearance Center, Inc.

golfers included, try many methods to trigger their most effective mind-set. Many golfers whom I've worked with use music to help them find the right mind-set. Some golfers listen to spiritual music, some to rap music, some to pop music with rhythm. Considering that music can affect how we feel and that it is based on rhythm, a good playlist can help move the internal needle higher or lower.

Another aid to triggering an effective game face is to use motion to create emotion. If you're a football fan, you've no doubt seen teams collectively jump in huddles. Consistent with this principle, some innovative practitioners are pioneering a movement called meridian stretching, in which they help people stretch into various positions that relate to corresponding emotions. The movement is gaining both momentum and credibility. To give you an idea of what I mean, look to the sky and raise your arms in the air. Doesn't your mood improve immediately? We can often detect sadness or melancholy in people through their body language. These innovative practitioners of meridian stretching are doing the reverse: Rather than having body position reflect emotion, they are manipulating body position to influence emotion.

Anyone who has followed Luke Donald's rise to the top of the golf world will notice how frequently he refers to the importance of his body language. At the 2012 BMW Championship that he eventually won, he was asked about the work that he has done on his body language and (non-golf-swing) posture.

Well, personally, I just feel like it's helped me. It's helped me to really be aware of my posture and how I outwardly project that feeling of positive-ness. It helps me, and you know, obviously sends a message to whoever I'm playing with.

These lessons relate to the types of qualitative changes that we discussed in our previous chapters, and they speak to your becoming more in tune with your body and internal states. Although a variety of methods and techniques are available to help people monitor and control the reactions of the body, I use one that is both simple and effective, called Jacobson's progressive muscle relaxation (Jacobson 1938). Here are the basic instructions:

Sit in a comfortable chair. Reclining armchairs are ideal, but a bed is OK too. Get as comfortable as possible—no tight clothes or shoes and don't cross your legs. Take a deep breath and let it out slowly. Do it again. What you'll be doing is alternately tensing and relaxing specific groups of muscles. After tension, a muscle will be more relaxed than it was before the tensing. Concentrate on the feel of the muscles, specifically the contrast between tension and relaxation. In time, you will recognize tension in any specific muscle and be able to reduce that tension.

Don't tense muscles other than the specific group at each step. Don't hold your breath, grit your teeth, or squint. Breathe slowly and evenly and think only about the tension–relaxation contrast. Each tensing is for 10 seconds; each relaxing is for 10 or 15 seconds. Count "One one-thousand, two one-thousand," and so on until you have a feel for the time span. Note that each step is really two steps—one cycle of tension and relaxation for each set of opposing muscles.

Do the entire sequence once a day until you feel that you are able to control your muscle tension.

Be careful. If you have problems with pulled muscles, broken bones, or any medical contraindication for physical activities, consult your doctor first.

Hands. The fists are tensed; relaxed. The fingers are extended; relaxed.

Biceps and triceps. The biceps are tensed (make a muscle, but shake your hands to make sure that you're not tensing them into a fist); relaxed (drop your arms to the chair). The triceps are tensed (try to bend your arms the wrong way); relaxed (drop them).

Shoulders. Pull them back (careful with this one); relax them. Push the shoulders forward (hunch); relax.

Neck (lateral). With your shoulders straight and relaxed, turn your head slowly to the right, as far as you can; relax. Turn to the left; relax.

Neck (forward). Dig your chin into your chest; relax. (Bringing the head back is not recommended because you could break your neck.)

Mouth. Open your mouth as far as possible; relax. Bring your lips together or purse them as tightly as possible; relax.

Tongue (extended and retracted). With your mouth open, extend your tongue as far as possible; relax (let it sit in the bottom of your mouth). Bring it back into your throat as far as possible; relax.

Tongue (roof and floor). Dig your tongue into the roof of your mouth; relax. Dig it into the bottom of your mouth; relax.

Eyes. Open your eyes as wide as possible (furrow your brow); relax. Close your eyes tightly (squint); relax. Make sure that you completely relax the eyes, forehead, and nose after each of the tensings.

Breathing. Take as deep a breath as possible and then take in a little more; let it out and breathe normally for 15 seconds. Let all the breath in your lungs out and then let out a little more; inhale and breathe normally for 15 seconds.

Back. With your shoulders resting on the back of the chair, push your body forward so that your back is arched; relax. Be careful with this one or don't do it at all.

Buttocks. Tense your buttocks tightly and raise your pelvis slightly off the chair; relax. Dig your buttocks into the chair; relax.

Thighs. Extend your legs and raise them about 6 inches (15 cm) off the floor or the footrest but don't tense the abdominal muscles; relax. Dig your feet (heels) into the floor or footrest; relax.

Abdomen. Pull in your abdomen as far as possible; relax completely. Push out your abdomen or tense it as if you were preparing for a punch in the gut; relax.

Calves and feet. Point your toes (without raising your legs); relax. Point your feet up as far as possible (beware of cramps; if you get them or feel them coming on, shake them loose); relax.

Toes. With your legs relaxed, dig your toes into the floor; relax. Bend your toes up as far as possible; relax.

Now just relax for a while.

At first, go through the entire sequence and keep to a schedule of doing the exercises daily. Eventually, your will become so in tune with your body that you can gradually reduce it to twice weekly. As the days of practice progress, you may wish to skip the steps that do not appear to be a problem for you. After you've become an expert on your tension areas (after several weeks), you can focus mainly on those problem areas. I typically go through the full sequence with my golfers about once per month to maintain good body awareness and to prevent tension buildup. My golfers are frequently amazed how quickly they lose that body awareness if they aren't diligent about our sessions. These exercises will not eliminate tension, but when it arises, you will know it immediately, and you will be able to "tense–relax" it away or even simply wish it away.

CHAPTER 24

Emphasize Rhythm, Not Mechanics

O ther than the transformation of time, perhaps the most prevalently reported experience that a golfer feels in the flow zone is a sense of perfect rhythm. The word *rhythm* came up repeatedly with every golfer I asked to describe flow.

When searching for the precise words to describe their flow state, golfers nearly always default to saying "perfect rhythm." Those of you who have been in flow know exactly what they mean. Playing in perfect rhythm has a signature: With relatively low tension levels, you move in rhythm. You don't find yourself rushing to catch up with your thoughts, or conversely trying to slow your thinking down. You think in rhythm. And because your body and mind are synchronized accordingly, your golf swing flows in rhythm. This, of course, is easy to contrast against the mental state in which thoughts are moving too quickly, a body that walks down the fairway at a rushed, hurried pace, and a golf swing that gets jerked away, quickens through transition, and looks out of sequence. The rhythm of golf goes beyond the tempo of a golf swing. It speaks to the rhythm of your warm-up, the rhythm of your walking, your routine, and everything that you do.

Figure 24.1 is a preround checklist I use to help my golfers get into rhythm.

Mind-set affects how I interpret things. Interpretation affects tension. Tension affects golf swing. Thus, *mind-set* is at the center of my golfing vision.

I realize that a good attitude precedes, rather than follows, good golf. ☐

During my warm up, I will establish the rhythm and tempo I want to keep for the day. ☐

I think of making every move about the move (not the result) ☐

My number one goal is to be the most committed, free golfer I can be. I will do whatever it takes to achieve that goal. ☐

My mind-set will be one of looking for solutions rather than problems. ☐

Beating myself up over the outcome of a golf shot is not an option. ☐

Pressure/nervous: "Soft hands. Rhythm. Release to the target." ☐

My sense of humor is an asset. I will use it to my advantage. ☐

I realize the "great ones" never overthink things. Keep it simple. ☐

While my opponents play each other, I play the golf course. ☐

My routine will consist of ☐

- Using my practice swings to capture the feeling of the shot I want to hit
- Loving the chance to hit a great golf shot
- Taking a deep breath before I walk into the shot
- Going all in on every shot
- Accepting, relaxing, moving on
- Grading the process not the outcome

(Preround) Am I prepared to . . .	Y	N
Commit to every shot?	☐	☐
Truly look forward to challenging shots?	☐	☐
Gladly try any shot, so long as it is the appropriate shot?	☐	☐
Focus on my process rather than outcomes?	☐	☐
Stay chill/relaxed?	☐	☐
Maintain my routine on each hole, each shot?	☐	☐

What's my strategy?

What's my target?

Figure 24.1 The preround checklist.

Jim Flick, who worked with Jack Nicklaus for much of his career, suggested that rhythm, not necessarily technique, was central to Jack's dominance. He said, "Jack's feet became the rhythm of his swing and taught him the transition from the ground up. It was a key factor in his development" (Tarde 2007). Of course, many outstanding teachers advocate the importance of footwork in the golf swing (a detail overlooked by many less advanced teachers whom I've watched). For instance, Sean Foley (who coaches Hunter Mahan, Justin Rose, and Tiger Woods) is an advocate of footwork, which is why he frequently has his golfers practice in bare feet. It is widely known that the great Sam Snead practiced in bare feet well into his 70s. The reason that barefoot practice promotes rhythm is twofold. First, it helps a golfer stay in balance, and a golfer who is in balance is much more likely to be in rhythm. Conversely, being out of balance has a falling, unstable aspect to it that often jerks the golfer out of rhythm. Second, and more important, although it is easy to overswing while wearing shoes, it is difficult to swing too hard while

Establish a routine for getting into a comfortable rhythm. Fred Couples, also known as "Mr. Smooth," plays with great rhythm.

in bare feet. Because the feet are the only thing touching the ground, the kinetic chain sequences at the proper rhythm.

When Tiger goes to the range at tournaments he is not so much working on his golf swing as he is practicing what he calls his natural rhythm. As he says, "I want to make sure I go out there with the right rhythm." Regarding the 28 that he shot on the front nine of his Friday round at East Lake for the 2007 Tour Championship, Tiger remarked, "I just felt it was a nice rhythm. The pace was good, walking pace was good."

IMPROVING YOUR SKILLS

Beyond spending some time practicing barefoot or in your socks to establish your rhythm, you can do several things to improve your game by focusing on rhythm. To begin, remember that along with tension levels and cognitive processes, rhythm is one of the first things to be affected by changing environmental factors. Thus, be sure to place rhythm at the top of your priorities when auditing your game.

Next, head to the range with the intent of working not on improving your golf swing, but on establishing your natural rhythm. Begin with your wedges and, after a few shots, try to determine whether your swing feels too fast, too slow, or perfectly matched with the rhythm of your thoughts. Usually, golfers feel that their swing is moving faster than is ideal, and if that's the case for you, work to slow down the tempo of your swing until your swing feels matched with the speed of your mind. After you've calibrated these two, begin working your way through the bag with your focus being not on your targets this time, but on the rhythm of your warm-up.

After you've made your way through the bag, end your range session with five routines. Your focus should be—you guessed it—the rhythm of your routine. At this point remind yourself that when you're on the golf course, the game isn't going to attack your golf swing as much as it will attack your rhythm. Therefore, establishing the rhythm of your routine is going to be the most important thing that you can do. So now, go through your routine in rhythm:

1. Take a deep breath in and exaggerate the exhale.
2. Ask yourself, "What's my strategy? What's my target?"
3. Make a free, committed, fearless swing.
4. Say to yourself, "I accept the outcome of that shot."
5. Take a closing breath with a deep exhale.

After you do this five times, you're ready to head to the golf course!

Your goal now is to see how many holes you can play in great rhythm. Through this process, you will likely begin learning some important lessons. First, you will become more aware that the game of golf really tries to throw golfers out of their rhythm. You will become more sensitive to the rhythm of the game, and as your round unfolds, you will no doubt begin to notice how the "lights and music" try to influence your thoughts and your inner state in a manner consistent with what we've discussed in previous chapters.

Whether you experience it in this first round of golf or not, if you are diligent with this exercise, you will experience not only the benefits that I've described earlier in this chapter but also the one thing that this book aims to drive you toward—the flow state. This exercise mirrors many of the things that I do in my Fearless Golf Academies here in Winter Park, Florida. With astonishing regularity, taking golfers through the process of focusing on the rhythm of every routine triggers the mechanisms required to get them into flow. As a result, even though they tend to come to me because they are in a slump, golfers are able to play good, mentally uncluttered, low-scoring rounds of golf. The secret (if there is such a thing) is to get out of mechanics, out of score, out of your way, and into your natural rhythm and the rhythm of the game.

Play Fearlessly

One of the contentions that I've put forth in this book is that the brain did not evolve with the game of golf in mind. Rather, it evolved to adapt in harsh environments to facilitate survival and reproduction. Therefore, we must craft the habits of the mind to evolve into the type of golfers we wish to be—the type who continually improve, enjoy the game, and are able to generate flow.

The principal mechanism for survival is the fear response. Fear is an adaptive mechanism in all sorts of situations, primarily those that are construed as dangerous. The fear reaction prompts people to flee danger while simultaneously preparing their bodies for trauma by redistributing blood, hormones, and chemicals throughout the body and tightening the muscles. These redistributions and physiological reactions help in a fight, and they help in a car accident, but they do not help while trying to finesse a pitching wedge to a firm, fast, tucked green that's running away from you. As I wrote in *Fearless Golf*, part of your challenge as an up-and-coming golfer is to address these reactions and turn them into assets in your mental arsenal.

Let me illustrate with a recent example. Recall that Justin Rose had gone nine years on the PGA Tour without winning. During that time, Justin was a fine golfer, no doubt. But what happened to Justin in pressure situations was what happens to just about every golfer who faces pressure and is unaccustomed to dealing with it: His survival instincts kicked in, and the resulting physiological process of fear degraded the very skills that put him in position to win.

On the eve of the 2012 Ryder Cup, as I watched Justin finish birdie-birdie to help the Europeans close out one of the greatest comebacks in golf history, I witnessed what this chapter is all about. The past three years that I worked with Justin were spent identifying the natural tendencies of the brain and developing the habits of thought, belief, behavior, and awareness that allow those same instincts to channel Justin to a place of focus, determination, and great golf.

Just as Justin learned how to play fearless golf, so too can you. But Justin did not just flip a switch three years ago. He works hard on all facets of his game, including his mental game. He is as close to the perfect student as I have met because he follows the directives laid out in this book. Simply put, Justin practices his craft of fearless golf by doing ordinary actions, consistently and carefully, so that they add up over time. Through this lens, his performance in the Ryder Cup was not an act of inspiration as much as the accumulation of a thousand little habits that he's practiced faithfully.

Playing fearless golf requires that you understand both the game of golf and yourself. As we discussed in chapter 6, feeling embarrassed by public failure is natural. We are hard wired to want, on some level, the approval and validation of others. Golf is a social game that has failure and setbacks built into it, so it can be a breeding ground for the embarrassing feelings that come with public failure. It is because golf is both social and chockfull of setbacks that Jack Nicklaus termed his setbacks in golf *so-called failures*. Setbacks—such as Adam Scott's second-round 80 in the 2007 Players Championship, or Woody Austin's plunge into a lake at the 2007 Presidents Cup—are part of the journey, part of the challenge, and part of the delicate beauty of the game.

Because always playing well is impossible, understanding the game for what it is rather than for what you might like it to be is of paramount importance. In golf, getting better doesn't mean an end to problems and challenges; it means only that you are facing different types of problems and challenges. As psychiatrist Theodore Rubin observed about life, "The problem is not that there are problems. The problem is expecting otherwise and thinking that having problems is a problem." Trying to outrun or outrace the inherent challenges in either golf or life is a waste of time. You are better served by preparing yourself to deal with them effectively.

The challenges encountered at advanced levels of competitive golf may be different from those at the beginning levels, but they are challenges nonetheless. As you improve your game, you are merely trading one set of challenges for a different, more delicate and refined, and often more tenacious set of challenges. In the early stages of development, your challenges are primarily mechanical as you learn to swing the golf club properly. You correct your slice by hitting more "inside" the golf ball, only to develop a hook, which you eventually correct by "covering" the ball. As you continue to develop, rudimentary mechanical challenges give way to working to become consistent and learning how to play different shots around the greens—learning to "score." At the advanced level, you trade mechanical challenges and scoring shots for mental and psychological challenges, such as dealing with fear and tension, fighting self doubt, and monitoring and fueling personal motivation. The mental game becomes more important, but learning how to be a complete competitive golfer requires the same dedication, commitment, and love for learning required to develop a sound, consistent golf swing.

As Aristotle suggested, the greatest battles that we ever win are the battles that we win over ourselves and our inborn tendencies

Jeff Robinson/Icon SMI

Accept occasional struggles and setbacks and learn to play with the fearlessness Rory McIlroy exhibits.

toward fear, self-doubt, indecision, laziness, anger, or impatience. Conquering these tendencies, including our inclination to be fearful, requires us to understand that the hardware in the brain is designed to respond to threats a certain way.

Thirty-five thousand years of evolution ensure that when perceived threats occur, your amygdala will fire and sound the proverbial alarm. Historically, these threats usually took the form of real danger: fire, violence, pain, aggression. The modern-day golfer doesn't face those threats, and although our evolved cortex can tell the difference, our overcautious amygdala cannot. To the amygdala, a downhill, 6-foot (2 m), left-to-right putt to decide the match can feel every bit as dreadful and threatening as violence. Hence, overcoming your instinctive response to that alarm requires the ability to step back, understand those processes, and to say to yourself, "Wait a minute. I know my stomach feels a little tight. I know I'm feeling a little off. I don't need to be afraid of what's happening here."

Although you may not be able to control the feelings in the heat of the moment, you can control how you choose to handle the feelings after you've identified them. You can decide to select a target, to soften your grip pressure to counter the increased tension levels, to go through your routine, and to trust the golf swing that you've spent hours routinizing into habit. Although you may not be able to stop the blood vessels in your hands from constricting (the body's natural response to fear), you can train yourself to resist the urge to grip the club tighter and thus be able to make a fearless swing. Being fearless involves a great element of choice!

IMPROVING YOUR SKILLS

In previous chapters I asked you to learn to play mastery golf, to remove mental barriers, to become more aware of your body, to emphasize rhythm, and to craft your environment. All those things have been designed to craft your thoughts, feelings, and behaviors so that you can feel confident in your process and be comfortable that you know what to do in a given situation. Preparation, practice, and learning are the prerequisites for playing fearless golf.

Having worked through the process, you are ready to tackle fear head on and set an explicit goal to ingrain the habit of fearlessness. The first step is to understand that the fear response is an automated thing and that your goal is to handle this response better over time. So, while being fully prepared for the difficulty of your task, your assignment is this: Immerse yourself in a type of situation that typically makes you feel inhibited or fearful on a golf course. If tournaments cause you to feel afraid, sign up for a tournament with the sole intention of learning how your body and mind react under pressure. If you've choked while playing with your boss, invite him or her to play again. If you've dunked four balls into the water on the 11th hole during your regular weekend tournament, sign up again and eagerly anticipate that hole. The best way to play fearless golf is to immerse yourself regularly in situations that trigger fear, learn how your body responds, and learn how to take control of your rhythm, tension, and ability to react with humor and acceptance

You should also revisit a recurring theme in this book—practicing how to control your focus. If you're afraid to play with your boss, after you've set up a tee time for both of you, try your best to play the golf course rather than your boss. Practice the habit of concentrating on the golf course rather than your boss's approval. If you feel yourself being evaluated by him or her, restructure your self-talk to ask yourself mastery questions. Shift from asking, "How am I appearing to my boss?" to asking, "What's the best way to play this hole? What's my target?" Keep defaulting to your fearless golf routine. Remember that the routine I've outlined in this book has been designed for precisely this situation. The opening breath will help lower your tension levels, the questions about your strategy and target will focus your attention on the golf course rather than your fear triggers, acceptance of the outcome of the shot will minimize the fear-enhancing pain being driven into your psyche, and the closing breath will counter the lights and music that quicken rhythm and increase tension levels.

After the experience is over, record the feelings that you had. Did you focus on grip pressure and rhythm? How did it turn out? Were you disciplined in your routine? If not, make that your goal the next time. In other words, the most important thing about this experience is not necessarily how you felt during it as much as what you are able to learn afterward. If you react like a mastery golfer and focus on the learning experience that you just had, you will have taken an important first step toward learning how to play fearless golf.

Having traveled with golfers as long as I have, I can tell you that there is no substitute for the experience that comes when you are scared on a golf course. Most people have the instinct to run away from these situations. But as every experienced winner in golf will tell you, they are the most valuable teachers. Immerse yourself in as many of them as you can, from the learning perspective of a mastery golfer, and have the goal of executing your routine in rhythm.

References

Quotations included in the text that are not listed here are from http://www.asap-sports.com or personal correspondence.

Beach, S. 2001. Good falling. How one childcare professional invites positive self talk. *Journal of Invitational Theory and Practice.* (7):2.

Burke, Monte. 2010. Ten minutes with Gary Player. *Forbes.* Retrieved from www.forbes.com/2010/05/27/gary-player-golf-lifestyle-sports-tiger-woods-pga_2.html

Chambliss, Daniel. 1989. The mundanity of excellence: An ethnographic report on stratification and Olympic swimmers. *Sociological Theory* 7(1):70–86.

Christakis, N., & Fowler, J. 2007. The spread of obesity in a large social network over 32 years. *New England Journal of Medicine.* July 26, 2007, (370-379).

Coyle, Daniel. 2009, *The talent code.* New York: Bantam Dell.

Csikszentmihalyi, M. 1997. *Finding flow: The psychology of engagement with everyday life.* New York: Basic Books.

Dingfelder, Sadie F. 2003. Tibetan Buddhism and research psychology: A match made in Nirvana? *Monitor on Psychology* 34:11.

Ericsson, K. Anders, Krampe, Ralf Th., and Tesch-Romer, Clemens. 1993. The role of deliberate practice in the acquisition of expert performance. *Psychological Review* 100(3):363–406.

Goldman, Robert and Stephen Papson. 1998. *Nike culture: The sign of the swoosh.* London: Sage Publications.

Jacobson, E. (1938). *Progressive relaxation.* Chicago: University of Chicago Press.

Jowett, S., and D. Lavallee. 2007. *Social psychology in sport.* Champaign, IL: Human Kinetics.

Marsh, H.W. 1994. The importance of being important: Theoretical models of relations between specific and global components of physical self-concept. *Sport Psychology* 16(3):306–25.

McDougall, Chris. 2009. *Born to run.* New York: Random House.

Miller, Bode. 2005. *Go fast, be good, have fun.* New York: Random House.

Nicklaus, Jack. 1997. *My story.* New York: Simon and Schuster.

Norman, Greg. 2006. *The way of the shark.* New York: Atria Books.

Reilly, Rick. 1986, April 22. Master strokes. *Sports Illustrated*, pp. 24–31.

Rowland, T. 2011. The athlete's clock: how biology and time affect sport performance. Human Kinetics: Champaign, IL.

Tarde, Jerry. 2007. A pair of jacks. [Editor's letter]. *Golf Digest.* Retrieved from www.golfdigest.com/magazine/2007-10/tarde

Weir, Kirsten. 2012. Smog in our brains. *Monitor on psychology* 43(7):32.

Woods, Tiger. 2001. *How I play golf.* Warner Books: New York.

Index

Note: The italicized *f* and *t* following page numbers refer to figures and tables, respectively.

A

acceptance 20-21, 67-68, 129-131, 144, 150-
152. *See also* mastery orientation
achievement domains 132-137
achievement goals 58
adaptive skills vs. traits 52-53
adversity or failure
    ego vs. mastery golfers 73-76
    as feedback 81-84
    positive response to 199-204
    in pro golfers 27-29, 76-79, 112-116
    role in confidence 89-91
    value in 80-81
Agassi, Andre 23
amygdala 89-90, 222
Appleby, Stuart 117-123
Aristotle 2, 171, 221
arousal 206, 208-209
association, in habit development 174
audience effect 113, 205
automaticity 14-15, 32, 40-44, 174
autotelic personalities 53, 67
awareness paradox
    concentration and automaticity in 38-44
    distractions in 35-36
    focus in 36-38

B

barefoot practice 215-216
beliefs 18-23, 66, 189
body control
    emotions and 205-208
    methods for 208-212
body language 210
Born to Run (McDougall) 102-104
brain activity 15-17, 89-90, 185-186, 222

C

Campbell, Chad 8, 39, 40, 197
Castro, Roberto 24
central governor hypothesis 186
challenges 54-55. *See also* adversity or
    failure
challenge-skill balance 48-50, 51-52
Chambliss, Daniel 188
change state 67-68
Cink, Steward 32
clearing 62
club, unison with 31-33
composure 208
confidence
    experience interpretation and 87-89,
        144-145
    importance of 46, 85-86
    role of failure in 89-91

role of success in 87-89, 91-94
    Stuart Appleby story 119-120
control paradox
    beliefs and perspective in 18-23
    brain activity in 15-17
    in Camilo Villegas story 131
    practice in 12-15
    racing metaphor 23-24
cortex 15-17, 222
Couples, Fred 79, 91, 170
Coyle, Daniel 126, 155, 174

D

difficulty of golf. *See* adversity or failure
distance runners 102-104, 185
distractions 35-36
Donald, Luke 170, 171, 173, 210
driving range vs. golf course 176

E

Earnhardt, Dale 140
effort paradox 29-34
ego-avoid mind-set 61-62
ego orientation 59-62, 108, 179-180. *See also*
    mastery orientation
Einstein, Albert 66, 71, 140
emergence 67-72
emotions
    body reactions 205-208
    influencing 208-212
energy expenditure 33-34
environment
    focus on 208
    impact of 191-194, 216
    routines and 195-198
Ericsson, Anders 28, 173
exceptionalism 65-66
expectations 110-111, 129-131

F

failure, so-called 79-80. *See also* adversity
    or failure
Faldo, Nick 164
Faxon, Brad 91
fear 62, 219
fearlessness 219-223
Flick, Jim 215
flow (term) 1
flow states
    adaptive skills vs. traits in 52-53
    challenge-skill balance and 51-52
    confidence and 94
    control over 1-2
    paradoxes in 2
    setting stage for 54-55

focus 36-38, 139-146, 208
Foley, Sean 106, 169, 176, 215
footwork 215
Franklin, Ben 164
Freud, Sigmund 66, 83, 144
Furyk, Jim 9, 24, 31, 41, 87

G
Garcia, Sergio 28, 42, 141
goals 55, 58
golf course
    vs. driving range 176
    playing against 59, 194-195
golf journals 181
Goosen, Retief 78
Granada, Julieta 78
gratitude 54, 62, 117-123, 131-132

H
habit 14-15, 55, 171-174
Hanin, Y.L. 209
Heron, Tim 41
Hogan, Ben 29, 55, 58, 172, 208
Howell, Charles III 10, 25, 34, 41-42
Huston, John 34

I
intrinsic rewards. *See* love of game
inverted-U model 209, 209f
Ishikawa, Ryo 28

J
Jacklin, Tony 89
Jacobson's progressive muscle relaxation
    210-212
James, William 171, 185, 206
James-Lange theory of emotions 206
Jobs, Steve 20-21, 66
Johnson, Dustin 6
Johnson, Zach 9, 60, 196
Jones, Bobby 126, 181
Jordan, Michael 79, 82

K
kaizen 46, 58, 113-114, 153, 180
kensho 44
Kim, Anthony 40
Kuchar, Matt
    awareness paradox 35-36, 40
    as exceptional 66
    love of game 97-104
    performance thresholds 187
    positive attitude 201-202

L
learning opportunities 112-116, 121
learning process 13-15, 126
Leonard, Justin 5, 41-42
limitations 183-190
Love, Davis III 25, 34, 95-96
love of game 45-46, 97-104. *See also* moti-
    vation

M
mastery orientation
    actualizing 62, 83

in adversity 73-76
    described 58-59
    developing 179-182
    effect on experience 63-64
    vs. ego orientation 59-62, 108
May, Bob 79
McCarron, Scott 10, 24, 30, 78
McDougall, Christopher 102-104
McIlroy, Rory 27, 28, 30, 31, 159, 170
McKenzie, Will 66
meridian stretching 210
Mickelson, Phil 4, 33, 176
Miller, Bode 127
Miller, Johnny 33
mind-set. *See* beliefs; mastery orientation
Molder, Bryce 9, 25, 147-153
motion, for mind-set 210
motivation
    clarifying 57-58
    extrinsic vs. intrinsic 45-46, 103-104, 108
    Justin Rose story 105-110
    Stuart Appleby story 119-120
music, for mind-set 210
myelination (muscle memory) 13-14
My Story (Nicklaus) 159

N
Nicklaus, Jack
    adversity 78, 79
    awareness paradox 38-39
    confidence 86, 89, 106
    on difficulty of golf 199
    emotions 206
    environment 208
    golf description 169
    on learning to win 157
    mastery orientation 59, 60
    motivation 57
    My Story 159
    on nature of game 136
    near wins 141
    practice 55, 170, 172
    rhythm 215
    routine 196
    self-talk 202
    time paradox 7
Norman, Greg 89, 141-142, 157-158, 159
Norman Slam 142

O
Ogilvy, Geoff 42-43
O'Hair, Sean 18-19, 67, 137, 139-146
Olazabal, Jose Maria 79
overcontrol 23-25

P
Palmer, Arnold 89, 141
paradoxes 2. *See also specific paradoxes*
patience 18, 19-22
peak experiences 1-2
Penick, Harvey 123
perfectibilism 183
performance fluctuations 125-137
performance thresholds 185-190

Perks, Craig 148
Perry, Kenny 30, 31
personal growth 50, 66, 68-72
Player, Gary 200-201
positive attitude 199-204
practice
    for automaticity 32
    debate on 169-170
    driving range vs. gold course 176
    lag effect of 18
    neurophysiology of 12-15
    psychology of 171-174
    success through 28, 53-54, 55
    types and drills 174-178
preround checklist 214
present moment focus 139-146
progressive muscle relaxation 210-212
Purkey,William 202

R
reactions 21, 144, 205-208
reading list, for success 160
relaxation exercise 210-212
repetition compulsion 83
resilience. See also adversity or failure
    ego vs. mastery orientation 73-76
    practice for 29
    in pro golfers 76-79
rhythm 144, 165, 176, 213-217
Roberts, Loren "Boss of the Moss" 43-44
role models 159, 161
Rose, Justin
    expectations 110-111
    failure as learning opportunity 112-116
    fearlessness 219-220
    motivation 105-110
    performance fluctuations 136
    practice 176
    time management 165
Rotella, Bob 207
routines 195-198
Rowland, Thomas 185-186

S
Saturday Slam 142
scores 35-36, 73-74, 179-182
Scott, Adam 10, 11-12, 31, 40
scripting 152-153
self, investment in 53-54
self-doubt 148
self-efficacy. See confidence
self-talk 201-204
setbacks. See adversity or failure
Singh, Vijay 166-167
six-shot drill 175-176
ski metaphor 48-49
Slater, Kelly 126-127, 127f
Snead, Sam 215
Snedeker, Brandt 41
stagnation 68-69
Strange, Curtis 25, 37

Stricker, Steve 69-71, 100
success
    perils of 120-121
    role in confidence 87-89, 91-94
    role of practice in 28, 53-54, 55
    study of 157-161
Sutton, Hal 10, 34, 79
swing mechanics 6, 148-149
synchronicity 14-15

T
Tantalus 140-142
Taoist parable 21
Tarahumara 102-104
tension 18, 122, 151
10,000-hour rule 28, 173
three–four rule 175
time, relational theory of 71
time management 163-168
time paradox
    perspectives on 8-10
    time transformation 4-8
Toms, David 8, 24
trust 19-22
Tucker Short Game Test (TSGT) 177-178,
    178f

V
Verplank, Scott 77-78, 149
Villegas, Camilo
    attitude of gratitude 131-132
    expectations and acceptance 128-131
    performance fluctuations 125-128, 128t,
        132-137, 197
visualization 91
Vygotsky, Lev 50-53

W
Watney, Nick 6
Watson, Bubba 41, 159, 202-203
Watson, Tom 24, 46
Weekley, Boo 89
whispering self 202
Woods, Tiger
    adversity 78
    associates 158
    automaticity 44
    confidence 87, 89, 91
    on difficulty of golf 199
    impressions of 27-28
    motivation 57-58
    patience 19
    practice 172, 176
    rhythm 216
    routine 196, 197
    time management 164
    time paradox 5

Z
zone of optimal functioning (ZOF) 209, 209f
zone of proximal development (ZPD) 50-53,
    51f

About the Author

Dr. Gio Valiante is one of the most prominent sport psychologists in the world. He has worked with many of the sport's top players, including Matt Kuchar, Justin Rose, Camilo Villegas, Sean O'Hair, Davis Love III, and Alexis Thompson. His clients over the past decade have won dozens of championships, and he has become the winningest sport psychologist on the PGA Tour during that time.

Valiante was named one of the 40 most influential people in golf under age 40 by *Golf* magazine in 2011 and was dubbed Guru of the Year by the Golf Channel in 2010. His book *Fearless Golf: Conquering the Mental Game* (Doubleday/*Golf Digest*, 2005) is a standard in golf psychology. He is a professor at Rollins College in Winter Park, Florida, and serves as the mental game consultant for the Golf Channel, *Golf Digest*, and the University of Florida.

Valiante lives in Winter Park, Florida.